The Children of Paul's

Published by the Press Syndicate of the University of Cambridge
The Pitt Building, Trumpington Street, Cambridge CB2 1RP
32 East 57th Street, New York, NY 10022, USA
296 Beaconsfield Parade, Middle Park, Melbourne 3206, Australia

First published 1982

Printed in Great Britain at the Pitman Press, Bath

Library of Congress catalogue card number: 82-4185

British Library Cataloguing in Publication Data
Gair, Reavley
The children of Paul's: the story of a theatre
company, 1553–1608.
1. Theater – London – History 2. Children
of Paul's – History
I. Title
792'.09424   PN2590.C/
ISBN 0 521 24360 2

The Children of Paul's:
the story of a theatre company,
1553–1608

REAVLEY GAIR

PROFESSOR OF ENGLISH, UNIVERSITY OF NEW BRUNSWICK

CAMBRIDGE UNIVERSITY PRESS

CAMBRIDGE

LONDON   NEW YORK   NEW ROCHELLE
MELBOURNE   SYDNEY

To Louise and Jonathan

Contents

Illustrations

1, 2, 4, 5 are taken from the Hollar engravings in W. Dugdale's *The History of St Paul's Cathedral*, 1658, by permission of the Syndics of Cambridge University Library.

3 is based mainly on the so-called Agas map of *c*.1562: street names are partially based on A. Proctor and R. Taylor, *The A to Z of Elizabethan London*, 1979.

6 is a drawing by Sidney Kingerley.

7 is based on a plan by F. C. Penrose, Guildhall MS. 460/*Pau* (2) pla., but the scale is much enlarged.

8 is a contemporary painting in the hands of the Society of Antiquaries of London: it is reproduced with their permission.

9 and 10 are based on the birth/marriage/death counts from the appropriate parish registers.

Preface

I am indebted to Mr A. R. Fuller, Librarian of St Paul's Cathedral, for his kind assistance on my various visits to that place and to the staff of the Guildhall Library for their help over Visitation Reports and parish records. Equally I am grateful for the encouragement of Cyrus Hoy, who urged me to write this book; to Richard Hosley for his help over matters pertaining to the playhouse and to Muriel Bradbrook and David Hoeniger for their interest and support. I wish also to express my thanks to Leonard Smith (of the Department of Classics of the University of New Brunswick) for his kind assistance with some difficult problems in the interpretation of various Latin documents. Similarly I am much in the debt of Don Rowan and Clayton Burns, of the University of New Brunswick, for their considerable assistance in ensuring the accuracy of the final typescript. Last, but not least, my wife's enthusiastic encouragement made the project feasible from its inception to its conclusion.

Some of the material, particularly from Chapter 4, was first presented as two papers to the Waterloo Elizabethan Theatre Conference (1975 and 1977) and these studies were published in *Elizabethan Theatre VI* and *Elizabethan Theatre VII*. I am indebted to George Hibbard, the editor and conference chairman, for his kind permission to re-work some of the content in this book.

In the very numerous quotations from manuscripts in this book, the original spelling, punctuation and abbreviation are all used; 'u'/'v' has, however, been modernised as has long 's'. Unless otherwise indicated, all plays are cited from first quarto editions with the original forms preserved.

W.R.G.

February 1981

Editions and abbreviations

Unless otherwise indicated, the place of publication of all books
is London.

Anon.
  The Maydes Metamorphosis, Q. 1600
  The Wisdome of Doctor Dodypoll, Q. 1600   *Doctor Dodypoll*

Beaumont F, and Fletcher J.
  The Woman Hater, Q. 1607.

Dekker T.
  Satiro-mastix, or The untrussing of the Humorous Poet, Q. 1602.
                                                              Satiro.

Dekker T and Webster J.
  West-ward Hoe, Q. 1607.   *W. Hoe.*
  North-ward Hoe, Q. 1607.   *N. Hoe.*

Chapman G.
  Bussy D'Ambois, Q. 1607.

Lyly J.
  Campaspe, Q. 1584.
  Sapho and Phao, Q. 1584.
  Endimion, The Man in the Moone, Q. 1591.
  Midas, Q. 1592.
  Gallathea, Q. 1592.
  Mother Bombie, Q. 1594.
  Loves Metamorphosis, Q. 1601.

Marston J.
  *Jacke Drums Entertainment: or The Comedie of Pasquill and
    Katherine,* Q. 1601   *J.D.Ent.*
  The History of Antonio and Mellida, The first part, Q. 1602.   *A.M.*
  Antonio's Revenge, The second part, Q. 1602.   *A.R.*
  Parasitaster, or The Fawne, Q. 1606.
  What You Will, Q. 1607.   *W.Y.W.*

Middleton T.
  Blurt Master Constable or The Spaniards Night Walke, Q. 1602.
  Blurt.

  Michaelmas Terme, Q. 1607. *M.T.*
  The Phoenix, Q. 1607.
  A Mad World, My Masters, Q. 1608. *Mad World.*
  A Trick to Catch the Old-one, Q. 1608. *Trick to Catch.*
  [?] The Puritaine, or the Widdow of Watling-Street, Q. 1607

Calendar(s) of State Papers *C.S.P.*

New Series N S

Notes and Queries *N. & Q.*

Plays and Masques at Court During The Reigns of Elizabeth, James and Charles, Cornell Studies in English, New Haven, Yale University Press; London, Oxford, 1926; reprinted New York, 1968. M.S. Steele. Steele.

Public Record Office P.R.O.

Quarto *Q.*

The Visitation Report of Bishop Robert Bancroft for the London Diocese 1598 (Guildhall MS., 9537/9). *V.R.*

Note: for Redford's *Wit and Science*, and *The Contention betweene Liberalitie and Prodigalitie*, the text cited is that of the Malone Society Reprints: for *The Marriage of Wit and Science*, it is that provided by T.N.S. Lennam in *Sebastian Westcott, The Children of Paul's, and The Marriage of Wit and Science*, Toronto, 1975.

The Children of Paul's and the English drama

This work originated as a development from the problems of editing Marston's *Antonio's Revenge* for the Revels series. I wished to create, with as much historical accuracy as possible, a commentary which would restore for the modern reader the play and its conditions as closely as the surviving information would allow. The present book is the result of that initial undertaking; it is designed as a social and literary history of England's first permanently based drama company and it seeks to challenge some of the orthodoxies about the theatre of the children. The Children of Paul's were a distinctive group with special qualities of their own and it is my intention to illustrate, as vividly as possible, this uniqueness.

This history, *The Children of Paul's*, seeks to illustrate the dramas performed by that company by studying the physical conditions of the playhouse, and the cathedral itself; by examining the personalities of the masters, the actors, the musicians and dramatists; and also by investigating the audience, to determine not merely who they were but what the players expected them to know and recognise. The physical context of this theatre, in the north-west corner of the Chapter House precinct, was a vital factor in determining both its success and its quality: for a period at least it was a local repertory theatre for people from the neighbouring parishes.

The focus of this study has been intentionally narrowed to illuminate the specific company studied, to stress the uniqueness of its character. This restriction necessarily inhibits a wider perspective on the development of the Elizabethan and Jacobean drama as a whole. In an attempt, therefore, partially to redress this balance, the following summary of the major developments in the wider corpus of dramatic history has been compiled. This précis is divided into three sections, each devoted to a different Master of Choristers, in order to cover the periods when drama flourished within the cathedral precincts. For the scholar it may be simplistic, but conversely it may act as a useful index and reference point for events at Paul's in relation to the wider context of the London drama outside its confines.

The Mastership of Sebastian Westcott
(1 February 1553–April 1582)

The scholars of St Paul's, both of the choir and the grammar school, may be associated with acting as early as 1378, when they petitioned Richard II

to prohibit some unexpert people from representing the History of the old Testament, to the great prejudice of the said Clergy, who have been at great expence in order to represent it publickly at Christmas.[1]

It is, however, to the Renaissance in England that their involvement with the drama properly belongs. The stimulus for the evolution of the acting and producing of plays may largely be ascribed to those scholars who argued for its educational function. In 1531 Sir Thomas Elyot in *The boke named the Governour* defended the plays of Terence and Plautus as a glass of conduct, arguing that

comedies . . . be undoutedly a picture or as it were a mirrour of mans life, wherin ivell is nat taught but discovered to the intent that men beholdynge the pmptnes [promptness] of youth unto vice: the snares of harlotts & baudes laide for yonge myndes: the disceipte of servantes: the chaunces of fortune cōtrary to menes expectation: they beinge therof warned: may prepare them selfe to resist or prevente occasion. Sēblably remēbring the wisedomes: advertisemēts: coūsailes: dissuasion from vice & other pfitable [profitable] sētences, most eloquētly & familiarely shewed in those comedies, Undoubtedly there shall be no litle frute out of them gathered: And if the vices in them expressed shulde be cause that myndes of the reders shulde be corrupted: than by the same argumente nat onely entreludes in englisshe, but also sermones wherein some vice is declared, shulde be to the beholders and herers like occasion to encreace sinners. (Gij)

The moral defence of the drama quickly gained extensive scholarly approval and by 1560 William Malim, headmaster of Eton, could take the argument a stage further, when he laid down the normal practice at the school for the month of December:

Around the feast of St Andrew the Master is accustomed to select, at his own discretion, the best and most accomplished plays, which the pupils may perform publickly, not without dramatic elegance, at the ensuing Christmas Season with spectators looking on. The art of acting is a slight accomplishment but in so far as it pertains to the learning of the action of oratory, and the gestures and movements of the body, nothing else accomplishes these objects to so high a degree. At times the master may also present plays in the English language, provided they are written with wit and humour.[2]

Whatever the theoretical justification for plays, however, the authorities long remained cautious, as a statute of Henry VIII in 1543 makes clear; while

it shall be laufull to all and every persone and personnes, to sette forth songes playes and enterludes, to be used and exercised within this realme, & other the kynges dominions, for the rebukyng and reproching of vices, & the setting forth of vertue: So alwayes the saide songes playes or enterludes medle not with interpretacions of scripture, contrary to the doctryne set forth or to be set forth by the kynges maiestie . . .[3]

The English drama and the actor, then, evolved in the latter part of the Renaissance poised between the theoretical justification of the scholar and the suspicion of the authorities that their activity was potentially subversive. Despite this insecurity of status, the travelling entertainers of the medieval period, who were as much minstrels and acrobats as actors and who never played in the same place twice running, were, in the first half of the sixteenth century, seeking to take advantage of the improvement in the social attitude towards drama in order to evolve into professional actors. Already by the 1560s there were more or less regular seasons of plays presented at the major London inns and the players quickly became aware of the desirability of finding a permanent playing-place under their own control. Such an investment, however, demanded a stability of position which they did not have, for the *Acte for the Punishment of Vagabonds* (1571/2) stipulated that all 'Comon players in Enterludes Mynstrels Iuglers . . . [who] wander abroade . . . [without] Lycense of two Justices of the Peace . . . shalbee taken adjudged and deemed Roges Vacaboundes and

Sturdy Beggers . . .'[4] The entertainers needed recognised social status to effect their metamorphosis from minstrels to actors.

This transition was achieved with the help of the court, which was consistently well-disposed towards actors, save in the case of subversive doctrine. The Vagabond Act of 1571/2, while ostensibly condemning all players, in fact makes a distinction between the best actors, who are licensed, and the rest who are truly rogues: this system of licence was to be the most important factor in the development of the player companies. In 1574 the City Fathers turned down a request for recognised playing-places in London, but later in the same year Elizabeth licensed James Burbage and others as servants to the Earl of Leicester 'to use, exercise and occupie the art and faculty of playeng comedies, tragedies, Enterludes, Stage playes, and such other like as they have alredy used and studied, or hereafter shall use and studye, aswell for the recreacon of o[r] loving subjects, as for o[r] solace and pleasure, when we shall thinke good to se them'.[5] The price for this royal support was, however, a measure of royal control, for they were forbidden to play during the time of common prayer or in the midst of plague visitations. In addition, in an Order of the Common Council for 6 December 1574, the players were warned not to perform any drama which had not met with the prior approval of the Lord Mayor and Aldermen.[6]

Despite the restrictions, the security was enough to justify the investment and by 1576 James Burbage had built a permanent playing-place in Finsbury Fields, The Theatre. This first outdoor public playhouse was erected at a time when Sebastian Westcott and the Children of Paul's had already shown what had probably been long suspected by Burbage, that there was a permanent year-round market in London for stage spectacles. In the same year the Children of the Chapel Royal at the Blackfriars began a sequence of regular shows indoors within a specially modified hall in their precinct. The next year, 1577, saw the building of The Curtain, adjacent to The Theatre in Shoreditch.

This rapid proliferation of heavily capitalised playing-places did not escape the wrath of the preachers, for they remained convinced opponents of the stage. Thomas White thundered from the pulpit of Paul's Cross on 3 November 1577:

4

. . . beholde the sumptuous Theatre houses, a continuall monument of Londons prodigalitie and folly. But I understande they are nowe forbidden bycause of the plague, I like the pollicye well if it holde still, for a disease is but bodged or patched up that is not cured in the cause, and the cause of plagues is sinne, if you looke to it well: and the cause of sinne are playes: therefore the cause of plagues are playes . . . without doubt you can scatly name me a sinne, that by that sincke is not set a gogge . . . theft and whoredome: pride and prodigality: villanie and blasphemie: these three couples of helhoundes never cease barking there, and bite manye so as they are uncurable ever after, so that many a man hath the leuder wife, and many a wife the shreuder husband by it.[7]

One may perhaps wonder whether White had the Children of Paul's very much in his mind when attacking the theatres, with his reference to 'pride and prodigality'[8]: like his fellow Calvinistically inclined priests, he saw only a direct challenge to the divine will in the existence of playhouses. White, unlike Elyot, has no doubt that plays are a positive element in the degeneration of the young.

During the period of the Mastership of Sebastian Westcott, then, the Children of Paul's co-existed with the rapid growth of the professionally organised London player companies and the development of buildings specifically designed for the performance of plays. Although Westcott's children had significant competition from the Children of the Chapel Royal, they remained Elizabeth's favourite entertainers, but when he died they were already beginning to be eclipsed. By 1582, despite the hostility of the preachers, in both the popular and the courtly imagination the professionals of the city were overtaking the choristers. It is towards the time of Sebastian Westcott's death, also, that it becomes obvious that the style of plays in England is moving away from the Morality tradition so popular at Paul's, with Legge's *Richardus Tertius* (1580), Peele's *Arraignment of Paris* (1581), Watson's *Three Ladies of London* (1581), and [?] Munday's *The Rare Triumphs of Love and Fortune* (1582).

The Mastership of Thomas Gyles (22 May 1584–July 1600)

During the period of Gyles' probation as Master, the Children of Paul's and the Children of the Chapel Royal performed as a joint company, but when this co-operative broke up the Blackfriars theatre appears to have closed (1584). This eclipse of the first Blackfriars company was symptomatic of the way in which the professionals were very rapidly overtaking the early lead in popularity gained by the chorister companies, and while Paul's, under Lyly, remained active and inventive, Gyles' mastership was wholly overshadowed by the brilliance of the professional, adult, London open-air theatres and their repertoires.

The professionals, however, were in conflict with the City Magistrates who, under the influence of the preachers, were seeking to close down the playing-places within their jurisdiction. Any excuse was sufficient; so on 13 January 1583, when a scaffold collapsed at a bear-baiting causing eight deaths, the playhouses were promptly ordered shut. The court, however, probably under the influence of Elizabeth herself, refused to allow the players to be intimidated and on 26 November 1583 the Privy Council directed the Lord Mayor that, 'Forasmuch as (God be thanked) there is no . . . infection within . . . [the] citie at this presente, but that hir maiesties playeres may be suffered to playe within the liberties as heretofore they have done, especially seeing they are shortly to present some of their doeinges before hir maiestie, we . . . pray your Lp. to geve order, that the said players maybe licenced so to doe within the Citie.'[9] At the same time there was created the Queen's Players Company, drawn from the best acting talents in London and including Robert Wilson, Richard Tarlton and John Laneham.

Although this group, the Queen's Men, remained the dominant company until about 1588, they were in competition with Worcester's Men from whom emerged the leading actor of the 90s, Edward Alleyn. By 1590 the companies had reshuffled and renamed themselves and the dominant position was assumed by the amalgamation of the Admiral's and Strange's Men, and this lasted until 1594. It was during the 80s and early 90s that there began to emerge, with the professional companies, the dramatists and the plays which have remained the hallmark of the Elizabethan drama. Kyd's *Spanish Tragedy*, Marlowe's *Tamburlaine I* and *II*, Peele's *David and Bethsabe* and the works of Lodge, Wilson, Tarlton, Greene were all first presented by the London open-air theatres in this period, before the Marprelate controversy caused the closure of Paul's in 1590/1. Business was good enough for an extra playhouse to be built. This was The

Rose (*c*.1587); situated on the south bank of the Thames in Surrey. The Rose, Theatre, Curtain and other public play-houses were usually round or polygonal timber-frame buildings with thatched side roofs. There were normally three ranges of gallery seating, reached by steps or doors from the main open yard. The prices increased the higher one climbed, a penny being paid at each level. There were special courtiers' galleries above the stage, which was a platform (up to 40 feet wide) projecting into the middle of the yard. At the rear of the stage was the tiring-house with two or more doors on to the main acting area. The 'above' (the first gallery level) had a balcony and there was a trap on the main stage. The acting area was largely covered by a roof, the heavens, to shelter the actors' expensive costumes and to offer a place from which descents could be made. Performances were always scheduled during daylight hours.

Coincident with the closure of Paul's (1590/1) is the clear emergence of Shakespeare as the dominant dramatic talent, with his *Henry VI*; then, in 1592, came Marlowe's *Dr Faustus* and *Edward II* together with Shakespeare's *Comedy of Errors*. But at this point London began to suffer a severe infestation of the plague and on 28 January 1593 the Privy Council directed the Lord Mayor and Aldermen that 'Forasmuch as . . . yt appeareth the infection doth increase . . . we thinke yt fytt that all manner of concourse and publique meetinges of the people at playes, beare-baitinges, bowlinges and other like assemblyes for sportes be forbidden.'[10] The plague continued unabated until late 1594 and it was not until 8 October in that year that Lord Hunsdon requested permission for his company (Shakespeare's) to be given permission to resume a winter season at 'the Crosse kayes in Gracious street'.[11] This long interruption caused a major reconstruction of the player companies. There were now no children's troupes, and after a short while it became apparent that the theatrical scene was to be dominated by two major companies who were to remain pre-eminent until the end of the reign. These were the Admiral's Men (under Philip Henslowe at The Rose) and the Chamberlain's Men (Shakespeare's group at The Theatre). Playing was now so successful that it was felt worth-while to build yet another playhouse beside The Rose on the south bank, The Swan (*c*.1595). These were stable and secure years for the companies, with playing normally running in an unbroken sequence of forty-two weeks, save for a lenten break, with an occasional summer tour of some eight weeks in the provinces.

In 1597, however, occurred an event which disturbed the profitable calm of this golden period. A new company, Pembroke's Men, performed a (lost) play *The Isle of Dogs* at The Swan, but this 'lewd plaie' was found by the Privy Council to contain 'very seditious and sclanderous matter' and, as a result, they 'caused some of the players to be apprehended and comytted to pryson, whereof one of them was not only an actor but a maker of parte of the said plaie'.[12] This was Ben Jonson, but he managed to establish his innocence by blaming his collaborators for the offensive parts of the play and thus escaped the loss of his ears. As a direct result of this political indiscretion the Privy Council, on 9 February 1598, sanctioned the existence of the Admiral's and the Chamberlain's Men, thus recognising their pre-eminence, but ordered the suppression of all other companies.

By now Shakespeare's fame had grown, as the testimony of Francis Meres makes clear:

As *Plautus* and *Seneca* are accounted the best for Comedy and Tragedy among the Latines: so *Shakespeare* amongst ye English is the most excellent in both kinds for the stage; for Comedy, witnes his *Gentlemen of Verona*, his *Errors*, his *Loves labours lost*, his *Loves labours wonne*, his *Midsummer night dreame*, & his *Merchant of Venice*: for Tragedy his *Richard the 2. Richard the 3. Henry the 4. King Iohn, Titus Andronicus* and his *Romeo and Juliet*.   (*Palladis Tamia*, 1598, p. 282)

The position of the Chamberlain's Men, with Shakespeare as chief purveyor of plays and three pre-eminent actors, Burbage (for tragedy) and Kempe and, later, Armin (for comedy), and the Admiral's, with an astute business manager in Philip Henslowe and a powerful dramatic talent in Edward Alleyn, seemed unassailable. As Gyles' health declined and his charges became more unruly and dishevelled only a seer might have predicted that within two years the Children of Paul's and the Children of the Chapel would once more seek to challenge the heavily capitalised and expansionist dramatic industry of the professional players.

The Mastership of Edward Pearce (11 May 1599–June 1612)

As the old year (1598) waned and the new began, so the Chamberlain's Men began to pull down The Theatre in Shoreditch and carried its timbers across the river to the south bank, where they used the materials to build the first Globe: for this location virtually all of Shakespeare's subsequent plays were designed. By the time this playhouse was fully functional, Paul's were on the verge of recommencing their dramatic activities under their new *de facto* master, although their former one was still installed in the almonry house.

As the 90s passed, so departed the calm and peaceful conditions which the playhouses had enjoyed. The new century opened competitively, for the Children of the Chapel Royal were re-established in a new building at the Blackfriars (1600) and the Admiral's Men, to meet the competition from the new Globe, built The Fortune playhouse within the city limits, between White Cross Street and Golding Lane. A contest of popularity emerged between the chorister and city companies and for a while the novelty of the children's revival made them the more successful. But the adults were by now established too firmly to be seriously inconvenienced: by 1602, when another company, Worcester's Men, was established at the Boar's Head, the Poets' War had been decisively won by the open-air professional stage. Before the old Queen died, however, a new conflict between stage and state arose, and this was even more serious than the *Isle of Dogs* affair.

On the night before their abortive insurrection, 8 February 1601, the supporters of Essex paid the Chamberlain's Men at The Globe for a performance of Shakespeare's *Richard II*: presumably they were attempting both to give themselves moral courage and to induce others to share their faith that the time was ripe to replace an old and ineffectual ruler by a young and vigorous pretender. The failure of the coup, an embarrassing fiasco, and the subsequent investigation caused a prohibition on playing and some probability that Shakespeare and his fellows would be arraigned for treason. They were, like Jonson earlier, successful in arguing their way out of trouble.

The Privy Council, however, grew sterner in its attitude to the playhouses, but still made an exception of the Admiral's and the Chamberlain's Men; in a sense these two companies were enjoying the unique privilege of an existence which the state was attempting to turn into a monopoly. On 31 December 1601 the Council reiterated its instructions to the Lord Mayor and Aldermen for 'th'expresse and streight prohibition of any more play howses then those two . . . charging and streightlie comaunding all suche persones, as are the owners of any the howses used for stage plaies within the cittie, not to permitt any more publique plaies to be used, exercised or shewed.'[13]

The return to favour of the player companies in general was not accomplished until the new reign began. In 1603 the Chamberlain's Men became the King's Men; the Admiral's Men, Prince Henry's Men; Worcester's Men, Queen Anne's Men and the Children of the Chapel Royal, the Children of the Queen's Revels – Paul's were not included in this general promotion. For the professional actors, however, royal recognition had now progressed so far that they were officially unfeed royal grooms. On 9 April 1604 the Privy Council directed the Lord Mayor and Aldermen that 'we thinke it . . . fitt, the time of Lent being now Passt, that your L. doe Permitt and suffer the three Companies of Plaiers to the King, Queene, and Prince publicklie to Exercise ther Plaies in ther severall and usuall howses for that Purpose, and noe other, viz. The Globe scituate in Maiden Lane on the Banckside in the Countie of Surrey, the Fortun in Golding Lane, and the Curtaine in Hollywell in the Cowntie of Midlesex, without any lett or interruption'.[14]

The ascendancy of the three adult companies at court was never seriously challenged by the choristers and quickly the two kinds of playhouse, the public (or those of the adult open-air theatre) and the private (those of the indoor chorister and ex-chorister company) became indistinguishable in terms of the age of the actors and the style of the plays. The royal recognition which they were all now enjoying, however, had its penalties, and in 1606 there came *The Act of Abuses*. This laid down a fine of £10 for any person or persons who in a stage play, 'Interlude, Shewe, Maygame, or Pageant jestingly or prophanely speake or use the holy Name of God or of Christ Jesus, or of the Holy Ghoste or of the Trinitie, which are not to be spoken but with feare and reverence'.[15] This led to the alteration of play texts, old and new, to avoid blasphemy; and in the following year the control further tightened when the Master of the Revels (the court official responsible to the sovereign for the regulation of entertainments both courtly and public) was given the power to license plays for publication, a practice formerly undertaken in a very amateur way by the Stationers' Company.

These were not easy years for the playhouses; frequently their seasons were badly interrupted by plague (as in 1603) and they were under increasing pressure from the preachers who campaigned, ever more urgently, for their suppression. In the case of Paul's the preachers may largely claim a victory. None the less, by 1605 a new playhouse (the Red Bull in Clerkenwell Fields) was built and in the following year the Whitefriars was established, just off Fleet Street. This was also the age of the finest flowering of the English drama, with Shakespeare's tragic period and the best plays of Marston, Jonson, Chapman, Middleton, Dekker, Webster, Tourneur. The majority of the finest of these dramas were owned and played by the King's and Prince Henry's Men.

In late 1596 James Burbage had bought premises within the precinct of the Blackfriars, and he intended 'to convert and turne the same into a comon playhouse'. The local residents, however, complained to the Privy Council, alleging 'a generall inconvenience to all the inhabitants of the . . . precinct, both by reason of the great resort and gathering . . . of all manner of vagrant and lewde persons . . . and allso to the great pestring and filling up of the . . . precinct, yf it should please God to send any visitation of sicknesse . . . besides the . . . playhouse is so neere the Church that the noyse of the drummes and trumpetts will greatlie disturbe and hinder both the ministers and parishioners in tyme of devine service and sermons'.[16] Burbage's endeavour was thus thwarted and he leased the premises to Henry Evans who contrived to evade the objections by establishing the 'private' Blackfriars house.

By 1609, however, the King's Men, who had long recognised the gradual changes taking place in public taste, were able to re-acquire the leasehold, and after the closure of Paul's and the failure of the Woodford/Rossiter Whitefriars venture they began playing at the Blackfriars and at The Globe. With Pearce quietly pensioned off and ownership of the Blackfriars premises now secured, they were wholly immune from competition from children's companies. Ironically, by the time Pearce died in 1612

The Globe had only one more year to exist; it burnt down in 1613 during a performance of *Henry VIII*. By this time Shakespeare had, of course, already retired. At no point during the ensuing Jacobean and Caroline periods, until the final closure of the theatres in 1642, did the children's drama re-emerge as a significant challenge to the established professional companies.

1

The decay of St Paul's

On 22 February 1631 the Bishop of London, William Laud, appealed to the Worshipful Company of Carpenters for a contribution towards

the repayre of ye decayes of St. Paules Church here in London . . . A greate dishono^r it is, not onely to this Cittye, but to ye whole State, to see yt ancyent and goodly pyle of buildinge soe decayed as it is, but it will be a farr greater, if care should not be taken to prevent ye fall of it into ruynes.[1]

That care was not taken and the decay progressively worsened; by January 1646 the condition of the parish church of St Gregory (attached to the south-west wall of the cathedral) was so serious that the Vestry instructed masons to 'demolysh all that part of the . . . church that is now standing and the same with the steeple being taken downe soe lowe as the Ground'.[2] Well might William Dugdale lament that the cathedral church of St Paul, 'rais'd, inricht, and beautified by the piety of our . . . Ancesters',[3] had become 'a wofull spectacle of ruine'.[4] Just how serious its condition became can be gauged from the description by Colonel William Webb, Parliamentary Surveyor-General for Bishops' Lands, of the Chapter House and its surrounding cloister, prepared in 1657:

The Roofe and ffloore of the . . . howse is fallen downe to the grownd, and lyeth on a heape wthin the Shell thereof wch only remaynes, The windowes broken to peeces, The Iron and leade Imbeziled, The whole building exceeding ruinous and very dangerous, And the wast grownd betweene the ffoundacon of the . . . cloysters and the . . . howse (for the most part) overspread wth soft stone and rubbish.[5]

This 'woeful spectacle' had gradually reached its hopeless condition by a combination of fire, rapacity, greed, encroachment by building, usage as a public thoroughfare, for 'the common highe waye' led 'owte of Powles churche yarde into Paules churche',[6] and the negligence of those entrusted with its preservation.

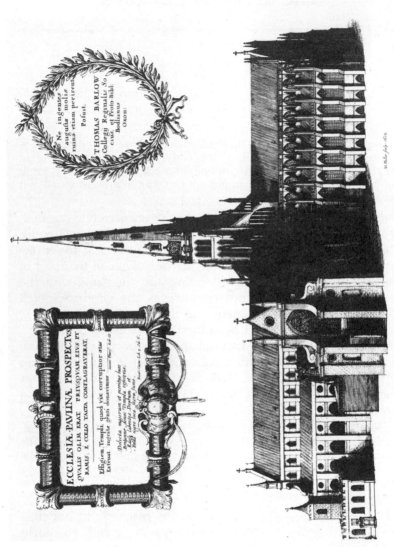

1 St Paul's Cathedral before 1561 (south face)

W. Hollar delin: et sculp

2 St Paul's Cathedral after 1561 (south face)

On 4 June 1561 'between one and two of the clock at afternoon, was seen a marvellous great fiery lightening'[7] which struck and damaged the steeple and roof of St Martin Ludgate [a church adjacent to the cathedral, to the west of Ave Mary Lane] and some witnesses affirmed 'that they saw a long and spear-pointed flame of fire, as it were, run through the top of the broche or shaft of Paul's Steeple'.[8] About two hours later smoke was seen coming from the steeple and suddenly 'the flame brake forth in a circle, like a garland, round about the broche . . . and increased in such wise that, within a quarter of an hour, or little more, the Cross and Eagle on the top fell down upon the South cross Ile'.[9] Various suggestions were advanced to stay the flames; some urged the use of gunpowder to demolish the steeple, others argued that part of the main roof of the church should be hacked away to create a fire break. The latter, more prudent, counsel prevailed, but it was to no avail, for 'the Church was of such height that they could not scale it, and no sufficient number of axes could be had: the labourers also being troubled with the multitude of idle gazers'.[10] It is perhaps not surprising that the workers could not scale the walls, for, according to John Stowe, the total height of the steeple was 520 feet, with some 260 feet being the height of the main facade.[11]

As a result of the failure to create a fire break, 'the fall of the Cross and Eagle fired the South cross Ile; which Ile was first consumed. The beams and brands of the Steeple fell down on every side and fired the other three parts: that is to say the Chancel or Quire, the North Ile, and the body of the Church. So that, in one hour's space, the broche of the Steeple was burnt down to the battlements; and the most part of the highest roof of the Church likewise consumed'.[12] Luckily the fire, despite burning fragments raining down like hail and drops of molten lead being blown across the neighbouring parishes, was contained within the churchyard of the cathedral. None of the vaults collapsed and while most of the timbers throughout the church were consumed and the lead melted, at least the two lower aisles of the choir and parts of the north and south aisles escaped entirely.[13]

A fund for the repair was initiated immediately by a donation of 1,000 marks from the Queen: in all, according to Dugdale, £6,702 13s 4d was collected.[14] At first the work was speedily executed, and 'within one moneth next following the burning . . . the church was covered with boordes and lead, in manner of a false Roofe against the weather, and before the ende of . . . the yeere, all the . . . Isles of the church were framed out of new timber, covered with leade, and fully finished'.[15] For the first month services were held in St Gregory's (which had escaped the fire), but the whole cathedral was permanently re-roofed by April 1566. There is, however, no doubt that a complete refurbishment of the church was not completed in the ensuing years, for when Sir Christopher Hatton wrote on 22 October 1584 requiring an inventory of all the 'timber, leade, Iron . . . tooles of Iron, weightes of brasse, and divers other pvisions [provisions] made for worke remayninge . . . after the fire'[16] the vergers replied that together with three beams of 30 feet, there were some 'fifteen loades or better' of timber and boards in one of the side chapels and an additional seventeen loads scattered in a variety of other stores, as well as quantities of lead, bell metal, iron, pulleys, ropes and scaffolding.[17] There seems to have been great assiduousness in the collection of the materials for the repair but less perseverance in the completion of the work, for while 'all the Roofs of timber . . . were perfectly finished and covered with lead . . . the Steeple, though divers modells were then made of it, was let alone'.[18] Similarly, some of the donated building materials were either lost or pilfered, and in 1598 Bishop Bancroft could still point out

that uppon the repaier of powles after itt was burnt there was much tymber left lead Iron and many ingions, pullies and other necessarye thinges to be used in buildinge, as also there beinge left greate store of Bell mettle and kept for the use of the Churche.[19]

Richard Smythe, verger, informed him that the bell metal 'that was found in St. Johns Chaple was sould [in 1593] to buy a Bell to hange in the steple';[20] and while some of the timber was given, lent or sold by Bishop Aylmer to the Lord Mayor, some yet remained, for in 'longe Chaple there is lyinge ould furr pooles and other ould lumber wch was laid there After the mendinge of the Churche when it was burned'.[21] This lumber had, apparently, not been moved for three or four decades. Some of the building materials, however, seem to have found themselves in the possession of the various cathedral officers, like the Master of Choristers who, in 1598, 'hath the possession of a great vaute under ye south side of the Churche wch he useth to laie in wood and other old lumber'.[22]

The problems that were encountered in maintaining the fabric of the cathedral and restoring it to an effective condition after the fire of 1561 were exacerbated by the fact that, since before the Reformation, the Dean and Chapter had been in the habit of leasing empty space in the churchyard to a profusion of merchants, shopkeepers, and priests. A lease typical of many was granted on 30 June 1545, by the Dean John Incent, to one William Bowman, citizen and stationer; for thirty years, in consideration of 5s per annum, he was allowed

all that theire voyde place and ground lying in Paules churche yarde, betwene the shede or shoppe of the bysshoppe of London adioynyng to the Southe dore of Paules by saynte Katheryns chapell wall on the northe ende, and the newe tenements of the sayd bysshope of London on thest ende, a longe by the southe ende of the said Saynte Kathernes Chappell walle and conteyneth in lengthe from the weste ende to the est ende xix foote, And in brede at the west ende frome the wall to the kynge hight way viij foote and an half. And at the est ende ij fote in brede from the wall towardes the kynge highe waye in wichye voyde place and grounde yt shal be leafull to . . . Willm Bowman to byld or make A Shedd or a shope, w'out hurting of the wall or wyndowes or the light of the same of the said Sainct kathernes Chapell.[23]

This small irregularly-sided area, of slightly less than one hundred square feet, was not strictly typical of the size and shape of the shops that were usual in the churchyard; most were smaller than this. The same Bowman was given a thirty-five year lease of another area, trapezium shaped, 11 feet, by $8\frac{1}{2}$ feet, by 9 feet, by 7 feet, in 1552 at the rate of over 1d per square foot, but this already had a shed upon it.[24] By the beginning of the reign of Elizabeth in 1558 most of the empty space, including the area inside the buttresses, had been leased and the values seem to have been fixed (they remained relatively constant during the next half century) at approximately 1d per square foot for 'voyde grounde'. Leases were granted for varying periods, but the term was not normally less than thirty-five years. Often stationers, leather-sellers, shirtmakers and others would pay this rate each year for the right to set up a stall in a space usually no larger than 12 feet by 6 feet.[25] This granting of numerous leases by the Dean and Chapter was clearly designed as a means of personal enrichment, although some of the revenues were used for the furtherance of the cathedral's business. They persisted in the practice despite the fact that,

while at the Reformation they had lost their 'endowed chari-
ties, obits, oblations at shrines, vestements, plate' and other
treasures, their estates and revenues had remained more or
less intact.[26] The result of their rapacity was further decay to
the cathedral fabric and annoyance to the worshippers within.

On 2 March 1586 John Pettley, carpenter, was leased an area
called The Green Yard as a reward for his work 'vewinge and
surveyinge of the decayes of the houses and tentes
[tenements]' of the Dean and Chapter. It was a twenty-one
year lease at 30s per annum and on the south side of the
church close to the east end. The lease included 'the neither
pte of the workinge howse, or store howse there and one
upper roome or chambre at and over the south ende of the said
workinge howse wth the stayers and stayre roome leading up
into the same roome or chambre and alsoe the saw pitt in the
same yard'.[27] By 1598, however, it was found that 'he hath . . .
made a Cesterne to receave the water w[ch] falleth from the
leades of the Chauncell w[ch] by reason that it hath not full
Current to passe throughe the greene yard by sutch yssue as it
hath done in former tyme yt sinketh into the walls of St
ffaithes Churche to the great annoyance of the foundation'.[28]
This water seepage was clearly a serious cause of the decay –
perhaps subsidence – of the fabric, but in Dugdale's view the
worst problem was created by 'the corroding quality of the
Coale smoake', from the chimneys of the shops and tenements
in the yard, and in his opinion it is to the latter that the decay
of Paul's was primarily due.[29]

All of the principal dignitaries of the cathedral, including the
Master of the Choristers, either owned outright or had a partial
share in various properties in the churchyard during the second half of the sixteenth century. On 28 November 1556
Sebastian Westcott, together with the other vicars choral, was
granted, 'for the better maintenance of them and their successors', for ninety-nine years 'a howse messuage or tenement
. . . adyoyning and lying unto the howse or mansyon of the
offyce of penytencyarye . . . sett lying and being in the west
pte of the churche yarde'.[30] The Master of the Choristers was
further enriched by a grant in the following year of a thirty
year lease for £20 6s 8d per year of Wickeham Paul manor in
Essex. This estate, fully planted with wheat, barley, oats and

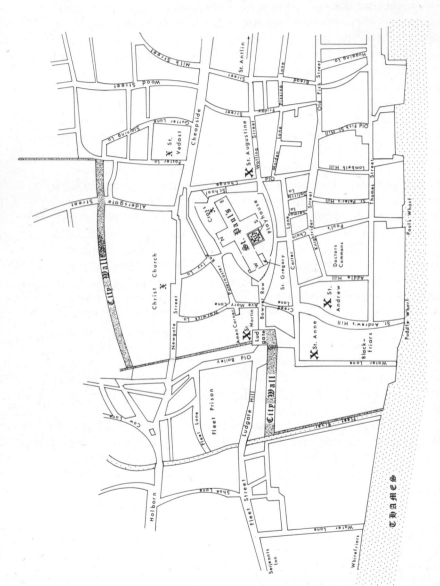

3 The setting of St Paul's Cathedral and playhouse in relation to the surrounding parishes

peas, of over three hundred acres, included five houses, each valued at £10, four oxen and sundry other farm animals.[31] From 1559, Westcott also enjoyed the use of the 'Almoner howse' which was 'situated and placed in the South part of the cathedral church of St Paul in London';[32] this grant was for sixty years or the term of his natural life and it became established, from this time onward, as a perquisite of the office of the Master of Choristers. It is this house to which he refers in his will of 14 April 1582, bequeathing to the use of the Masters of Choristers who shall subsequently live in it:

my cheste of vyalyns and vialles to exercise and learne the Children and Choristers there. And also one Table in the hall withe the frame, a settle of ioyned work, a payre of great iron Aundirons, there, the table, frame and settles, hanginges, wainscott, and Cupborde in the parlour there. The hanginges in mine owne chamber, the hanginges in the Chamber over the kytchen, The great chest and greate presse there the Cupboard and the greate chest at the stayers heade fyve bedsteedes fyve mattresses, fyve paire of blankettes, fyve bolsters of floxe fyve coverledes such as are accustomablie used for the Tenne Choresters . . .[33]

Clearly at this time the choristers resided in the almonry house along with their Master, who acted not merely as music instructor but also, in the modern sense, as 'house master'.

Westcott's successor, Thomas Gyles, however, allowed some encroachment upon this mansion for on 2 July 1596, the 'Almener especially movinge', a lease was granted to one William Creek, a lawyer and 'one of the procters of the Arches', of

three Chambers or Roomes as hee the said William hath now divided them, One belowe on the ground and twoe above (which said upper roomes are next the tyles and such whereof before nowe none was had or made) beinge parcell of the howse wherein . . . Thomas Giles now dwelleth belonginge to the Almener . . . and are situate lyinge and on ye west side of the . . . Almeners howse abutting on the Narrow streate or lane that leadeth downe from the lyttle sowthe dore of St. Paule . . . and adioyinge close to a Tenement which one Richard Smyth one of the ringers of the . . . Cathedral churche now holdeth occupieth and possesseth beinge lykewise parcell of the Almeners howse.[34]

The quarters of the choristers, assuming that there had been no change in the practice whereby they lived in the same house as their master, were becoming smaller and more crowded. Gyles also controlled five out of ten sheds or shops which were 'incroched in the Alley wch leadeth to the Churche at the little sowthe dore wch straights the passage on both sides of the waie'.[35]

These encroachments were serious and had been made despite an official clause in the document of appointment of the Master forbidding such subleases or redivisions of space within the house. In the document of appointment of Gyles' successor, Edward Pearce, the Master was specifically forbidden, 'under payne of forfeiture' of his office, to 'sett nor lett anie part . . . of the howse belonging to the Almener wherein Thomas Gyles the nowe Almener . . . nowe dwelleth'.[36] This prohibition against subletting did not, however, deter Pearce from obtaining from the Dean and Chapter a lease granted to John Bartholmew (alias Martyn), a saddler, on 15 May 1601 of a 'certayne shopp at the sowthwest end of the mansion howse belonginge to the Almener of Paules and being parcell of the said Mansion howse, situat lyinge and beinge wthin the parish of Sainte Gregorie'.[37] This was a small shop of some 6 feet square; it was 8 feet 10 inches high and the lease included two small stalls only 2 feet wide on each end. The leasehold was assessed at 33s 4d per annum for twenty-one years. By the beginning of the seventeenth century, then, the ground rent, at least in particularly choice locations (the stalls would be in the main thoroughfare up to the little south door) had risen very sharply. In this case a saddler's shop cost 6½d per square foot per year to lease. This sublease was not, of course, an infringement by Pearce on the almonry house itself for the stalls were outside it, but using its walls as their rear. No other encroachments were effected by Pearce on the house of the almoner during his tenure of that office and the Mastership of the Choristers.

The churchyard was enclosed by a wall, begun, according to Stowe, in 1316/17 in an attempt to reduce 'the murthers and robberies that were there committed': it was completed in the reign of Edward III, about 1343, 'and to this day [1598] it continueth. Although now on both the sides (to wit, within and without) it be hidden with dwelling houses'.[38] Paul's yard, during the second half of the sixteenth and the first half of the seventeenth century, was a cluster of jumbled shops and sheds (some little more than canvas-covered market stalls), tenements, and mansion houses (mostly subdivided into numerous narrow lodgings) which were often in a serious state of disrepair. In 1598 the house of the Sub-Dean, Hugh Andrews, was so 'greatlie decaied and in such bad Repacons that ye plummer will not mend the leades thereof for thirty poundes'; in addition the timbers were rotting and the 'kitchen . . . readie to dropp downe'.[39] Many of the buildings in the churchyard 'both houses shedds and shoppes built and inlarged since ye beginninge of her ma^ts Raigne . . . have incroched upon aunctient buriall ground',[40] and this encroachment was both above and below ground for some houses had added to their square footage by digging cellars under the church walls.[41] In 1598 John Stowe found that 'the South side of Saint Paules Churche, with the Chapter House (a bewtifull peece of woorke, builded aboute the rainge of Edward the third) is now defaced, by means of Lycences graunted to Cutlers, Budget makers, and other, first to build lowe sheddes, but now higher Houses which do hide that beautifull side of the Church, save only the toppe and South Gate'.[42] For at least one foreign sightseer in England's capital in 1592, St Paul's, the principal church of Anglican Christendom, although 'large and remarkable' with two churches one over the other (St Paul's and St Faith's), had otherwise 'nothing of importance to be seen'.[43]

Stowe's complaint that the perspective of the church had been destroyed by the gradual rise in the height of the buildings in the churchyard is amplified by the vergers in 1598 who point out that the windows of the side chapels were seriously obscured and often the carpenters, whose yards were on the outside walls of the cathedral, broke the glass in the windows while moving their lumber.[44] Further cause for complaint was that many of the original lessees had, instead of stalls and without permission, built dwellings on their 'voyde grounde' in the churchyard, and these were 'verie offensive for that they have digged sellers and made privies and raysed Chimneys in them'.[45] In addition to the building of these private facilities, another result of the gradual encroachment was that 'at the east end of the Chauncell a Comon privie [was] taken awaie, whereunto the schollers of Powles schoole, and the inhabitants there aboute used to resorte, whereby the Churche yard nere about the Crosse [i.e. the preaching cross, on the north-east corner] lyeth more like a laystall then a churche yarde'.[46]

On occasion Paul's churchyard was the scene of violence, sometimes officially approved, more often lawless. Henry Machyn records on 14 July 1562 that there 'was a grett sh[ooting of the] parryche of sant Gregores in Powlles Chyrche-yerd, [the one] halff agaynst the thodur; on syd had yelow [scarfs, and] thodur red skarffes, and a vj drumes and iiij fluttes'.[47] Some used it as a location for the settlement of private disputes: duels and deaths were not uncommon. In 1594 St Gregory's records the burial of Francis Bowd, gentleman, 'slayne in St. Pawles Churchyard'; the next year was buried 'John Pendringe, gentleman, who receaved his deathes wound by Poules cheyne in yᵉ street' and then, in August 1595, was 'John Partlett servingman slayne at the west ende of St. Pawles churche'.[48] Similarly in a place of such extensive public resort, unwanted children could be disposed of; there were many, like Nicholas, who was 'found upon a stall' in September 1575.[49] Those connected with the choristers were by no means immune from the violence about them. In 1598 Ambrose Goulding, Senior Cardinal and spiritual adviser and teacher of the choristers, advised Bishop Bancroft that his junior partner, William Maicocke, 'often tymes sollicited sondrie younge maides . . . amongst others one Elizabeth Brooke [the Goulding's maid servant] and hath groaped her forcibly sondrie tymes . . . and in like sorte hath watched her from tyme to tyme to ravish her in pardon Churche yarde'.[50] In addition on 5 May 1598 this same Maicocke 'did most outragiouslie beat . . . Jane [Goulding, the Senior Cardinal's wife] wᵗʰ such unpittious blowes as that she fell down dead [i.e. unconscious]' and his wife Marie did 'strike and wound . . . Elizabeth [Brooke] wᵗʰ a knife in the arme'.[51] Although allowance must obviously be made for the exaggeration of invective, since Ambrose Goulding's dispute with his junior partner was a quarrel with a long history and much notoriety,[52] it was through the churchyard that Hugh Andrews, the Sub-Dean, was often carried in the last decade of the sixteenth century, for he was

soe notorious a drunkard, as that in steed of subdean men Call him Cup deane, he is a Comon hawnter of Taverns wᵗʰout all moderacon, not for bearinge the daies wherein he administreth the holie Communion, he is many tymes so drunke, as that he is ledd, and divers tymes hath fallen downe the stayers . . . he hath byn so extreame drunke as that he hath byn faine to be brought home in a Porters baskett.[53]

24

Not an edifying spectacle for the choristers, who, perhaps as a result, were in the habit of going to taverns themselves.[54] Certainly the vicars choral had a reputation as carousers, for in *The Owles Almanacke* (1618) Dekker (if he is the author) remarks 'If the singing men of the Chappell of Powles, and of Windsor meete this yeare together in any one of the Court-cellers, I set it downe infallible as Fate, some hogshead or other must that day be knockd soundly' (p. 29). A hogshead contained over fifty gallons. Complaints about drunken musicians are a commonplace in the contemporary drama and the plays for Paul's are no exception, as in *The Wisdome of Doctor Dodypoll* where 'one of the Haultboyes' was 'out of tune' because the player was 'drunke' (B2). In *Jacke Drums Entertainment* 'liquor' has 'tript up' the 'heeles' of the Morris (B); in *West-ward Hoe* the fiddlers are too drunk to play (G3) and in *The Puritaine* the Captain tells Edmond to call in the musicians and 'licquor 'em a little'; Edmond agrees and declares that he will 'make ech of them as drunck as a common fiddeler' (H2).

A visitor to the cathedral, entering by either the great or little south door, would at once have been conscious that it was 'kept verie ill for Comonlie it is never wthout a muckhill in it as this last summer [of 1598] there was at ye steple dore a doinghill of the quantitie of iiij or v loades and likewise whensoever the churche is made cleane the muck is not Conveyed out'.[55] Clearly little attention was paid at Paul's to the *Homily for Repairing and Keeping Clean and Comely Adorning of Churches* of 1562, which argued and exhorted:

forasmuch as your churches are scoured and swept from the sinful and superstitious filthiness wherewith they were defiled and disfigured, do ye your parts, good people, to keep your churches comely and clean: suffer them not to be defiled with rain and weather, with dung of doves and owls, stares and choughs, and other filthiness, as it is foul and lamentable to behold in many places of this country. It is the house of prayer, not the house of talking, of walking, of brawling, of minstrelsy, of hawks, of dogs. Provoke not the displeasure and plagues of God for despising and abusing his holy house.[56]

The disorder inside St Paul's at the end of the sixteenth century had altered little from its state in the preceding decades, except to grow rather worse. It was traditionally the responsibility of the bellringers, under the jurisdiction of the vergers, to keep the church clean. Bishop Aylmer had, however, taken from them their principal source of income, the right to charge visitors an entrance fee to the steps leading up to the steeple (or blunt tower as it was after 1561). This fee farm had been given to one of Aylmer's own servants, 'By meanes of wch losse the bellringers became carelesse in their places, not givinge such attendance as before ty~ne was used and soe the . . . Churche, in verie short tyme wa͟ ͵ dailie pestered wth all kynd of abuses'.[57] By 1598 the bellringers had recovered this fee farm and their wives used to collect the money, but they did not resume their former responsibilities – the church remained unkempt.

One of the main obstacles to the better management of the cathedral was the continued use of the main aisles as a public 'throughfare of all kynd of burden bearing people as Colliers wth sackes of Coles Porters wth basketts of flesh'[58] and 'whoe not . . . suffered in speciall tyme of service, to Carrye and recarrie whatsoever, no man w^thstandinge them or gaynesayinge the[m]'.[59] Apart from this clutter of business, the whole cathedral stank; there was a 'verie ill savour greatlie preiudiciall to mens health',[60] a smell made up of a variety of odours: smoke from the chimneys of adjacent buildings, the smell from their privies, from the 'doggs [which] . . . Come in to defile the matt' upon which the vicars choral knelt to sing the Litany;[61] and the unpleasantness caused by the fact that 'drunkards [do] lie and sleepe upon the formes and aboute the quier dores, and other Idle and masterlesse people, where they doe verie often tymes leave all that is w^thin them verye loathsome to behould'.[62] The atmosphere was not made more savoury by the habit of 'boies . . . pissinge upon stones in the Churche, by st. ffaithes dore, to slide upon as uppon ysse'.[63] This behaviour was apparently emulated by the general public, for the Butler of the College of the Minor Canons was in the habit of 'suffering Captaines, Gamlers, and stranigers to drinke both bere and ale and tobacco in the petticannons haule in service tyme, and sermon tyme', with the result that 'by meanes of such resorte there is such fullsomenes as pissinge and other inormities that ye passages in and out to the College is both lothsome and verie unholsome and wilbe also verie danigerous to the health of us all especially yf any hotte weather Come for breedinge the infection of the plague'.[64] Some of these customers were well-to-do, for tobacco was not cheap;

the average price was 3d per pipeful, which is the price charged by Ursula, the pig woman, of *Bartholomew Fair* (II.ii.90).

It was in these conditions that divine service was celebrated – morning prayer was at 6 a.m. in the winter and at 5 a.m. in the summer.[65] The performance of the choristers, at least in 1598, was much hampered by the fact that the organ bellows were broken and, as a result, 'the wind is not sufficient to give sound to the Instrement'.[66] The boys' concentration could hardly have been improved by people walking in the upper choir, who stood in front of the Canons in their stalls,[67] 'wth their hatts on their heads Comonlie all the service tyme';[68] sometimes one of the choristers would be sent to find a verger to try to evict these idlers.[69] Other visitors, having paid the bellringers' wives, were suffered to 'goe up into the Steple where in tyme of divine service, they hallowe, throwe stones, and make great noyses, hard downe plainelie into the quire'[70] and there they would damage the fabric by carving their names in the wood, stone or lead, 'indeed the top of *Powles* conteins more names then *Stowes* Cronicle'.[71] But this thirst to preserve one's name 'in a coffin of lead' was not without its perils, for Dekker warns 'when you are mounted there, take heede how you looke downe into the yard; for the railes are as rotten as your great Grand-father'. From the vantage point of the steeple the thronging crowds of the aisles may well have struck some as a vista from Bedlam, sometimes etched more finely by the intrusion into the choir of 'lunatike psons [persons] and diseased psons, and Children, leaping and playinge'.[72]

The cathedral was thronged not by worshippers but by those who came to transact business; the crowds were attracted by the many services that Paul's could offer. Falstaff mentioned slightingly that he 'bought' Bardolph 'in Paul's' (*2 Henry IV*, I.ii.47) and servants were commonly hired there; it was usual for would-be servants or clergy to advertise their availability on the *Si-quis* door—as Joseph Hall rebukes his contemporaries,

> Saw'st thou ever *Siquis* patch'd on *Pauls* Church dore,
> To seek some vacant Vicarage before? . . .
> Come to the left-side alley of Saint Poules.[73]

There was other flesh for hire too. In 1598 the vergers expressed disquiet that the wife of Reignold Chunnell (one of the bellringers), 'a younge proper woman', along with the wife of Robert

Parker, the other bellringer, used to 'sett or stand openlie in the south yle of . . . the . . . Churche daile to take everie manns money for goinge up into the Steple, by reason whereof there is great occasion of suspicon: wch is not onelie a greate discreditt to ye younge women, but also a scandall to the Churche, Consideringe they be not ye best sorte of people that travaile that waie'.[74] This rather coy objection is probably the result of an unwillingness to admit that soliciting was practised in the cathedral. Certainly there seem to have been bawdy houses in the churchyard. In 1592 Edward Guilpin in *Skialetheia* remarks 'There in the window mistress minkes doth stand, / And to some copesmate beckneth her hand' (Diiii), and this takes place in Paul's yard. As far as the boys themselves were concerned, Philip Stubbes in 1583 had already suspected them (and players generally) of numerous fleshly offences; they 'in their secret conclaves (covertly) . . . play the Sodomits or worse'.[75] Later, in 1619, a certain I.H. in *The House of Correction*, said of a whore: 'Faine would she have beene a *Quorster* at *Paul's*, but that she loves not to stand in a *Surplesse*: yet many times she repayres thither, especially unto the *lower end of the Middle Ile*.'[76] While not willing to don the white shroud of the penitent, she would have been well placed as a chorister to solicit custom. This suggestion that soliciting was an activity not unknown to the boys themselves is not, to my knowledge, corroborated by any other witnesses. On the other hand the dramatists were well aware of the homosexual appeal of the youth and beauty of the Children of Paul's and this consciousness ranged from the crudity of Marston, in *Antonio and Mellida*, who named two of the youngest actors Dildo and Catzo – both Italian terms for penis – to the delicate fantasia of Lyly with his transformation of Gallathea from a boy/girl to a girl/boy. However, as Middleton pointed out, Ganymede was 'Ioves own Ingle' (male-bawd: *Blurt*, G4^v), and in *Poetaster* Tucca refuses to hire his players to Histrio because 'you'll sell 'hem for enghles' (III.iv.276) and Ovid Senior fears his son, who is stage-struck, is become 'an enghle for players' (I.ii.16). I.H. may be right.

The choristers were certainly personally involved in the general atmosphere of barter and aggressive commercialisation, for instead of studying their prayer books or bibles during the services they spent their time talking, playing and 'huntinge after spurr money where on they sett their whole mindes, and doe often abuse dive[rs] yf they will not bestowe some what on them'.[77] The boys went so far as to interrupt those at their prayers with their demands and refused to be put off, being aggressive enough to drive men out of the choir if they denied them their spur fee. This demand for spur money was a traditional right of the choir, who required all those entering the cathedral wearing spurs to pay a fine. Probably it was a lucrative source of income since in the last decade of the sixteenth century Creed Lane, on the south-west corner of the church-yard, was undergoing a metamorphosis into Spurrier Row – the London centre of the spurriers' trade.[78] What more natural a reaction to the purchase of a new pair of spurs than a walk through the adjacent main aisle of St Paul's where all of London congregated? Dekker's ironic advice to a gallant how to behave in Paul's Walk, in *The Guls Horne Book*, while exaggerated for effect, offers a vivid picture of the multitude of distractions for the choristers during the services:

Never be seene to mount the steppes into the quire, but upon a high Festivall day, to preferre the fashion of your doublet, and especially if the singinge boyes seeme to take note of you: for they are able to buzze your praises, above their *Anthems* if their Voyces have not lost their maiden-heads; but be sure your silver spurres dogge your heeles, and then the Boyes will swarme about you like so many white butter-flyes when you in the open *Quire* shall drawe forth a perfumd embrodred purse, (the glorious sight of which, will entice many Countrymen from their devotion to wondring) and quoyt Silver into the Boyes hands, that it may bee heard above the first lesson.[79]

Dekker may not be exaggerating much, for the 1598 Visitation Report makes it clear that the choristers might well have dropped their books in unison and run off to challenge an obvious rich 'mark' in spurs.

Francis Osborn speaks of how it was the fashion in the reign of James I for 'men of all professions not merely Mechanick, to meet in Paul's Church by eleven, and walk in the middle Ile till twelve, and after dinner from three to six, during which time some discoursed of Businesse, others of Newes'.[80] William Dugdale points out that it was here 'where each Lawyer and Serjeant at his Pillar heard his Client's Cause, and took notes thereof upon his knee'.[81] It is hardly surprising that so usual and familiar a location should often be the scene for the action in contemporary plays: Act I Scene i of Middleton's *Michaelmas Terme* and Act II Scene i of Dekker and Webster's *West-ward Hoe* are set in the middle aisle at Paul's; both of these plays were in the repertoire of the Paul's Boys Company. Middleton's Rearage and Salewood, in *Michaelmas Terme*, plot to pluck Easy, an obvious 'pigeon', in Paul's, and in the same play Mother Gruel comes to Paul's looking for her wayward son. It was a place of sanctuary, however, as well as exploitation, for, as Dekker points out, in Paul's Walk (especially close to Duke Humphrey's tomb – actually, the tomb of Sir John Beauchamp – which was in the main aisle) there was security from creditors:

the Dukes Tomb is a Sanctuary, and will keepe you alive from wormes and land-rattes . . . there you may spend your legs in winter a whole after-noone, converse, plot, laugh, and talke anything, iest at your Creditor, even to his face, and in the evening, even by lamp-light, steale out, to cozen a whole covy of abhominable catch-pols.[82]

Criminals could hide in the church too: Greene makes this clear in *A Dispute Betweene a Hee Conny-catcher, and a Shee Conny-catcher*. When officers attempt to arrest a farmer at the west end of the church, a cut-purse who has engineered the arrest as part of an elaborate theft, raises a hue and cry, exclaiming:

you are wrongd honest man, for hee hath arrested you here in a place of priviledge, where the Sherifes nor the Officers have nothing to do with you . . . yet shall hee not offer the Church so much wrong, as by yeelding to the Mace, to imbollish Paules libertie . . . the Prentises arose, and there was a great hurly burly.[83]

Cut-purses had much custom in Paul's Walk and they were safe from arrest. This must have added to the hazards of doing business there. Greene describes, in *The Blacke Bookes Messenger*, how one Ned Brown operated:

as soone as the throng grew great, and that there was Iustling in Paules for roome, I stept before the Gentleman and let fall a key, which stooping to take up, I staid the Gentleman that he was faine to thrust mee, while in the presse two of my freends foisted his purse, and away they went withall.[83]

It was hazardous in these conditions to risk a visit to the theatre, for

at plaies, the Nip [Cut-purse] standeth . . . leaning like some manerly gentleman against the doore as men go in, and there finding talke with some of his companions, spieth what everie man hath in his purse, and where, in what place, and in which sleeve or pocket he puts the boung and according to that so he worketh either where the thrust is great within, or els as they come out at the dores.[83]

Aside from those seeking professional advice or sanctuary, there were many who came to the cathedral to shop, for not merely were there numerous retail businesses in the churchyard (by 1582 there were at least twenty-five booksellers established there[84]) but also a number of shops inside the cathedral itself. They ranged from that of a glazier set up in a chapel at the extreme end of the south aisle, who was in the habit of bringing his raw glass into the church during the services with a horse and cart, which damaged the steps so badly that 'many men and woemen have had shrewde fales divers tymes especialie in frostie weathe[r] where the stepp be slipperie and the stones lying aslope',[85] to trunkmakers who had hired the lower cloisters (around the Chapter House) from the Master of the Choristers and turned them into a 'Comon laystall for boardes trunckes and Chests . . . whereby meanes of their dailie knockinge and noyse, the Churche is greatlie disturbed'.[86] Most of the side chapels were let as shops: there were bookbinders, schoolteachers, joiners, carpenters, stationers, mercers and hosiers. At least some of their shops were open for business on Sundays and during weekday services, and after shopping one could refresh oneself with tobacco, beer and ale in the minor canons' buttery. Alternatively one might well combine business with pleasure: after consultation with a client, a young lawyer would have had little hesitation in stepping into the adjacent theatre.

The cathedral, then, functioned as an Elizabethan version of an indoor shopping mall. While the shoppers were protected from the worst of the weather, despite the fact that most of the side-chapel windows were broken,[87] walking was somewhat hazardous, for, apart from the stones thrown by those in the steeple, 'the pavinge of the great middle Ile of the Churche is broken and lyeth verie uneven'.[88] According to Dekker, this did not deter people from across the whole spectrum of contemporary society from congregating there:

For at one time, in one and the same ranke, yea, foote by foote, and elbow by elbow, shall you see walking, the Knight, the Gull, the Gallant, the upstart, the Gentleman, the Clowne, the Captaine, the Appel-squire, the Lawyer, the Usurer, the Cittizen, the Bankerout, the

Scholler, the Begger, the Doctor, the Ideot, the Ruffian, the Cheater, the Puritain, the Cut-throat, the Hye-men, the Low-men, the True man and the Thiefe: of all trades and professions some, of all Countryes some.[89]

The authorities were conscious of the abuses to which St Paul's was subject and frequent edicts were pronounced to remedy the worst of the ills. On 5 August 1554, the Lord Mayor had declared:

Forasmuch as the material temples or churches of God were first ordained and instituted and made in all places for the lawfull and devout assembly of the people there to lift up their hearts and to laud and praise Almighty God, and to hear His Divine Service and most holy Word and Gospel sincerely said, sung and taughte and not to be used as market places, or other profane places, or common through-fares with carriage of things; and that now of late years many of the inhabitants of this City of London and other people repairing to the same, have and yet do commonly use and accustom themselves very unseemly and unreverently; the more is the pity to make the common carriage of great vessels full of ale and beer, great baskets full of bread, fish, fruit, and such other things, fardles of stuff and other gross wares through the Cathedral Church of St. Paul . . . and some in leading of horses, mules, or other beasts through the same . . . Be it therefore . . . ordained . . . that no manner of person or persons, either free of the . . . city or foreign, of what estate, condition, or degree soever he or they be, do at any time from henceforth carry or convey, or cause to be conveyed or carried through the . . . Cathedral Church of St. Paul any manner of great vessel or vessels, basket, or baskets, with bread, ale, beer, flesh, fruit, fish, fardells of stuff, wood billets, faggots, mule, horse, or other beasts, or any other like thing or things.[90]

Although fines were laid down, from 3s 4d for a first offence to 10s and two days' imprisonment for repeated violations, the edict had no effect: a main traffic artery of London simply refused to be regulated. The description of the cathedral emerging from the complaints of the officers to Bishop Bancroft in 1598 makes it clear that, while details would vary from time to time, in the main the situation as described then held good for the state of the church in the second half of the sixteenth century and, as other witnesses confirm, in at least the opening years of the next century. As Thomas Harrould grumbled in 1599 to Bishop Bancroft:

The nursing faulte of all theis disorders is because after oᵣ complaynt the followeth no amendinge, as thoughe yoᵣ visitation were held rather for forme sake then to reforme, for theis disorders have byn most oft the Complayned on at everie visitacon and yet Continue in their ould irregularitie.[91]

The transition from an early childhood in rustic isolation to this environment by forced impressment must often have been traumatic for boys who were no more than six or seven. The Masters of the Choristers were empowered to 'take upp suche apte and meete children, as are most fitt to be instructed and framed in the arte and science of musicke and singing, as they may be had and founde out with in anie place of this our Realme of England or Wales'. This was the authorisation granted to Gyles in 1585, and Westcott's was similar: no refusal by child or parent was tolerated, no 'letts, contradictions, staye or interruption'[92] was allowed to interfere with the 'press' by Gyles and his deputies. Thomas Tusser, born and brought up initially in Wallingford, Oxfordshire, tells how,

> . . . for my voyce, I must (no choice)
> Away of force, like posting horse,
> For sondrie men had placards then
>   Such childe to take:
>
> The better breste, the lesser reste,
> To serve the Queene, now there, nowhere
> For tyme so spent I may repent,
>   And sorrow make.

His grief at this sudden wrenching from a familiar environment was, at least in later life, assuaged by a consciousness of the opportunities for advancement that had been presented:

> But mark the chance, myself to 'vance,
> By friendship's lot to Paule's I got;
> So found I grace a certain space
>   Still to remain
>
> With Redford there, the like nowhere
> For cunning such, and virtue much,
> By whom some part of Musick's art
>   So did I gain.[93]

Having passed his audition, Tusser was taken under the tutelage of John Redford, who preceded Sebastian Westcott as Master of Choristers, and he obviously showed Tusser kindness and offered him a musical education of outstanding quality. Tusser would, no doubt, have been one of those choristers under Redford who sang, between Christmas and Easter,

> Be as merye as you ca[n]
> So you maye please both god and man

and then, from Easter to Whitsuntide,

> Let us all now joye & singe
> Be merye all in Christs risinge.[94]

Both choral phrases were composed and conducted by Redford for his pupils.

This close attention to the musical education of the choristers, both vocal and instrumental, was continued by Redford's successors. It was Sebastian Westcott who was appointed to take over from him at the beginning of the reign of Mary and he was granted the office of 'Elemosinarie' [i.e. Almoner, which was held jointly with the Mastership of Choristers] as a reward for the excellent service he had already given both as a vicar choral and as music teacher to the boys. He had clearly proved his worth as Master of Choristers prior to the offer of appointment: the office was granted 'pro termino vito suo naturalis in tam amplis modo et forma' as John Redford had enjoyed. He was confirmed in this office at the beginning of the reign of Elizabeth in 1559, and his document of appointment was at this time further elaborated to include the possession of the almoner's house[95] in exchange for which he was required to provide, at his own expense, food, clothing and all other necessities for the choristers during the whole period of their residence in the cathedral choir.[96] This requirement was one which had been traditionally assumed by the Master of Choristers, but it was now given a new official status.

In his will Sebastian Westcott makes special provision for superannuated choristers: those whose singing days were over were left a legacy of 20s each (they were still, in 1582, maintained by the Master). In this concern for boys whose usefulness as choristers has ceased, Westcott is continuing the medieval practice which from the early fourteenth century had recognised the need to provide for their maintenance, at least for some limited period. In 1318 the will of Richard de Newport, Bishop of London, provided funds to maintain one or two of these superannuated boys, 'when they shall change their voices provided they have no other exhibition'.[97] Similarly, during the reign of Henry IV, in the first decade of the fifteenth century,

Thomas Evere gave 30s 'to the poore choristers of Paules towards their exhibicion in the University'.[98] The pre-Reformation practice recognised the responsibility of the Master and the Dean and Chapter in caring for choristers after puberty, by making provision for their maintenance and for their subsequent education; there is every reason to believe that this practice continued in almost exactly the same way after the Reformation. Thomas Tusser went to Eton after his days as a singing boy were over, apparently as a result of the efforts of John Redford.[99] Thomas Morley, who was a chorister under Westcott and listed in the choir in 1574, was at that time seventeen: clearly he was one of the superannuated boys but he was still maintained and, although this was perhaps exceptional, continued to be listed as one of the ten choristers on the foundation. Thomas Ravenscroft, another musician of later fame, left the choir in about 1604 and went up to Cambridge to read music.[100] It remained, then, normal practice for the Master of Choristers, during the tenure of Redford, Westcott, Gyles and Pearce, to provide for their charges after their singing days were finished, and it was also customary for at least some of these older boys to continue to be maintained for two years or more, until provision for their future could be secured. As far as plays were concerned this provided a source of older, well trained ex-choristers. When they eventually left the St Paul's cathedral establishment some may well have become full-time scholars of St Paul's Grammar School, others went straight to the universities.[101]

Sebastian Westcott's will with its legacy of violins and viols (a six or seven stringed instrument played with a bow) for the boys' musical education makes it clear that he did not neglect their training. Claude Desainliens (alias Claudius Holyband) in *The French Schoole-maister* of 1573 testifies that the Paul's choir was outstandingly good: in his dialogue of a tour in London, with a facing French translation, his foreign visitor, entering St Paul's, exclaims, 'Harken, I doo heare a sweet musick: I never heard the like.' His English guide responds by urging, 'See whether wee may get to the quier, and wee shall heare the fearest [fairest] voyces of all the cathedrall churches in England.' His visitor is easily persuaded: 'I beleeve you: who should have them, if the Londonners had them not?', and concludes by agreeing that to 'tell the trueth, I never heard better singyng' (pp. 74–6). Later, when Bishop Bancroft inquired about the competence of the choir in 1598, he was assured that 'those that have skill in musicke'[102] would testify to its excellence: Thomas Gyles, whatever his other failings as Master, did not neglect the musical education of his charges. It was in his document of appointment that it was first laid down as a specific condition that he should instruct the boys 'in the arte and knowledge of musick, that they may be able, thereby, to serve as Quiristers in the . . . Churche'.[103] Gyles' assiduous attention to this injunction was emulated by his successor, Edward Pearce. Thomas Ravenscroft, the lutenist and composer, describes, in the Preface to his *Briefe Discourse* of 1614, his early experiences as a chorister at Paul's:

Maister *Edward Pearce* the first, sometimes Maister of the Children of Saint *Poules* in London, and there my Master, a man of singular eminency in *his Profession*, both in the *Educating of children* for the ordering of the *Voyce* so, as the Quality might afterward *credit* him and *preferre* them: And also in his those his *Compositions* to the Lute, whereof, the world enioyes many, (as from the *Maister* of that Instrument) together with his skilfull Instructions for other Instruments too, as his fruits can beare him witnesse.[104]

This testimony, although spoken of Edward Pearce, would equally have applied to any of his three predecessors: in whatever other ways they were venal or remiss, in their care for the choral and instrumental music in the cathedral the Dean and Chapter fulfilled their office as faithful servants. It was usual, indeed, for the Master of Choristers not to be officially appointed until he had proved his ability by teaching the boys without the perquisites of office. Westcott had done so, and so had Gyles, who seems to have acted as unpaid Master of Choristers for the two years between Westcott's death in April 1582 and his own official appointment on 22 May 1584.[105] Pearce's case was different, for he was given official status as Master while Gyles was still living but so ill as to be unable to carry out his functions.[106] Gyles retained most of the emoluments of his office and continued to live in the almonry house until his death in 1600. In effect, Pearce, although regularly appointed, acted as Master but without all the perquisites of his office from 11 May 1599 until July 1600, but did not relinquish his position in the Chapel Royal until 15 August 1600.

The formal requirement that the Master was responsible for the material welfare of the choristers first appears in 1559, with the confirmation of Westcott's position at the accession of Elizabeth, and its terms were further elaborated for Thomas Gyles, who was required

> of his owne proper cost and Charges, [to] provide as well convenient and cleane choyce of surpless as also all other manner of apparell as gownes coates cappes and dubletts Chaunge of sheetes, hosen shoes, and all other necessaries, holsome and sufficient diet, holsome and cleane beddinge, wth all thinges nedefull for them and in their sickenes shall see them well looked unto and cherished and procure the advise and helpe of Phisitians or Surgians if neede so requier.[107]

Gyles was unfortunate enough to lose four of his charges, despite the help of physicians, between November 1593 and September 1594, a period of severe plague infestation: William Noblett (alias Loblee), William Rawlyns, Thomas Quiddington and Giles Jennynges were all buried during this period from the parish church of St Gregory.[108] But only one other boy was lost by him, Anthonie Hitchman, who was buried on 20 April 1598. Pearce was more fortunate: despite the great plague year of 1603 when the old Queen died, he had lost none of his charges to disease by 1606.

The need for the developing elaboration of the terms and conditions of the Masters' obligations stems from the gradual attempt by the Dean and Chapter to correct the deficiencies left in the organisation of the choir by the despoiling of the church at the Reformation. In 1507 it had been the responsibility of the Guild of Jesus to clothe the choristers, and their statutes enjoin that the Wardens

> shall paie and yerely deliver unto the Maister of the Armery . . . at the ffest of Midsomer every yere iiij£, ffor and to thentent that the same Maister small emploie and bestowe the same iiij£ upon wollon clothe: and the same clothe he shall distribute and do to be made in tenne gownes, mete for the . . . tenne Queresters, to be worn at ffestivall dais.[109]

If the Master fails in his duty, he is to be fined 10s for every gown missing. In these pre-Reformation days the boys were paid 4d each for taking part in the processions on the day of the

Transfiguration – no doubt in later days they made up for this loss of revenue by extra efforts in the collection of spur money. During the brief re-embracement of England by Rome the Wardens' accounts for the Guild in 1553/4 record a payment to Westcott of 26s 8d for 'keeping of the *Salus* dayly in the . . . Crowdes [i.e. in St Faith's church] after Complyn doon in the . . . Cathedral Churche before the Images of Jhu, our blessed Lady, and Seint Sebastyan'.[110] Gradually, however, as the Elizabethan settlement took firmer effect the entire responsibility for the welfare of the boys was shifted to the Master.

By the latter part of the sixteenth century, the only survival of the pre-Reformation arrangements was the continuance of the requirement that the Senior and Junior Cardinals (two of the minor canons) should instruct the boys in the principles of the Christian religion: in 1598, at least, they were supposed to catechise the choristers weekly, but were negligent in so doing although they were frequently in their company.[111] They were further required to report any of the choristers who were delinquent to the Dean. In actual fact, however, it was the Master who was essentially responsible for the choir and it was his obligation to ensure that they were taught 'as well in the principles and groundes of Christian religion, contayned in the littell Catechisme [of Dean Nowell] set out by publique auctouritie and after when they shalbe older in the middle Catechisme and in writinge'. He was further enjoined to ensure that they be brought up in 'all vertue, civility and honest manners'.[112] In this respect the post-Reformation requirements did not differ greatly from the earlier practice, for the Master in the fourteenth century was required to bring them up 'in morum disciplina' and to ensure that they were taught both singing and 'literatura' so that they might be fit to serve as choristers in the cathedral church.[113]

There is effectively a conflation, in records of the first half of the sixteenth century and earlier times, between the boys who were pupils of St Paul's grammar school and the boys who composed the cathedral choir:[114] in the era before the Reformation there was a substantial overlap between them. After the refounding of Paul's School in the first decade of the sixteenth century by Dean Colet this association, obscured and interrupted as it was to be by the confusions of the Reformation, becomes once more clarified when, by the decade of the eighties and probably earlier, the practice was once more established whereby the choristers were part-time pupils of the grammar school. Gyles is instructed by the Dean and Chapter:

> when the children shall be skilfull in musicke, that they shall be able convenientlye to serve the Churche that then . . . Thomas shall suffer them to resorte to paules schole tow howers in the forenone and one hower in the afternone, from the feast of the annunciation of the blessed virgin St. Mary untill the feast of St. Michael tharchaungell every yeere, and one hower in forenone, and one hower in the afternone from the feast of St. Michaell the Archaungell ev^{r}ye yeere likewise (the howers for divine service onely excepted) that they may learne the principles of gramer, and after as they shall be forwardes learne the catechisms in Laten wch before they learned in Englishe and other good bookes taught in the . . . Schole.[115]

The 'other good books' for the lower school in 1559, during Westcott's Mastership, included Terence, Aesop's fables, Barbard's dialogues and a study of grammar; in the upper school they studied the epistles of Cicero, Vergil's Bucolics, Terence (but not, apparently, Plautus) and Baptista Mantuanus (whose works were still part of the curriculum in 1600). In addition they were taught grammar and practised translations from and into Latin; Greek was not, at this time, part of the curriculum.[116] Westcott's pupils would have read at least some of these books; and probably the syllabus in the time of Gyles and Pearce was similar, with the addition of Greek, for by 1568, under John Cooke (High Master 1559–73), this was added to the curriculum.[117] During his tenure the boys also studied Vergil's *Aeneid*, Ovid's *Metamorphoses* and Sallust's *Catiline*[118] as well as Dean Nowell's catechisms: *A catechism, or first instruction of christian religion* and *A catechisme, or institution of christian religion, to bee learned of all youth next after the little catechisme, appointed in the Book of Common Prayer*; the Latin version was the *Catechismus, sive prima institutio disciplinaq[ue] pietatis christianae*. Nowell's original Latin version was for senior choristers and the English versions (translated for general use by Thomas Norton) were for juniors. Since the choirboys had only three hours of schooling, apart from music, in the winter and two hours in the summer – perhaps even less when they were acting – their education must have been not merely more fragmentary but also rather more disconnected than that of the regular pupils of the grammar school. No doubt, however, a special shortened syllabus was established for these part-time pupils.

Gyles was also enjoined to ensure that his pupils were brought up with a respect for their social superiors and an acceptance of the moral values of their day. If the Dialogue written for the examination of the scholars of the grammar school in 1585/6 by the then High Master, John Harrison, may be used as an indication of Gyles' views of proper conduct, a boy is strictly forbidden to

sometymes go to the bowlinge alley, sometymes to beare baytinge, sometimes to see playes and tumblers for his recreation and sometymes beare his friends companie to ye taverne and such bawquets.[119]

The boy who spoke these words in the character of one Ludio added, rather wistfully, 'for my prt he shall have my voyce to take more libertye and lesse paynes yf he [the Master] woulde but give us leave to play oftener than we doe'.[120] Since this Dialogue was prepared for the annual testing of the boys (and their instructors) by the examiners appointed by the Mercers' Company, its value as testimony may be idealistic rather than real. In 1598 the picture that emerges from the *Visitation Report* prepared for Bishop Bancroft suggests that most of the injunctions of John Harrison were not being observed. Among other complaints John Howe, a verger, objected to 'the M[rs] of Powles Schoole, and other schoole masters nere adioyninge to the Churche for sufferinge their Children to plaie in the Churche yard whereby the windowes are broken, and well disposed people in the churche disquieted at the time of divine service'.[121] Ludio had, apparently, got his wish.

The choristers were among those who suffered the 'disquiet', for they were reasonably assiduous in attending the regular services,[122] but not so consistent in being present at all the special divinity lectures and sermons on Sundays and holy days. They were required to process into the church 'two and two in devout order' and were expected to wear clean surplices and have their other apparel 'decent w[th]owt tearinge and totters';[123] in fact it was reported, in 1598, that they were

well instructed and fitt for their places and they doe diligentlie keepe theire accustomed howers in repayringe unto divine service, they come to the Churche in decent order, but they have not their gownes lyned as in former tymes was used, their surplice are most Comenlie uncleane, and their apparrell not in such sorte as decencie becometh as we are informed they have sufficient allowance of meat and drinke.[124]

Gyles was neglectful of their outer garb, but did not starve his boys; this lack of attention to their appearance and conduct at this time finds further reflection in their habit of going to taverns, but at least they had not been overtly drunk or quarrelled much in the recent past.[125] One must assume, however, that drunkenness and quarrelling were not unknown among the choristers. In 1598, in addition to playing and seeking spur money during the services, the boys were often late in attendance and sometimes left in a body before the office was completed.[126] They were also, apparently, trying to gain extra allowances by failing to light enough candles to see their music for evening prayer. There is no direct evidence that they frequented bear-baiting, bowling alleys or tumbling shows but the general lack of supervision suggests that if they had so wished no obstacle would have prevented them. As for plays, there were some amateur players within the cathedral precincts in 1597, for it is reported that in January of that year

certain weoman would have a maske to make themselves famouse Robert Parkers wief the bellringer [who took pennies at the steeple door] Edward Smythes wife Edward Owens wife and ii of Mr. Sleggs daughters Marie and Honor [all residents of the tenements in the churchyard]. Theise daunced at Sleggs till about xii of the clocke in the nyghte and then came downe and daunced in the College yarde with their minstrells and in the end went to the College gate [the College of the Minor Canons] wch being locked accordinge to order theise maskers breake open most auditiouslie.[127]

The choristers in the almonry house may well have been disturbed by the ensuing commotion.

Gyles (like his predecessors and successors) had ten choristers under his control. For their support, apart from the almonry house, there was the sum of £50 per annum from the Dean and Chapter and £20 per annum from the rent of certain other almonry houses.[128] In addition he had at his disposal the letting of five sheds or stalls, all of which were 10 feet 7 inches by 23 feet 5 inches, in the alley leading up to the little south door;[129] £3 12s per annum from the rental of tenements in Paternoster Row;[130] part of the rent from a house at the west end of the Chapter House wall;[131] the use of a vault under the choir

41

and chancel on the south side of the church; he held keys to the cathedral and had exclusive control of the upper and lower cloisters and the Chapter House garth (these cloisters, a covered area of some 4,000 square feet, were let to trunkmakers).[132] Excluding the unknown value of the rent from the house at the west end of the Chapter House wall, and allowing a conservative value of 1d per square foot for the other rentals, this amounts to an additional £22 without any allowance made for the higher cost of leasing other than 'voyde ground', for the covered cloisters would surely have rented for more than the basic rate. The *Visitation Report* of 1598 makes it clear that most, if not all, of these fees were perquisites of the office of Master of Choristers, rather than personal possessions of Thomas Gyles. In view of this general affluence, the ragged state of the choir at the end of the sixteenth century was probably due to parsimony, and Gyles appears not to have been averse to making extra income from 'transfer fees' of certain choristers to other choirs, a practice against which his successor is specifically warned. Edward Pearce is cautioned

not at any tyme during his . . . estate and tenure [to] consēt to the selling or shifting awaye of anie Chorister of the . . . Cathedrall Churche for money or for anie other reward or consideracon.[133]

This recognition of the value of a chorister as worthy of sale or theft was known early, for before December 1575 'one of Sebastianes boyes being one of his principall plaiers [was] lately stolen and conveyed from him'; the Privy Council required that 'such persons as Sebastian holdeth suspected' should be examined.[134] The outcome is not known, but perhaps the boy was stolen in anticipation of the setting up of the first Blackfriars company in 1576. This testimony does, however, establish the existence of the Paul's company as actors known to a wide public, with principal players recognised prior to 1575. The lack of care by Gyles for these valuable properties in 1598 was due, he explained, to chronic illness; he was too sick to report on the choir to Bishop Bancroft and he never recovered.

It was out of this state of economic exploitation, the neglect and decay of office in pursuit of personal gain, and the gradual disintegration of the fabric about them, that there took place the metamorphosis of ten choristers into, first, the primary purveyors of dramatic entertainment to the court and the higher echelons of Elizabethan society and, second, popular entertainers of such success, fame and energy that the powers of both the Privy Council and the courts were needed to curb their enthusiasm. Although neglected and unruly at the end of the sixteenth century, it was this group of young men who, under their three masters, Westcott, Gyles and Pearce, played a formative role in the development of the commercial exploitation of the drama in Renaissance England.

2

Paul's playhouse

In the *Repertories of the Court of Common Council*[1] on 8 December 1575, a complaint was lodged against the Master of the Choristers at Paul's, on the grounds that

this Courte ys enformed that one Sebastian that wyll not communycate with the Church of England kepethe playes and resorte of the people to great gaine and peryll of the Coruptinge of the Chyldren with papistrie	
master Morton to goe unto the Deane of Powles	And therefore Master Morton ys appoynted to goe to the Deane of Powles and to gyve him notyce of that dysorder, and to praye him to gyve suche remeadye

therein, within his iurysdyccion, as he shall see meete, for Christian Relygion and good order.

This Westcott was clearly an obstinate heretic[2], dangerously likely to poison the minds of the choristers committed to his charge; also he was making money, since he had had the bright notion of 'keeping plays' – quite inappropriate for a Papist.

This complaint of December 1575 clearly refers to a practice already successfully and popularly established: thus Sebastian Westcott had by now organised a company of players performing regularly in the same location, on a professional basis. It is true, of course, that companies of players had preceded him in this kind of enterprise by hiring halls, inns or churches for seasons of drama and the investors in The Theatre (1576), and the (first) Blackfriars (1576) must have been planning their undertakings for some time before they actually opened; but Westcott seems to have established the first regular playhouse in the City of London.

These plays were successful enough to attract considerable audiences and to afford 'great gaine'; but where were they performed? Did the choristers, under Westcott, operate a playhouse in the sense we now know it? Did the Children of Paul's act in a building specifically designed or converted for the drama? If so, was this building used until 1582 when Sebastian

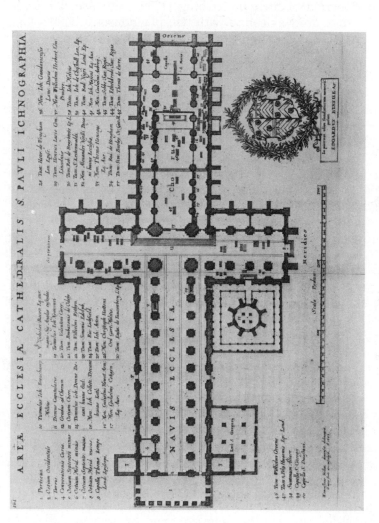

4 St Paul's Cathedral, ground plan

Westcott died and again by his successor, Thomas Gyles, until about 1590/1 when the dramatic activities of the choir were repressed by the Privy Council? Did the actors of Paul's in the second period of their flourishing (1599–1608) use this same structure or are we dealing with two playhouses at Paul's, like the two separate locations for the Blackfriars?

For some the multiplicity of questions and the scarcity of answers create an insoluble difficulty. H. N. Hillebrand declared, in exasperation:

When we try to fix the place in which the Paul's boys set up their theatre, we are met everywhere with the most baffling uncertainty . . . [but eventually he settles for an unspecified residence] in the northwest part of the south church-yard.[3]

He locates the playhouse in the same general area as the almonry house, but there is no sign that this was used as the playhouse, either in Westcott's will, or in the leases which relate to it under Gyles or Pearce.[4] Furthermore the almonry house continued to be used by Gyles as a residence while he lay dying between early 1599 and July 1600; the extensive renovations and alterations that were made to the playhouse at this time,[5] as well as the specific prohibition against subdivision or subletting of the almonry house in the documents of appointment of both Gyles and Pearce,[6] effectively rule out this building. The playhouse lay elsewhere.

To solve the riddle it is necessary to move forward in time from Westcott's initial venture of the 1570s to the period just prior to the re-opening of Paul's in 1599. In 1598/9 Bishop Bancroft of London 'visited' St Paul's Cathedral and among his Articles of Inquiry were a group of supplementary questions, administered on 23 April 1599. Two of them related to the Chapter House precinct:

11 how is the upper Cloyster by the Chapter howse imployed, and wheather is theire any extraordinary doore for any private mans use made into it, by whome and by whose consent.
12 In whose custody are the lower Cloisters, and the place Caled the shrowdes how are they imployd, and by whome and whose license and whether is there any doore of any pryvate mans use made into them, and for whose use.[7]

He received two separate responses. In the first Richard Smythe, a verger, declared that 'the upper cloister in the Chapter howse are not imployed to any use at this presente neither is there any dore for any private manns use but suche as were made at the buildinge of the same'.[8] The upper cloister, accessible only by a door or doors probably located at the sides of the second-storey bridge to the Chapter House, is unused, in early 1599. He adds that 'the lower cloisters and the place called the shrowdes are in the Custodie of M[r] gyles and by the license of the Dean and Chapter'.[9] Thomas Gyles, as Master of Choristers, is in control of the lower cloisters, garth and 'shrowdes' – a power recognised as belonging to the office of Master of Choristers by Dean Nowell and the canons in the document of appointment of Edward Pearce of May 1599.[10] The term 'shrowdes' was applied also to the church of St Faith which was in the vaults of St Paul's, at the east end under the choir. Here it is likely that it refers both to the 'shrowded' or shaded area of the garth (permanently in the shade of the high walls of the cloisters and Chapter House) and to the space beneath the Chapter House itself, which was built upon four pillars which were inside an open octagonal undercroft. John Howe, also a verger, affirms that 'the Shrowdes and Cloyster under the Convocation howse (were not longe since the Sermons in fowle weather were wont to be preached) are made a Comon laystall for boardes trunckes and Chests beinge lett out unto trunckmakers, whereby meanes of their dailie knockinge and noyse, the Churche is greatlie disturbed'.[11] Inclement weather had, in the past, caused this area to be used as an alternative site for the Paul's Cross sermons,[12] but this had, apparently, ceased since the letting of this covered area to trunkmakers by Gyles. This leasing of the Chapter House precinct was specifically forbidden, on penalty of forfeiture, to Edward Pearce.

A second response to Bancroft's questions was made jointly by John Howe, John Sharpe and Zachery Alley. These three witnesses confirm that the upper cloister is at present unused, and that there are no unauthorised entries into it, 'but onelie the dore to goe into the leades to clense and repaier them of which dore Mr Gyles hath a keye'.[13] The Master of Choristers also controlled access to the upper cloister. As to the lower cloisters, they are more specific:

the lower cloyster and the place called the shrowdes are in the keepinge of Mr Gyles which have a longe tyme byn used of the master of the Quoristers, there is not now any dore into them for any mans private use

DOMVS CAPITVLARIS S. PAVLI.
Meridie Prospectus.

5 The Chapter House precinct

but there is a house builte in the shrowdes by Mr Haydon sometyme petticannon of this churche which howse we take to be verie offensive in that it is close adioyinnge [adjoining] to the upper end of the chapter howse wall.[14]

The lower cloisters could be entered only from a small door at the north-east corner which gave access from the cathedral nave, immediately adjacent to the public thoroughfare, with its thronging crowds, in the north–south transept. Clearly the Master has had control of them for a considerable period as a perquisite of his office. Elsewhere John Howe affirms that he has 'certain knowledge' of the conditions in the cathedral for 'the space of theis fiftie yeres last past.'[15] The house here referred to was built in the garth (the only open area), extended into the undercroft (the 'shrowdes'), and reached the 'upper end of the Chapter house wall'. Which wall is this? The reference cannot be to the area between the buttresses as this is an archway; the meeting room of the Dean and Chapter was at the second-storey level, reached by a passage-way which led through the upper cloister above the entrance colonnade; this octagonal room had tall windows in each face.

The wall referred to is defined by Colonel William Webb, Surveyor-General of Bishops' Lands, in his survey of 12 November 1657; he describes the Chapter House precinct as 'a Square peece of about 100 Foote each syde, bounded wth the Mayne Wall of the Cathedrall on the North and East sydes thereof, and wth an high old Wall commonly called The Convocacon howse wall on the West and South sydes thereof'.[16] The Chapter House wall, then, is the enclosing wall of the precinct, particularly that on the west and south sides, but not, surely, excluding the north and east sides which are simultaneously the main wall of the cathedral and the Chapter House wall. The house is also at the 'upper end': end presumably means 'corner' and 'upper' is unlikely to refer to a direction away from the main body of the cathedral; also the main entrance to the Chapter House was from the west wall of the south transept. Haydon's house, then, lay against the main south wall of the cathedral, probably in the north-west corner of the Chapter House precinct. The house was also 'verie offensive' because it was 'close adioyinnge' to the Chapter House wall: this complaint implies that it extended into and across the cloisters on the west side and probably also on the north, for their outside boundary was the Chapter House wall. Its position would have seriously restricted movement around the precinct and its location was in itself an affront to the dignity of the cathedral, encroaching on the very centre of the preserve of the Dean and Chapter. It must, also, have been a fire risk to the Chapter House itself, just as various sheds were to the Apostle's Chapel, St Faith's Church and the revestry 'where a great pte of the evidences and recordes of the Churche doe lie wch shedds . . . are verie danigerous yf any mischaunce should happen to them by fire'.[17] If tall enough, the upper storey of the house may have obscured one or more windows of the Chapter House.

That the house was built by this 'Mr Haydon' is confirmed by Richard Smythe who declares that there is 'one little howse . . . builte by Mr Heydon in the lower place Called ye shrowdes wch howse Raynold Chunell Inioyeth by license of Mr Gyles wch howse was built by the Consent of Mr Benbowe beinge then Almner: and the said Mr Heydon one of the petticannons'.[18] This witness speaks of the 'shrowdes' as being a 'lower place', and the Hollar etching of the plan of St Paul's[19] shows a flight of steps leading down from the south-west transept into the garth: F. C. Penrose's excavations of 1879[20] reveal that the old cloister was some 14 feet below the level of the present cathedral – Haydon's house was, in a sense, 'underground'. In 1598/9, however, Thomas Gyles was permitting Reignold Chunnell (or Chune), one of the bellringers, to live in the house in the 'shrowdes': but the permission, 'by license of Mr Gyles', sounds more like 'grace and favour' than a regular lease. Chunnell's wife, a young woman, was one of those who took pennies as entrance fees at the steeple door. Chunnell himself, who died probably of the plague in October 1603, had a young family in mid-1599: a daughter Mary of two and an infant son, Thomas.[21] The house, at this time, was in sufficiently good repair and sufficiently large to be used as a family dwelling and presumably had a privy and a chimney – both reasons why it was 'offensive' in its location. It is quite possible that it was a two-storey building since the cloisters were each some 10 feet high and buildings outside the wall often reached to its top, like Richard Fenton's property, 'wch howses are offensive for that they have builte their howses soe highe as the upper pte of the

Cloyster wall whereby great annoyance happeneth both to the Cloister and to the leades of the same'.[22]

'Mr Benbowe', who is credited with being almoner at the time the house was built, was Thomas Benbowe who first became twelfth minor canon on 1 March 1570/1.[23] He was an active member of St Gregory's parish and continued in the employ of the cathedral until at least 9 July 1581 when his second wife, Joane, was buried.[24] After 1581 he appears to leave St Paul's, since there is no subsequent reference to him either in the cathedral's or in St Gregory's records. He reappears in 1592 when, on 23 November, he gave up his place at the Chapel Royal.[25] Benbowe's close association with the cathedral was essentially during the mastership of Sebastian Westcott, particularly in the decade 1571–81. That Richard Smythe should call him 'Almner' is curious; it may, of course, merely be a mistake since he is referring to a period some twenty or more years before and no other witnesses confirm the ascription. It is possible, however, that Benbowe did act as almoner on a temporary basis during a period of sequestration imposed upon Sebastian Westcott for his continued popish activities.[26] Westcott was in difficulties with the cathedral authorities both in the decade of the 60s and again in the 70s, but despite imprisonment remained obdurate and, indeed, kept his office.

The 'Mr Haydon' who John Howe affirms was 'sometyme petticannon' – a vague statement, suggesting some uncertainty about dates and perhaps indicating that this was in the remote past – and declares responsible for the house, is confirmed as its builder by Richard Smythe. Haydon, however, remains mysterious. There is no record of a Haydon as a minor canon (but the surviving lists are far from reliable); there are some Haydons associated with the neighbouring parishes, like the 'Mary Haydon the daughter of Richard Heydon' of St Vedast, who was buried in Paul's churchyard in 3 April 1595, but no identification exists of a Haydon (or Heydon) as a minor canon in any extant local parish record. The records for St Faith's (which covered the north-east section of the churchyard) are, however, lost, so he may have been associated with that parish. Since two independent witnesses affirm his responsibility for the house, I am inclined to believe that they are right, but when he built it and who he was remain obscure. The only facts about him which seem certain are that he was dead by 1598 and that, if he was a minor canon, he was a priest, for the rule of Pope Urban VI of 11 May 1374 that the twelve minor canons 'debent esse sacerdotes' remained in force after the Reformation.[27] Thomas Benbowe's residency at Paul's, however, offers date limits for the house in the 'shrowdes' in the decade of the 70s.

This house was, then, originally built at about the time Sebastian Westcott first began his commercial exploitation of the English drama. The house was large enough to be used as a dwelling house by a family, but its area was restricted by the size of the garth and undercroft. It was situated in the Chapter House precinct which was wholly under the control of the Master of the Choristers (but by permission of the Dean and Chapter), and access to the cloisters was by means of a single door from the west wall of the nave. The house was almost certainly two storeys and reached across the garth into the cloisters (on the west and probably also north walls) and in addition extended, at least partially, under the Chapter House into the undercroft. The total area involved was about 1,000 square feet for the undercroft itself, some 480 square feet in the garth, and an additional 550 feet in the north and west cloisters: even excluding the undercroft, this allows over 1,000 square feet, assuming the whole area was utilised.

Contemporary testimony as to the location of the Paul's playhouse is at once wholly specific and wholly vague. Stephen Gosson in *Plays Confuted* of 1582 speaks of '*Cupid and Psyche* plaid at Paules':[28] no distinction is made here between the cathedral and the location of the playing-place. The same holds true of the allusion in Nashe's *Have With You to Saffron Walden* (published in 1596), where he speaks of the 'Playes at *Powles*',[29] and the Middle Temple entertainment for Christmas 1597/8, *Le Prince d'Amour or the Prince of Love*, again speaks simply of 'any Play at *Paul's*'.[30] In all of these early references the general location is clear but the specifics remain tantalisingly obscure. Nashe, however, in his flyting of Gabriel Harvey of which *Have With You to Saffron Walden* is a part, offers, at least obliquely, some further details:

We neede never wish the Playes at *Powles* up againe, but if we were wearie with walking, and loth to goe too farre to seeke sport, into the Arches we might step, and heare him plead; which would bee a merrier Comedie than ever was old Mother *Bomby*.[31]

The court of Arches where Harvey made his pleas may be only one side of the pun; perhaps arches also existed in the playing-place at Paul's. In its first phase of operation, then, the Paul's playhouse was located in the immediate area of the cathedral church, perhaps where arches were prominent features.

The professional dramatic career of the Children of Paul's was interrupted between 1590/1 and late 1599: between these two dates their playhouse no longer functioned. The playing-place remained, however, within the cathedral precincts, as William Percy (1573–1648, younger brother of Henry, ninth Earl of Northumberland) testifies *c*.1600/1 in a Note affixed to a copy of his plays:

To the Master of children of Powles Memorandum that if any of the five and foremost of these Pastoralls and Comoedyes conteyned in this volume shall but overeach in lengh (The children not to begin before Foure after Prayers, And the gates of Powles shutting at six) the Tyme of supper, that then in tyme and place convenient, you do let passe some of the songs and make the consort the shorter, For I suppose these Plaies be somewhat too long for that Place—Howsoever on your own Experience and at your best direction be it. Farewell to you all.[32]

It is clear that the playhouse was inside the cathedral area, certainly within the churchyard wall and perhaps even further inside if by 'gates' he means not merely the yard, but the main building itself, which was locked from public access at dusk.

Further information as to the playing-place is found in a legal deposition made by Thomas Woodford (manager of Paul's, 1603–4) on 23 May 1603: he states that Chapman's *Old Joiner of Aldgate* 'was played by the children of powles in a pryvate house of a longe tyme keepte and used and accustomed for yt purpose'. At this time, too, one of the major canons, Thomas White, was able to require that the playhouse should be closed down for a period, because the players had become involved in a matter which was *sub judice*.[33] The Boys, then, during the second period of operation at the cathedral, were using a 'pryvate house' – the first clear evidence of a specific building used for plays – and this purpose-built or modified structure had been used for 'a longe tyme'.

Supplementary evidence as to the location of this house is supplied by Burbage, Heming and Condell in a rejoinder to the Replication of Robert Keysar, on 29 June 1610, but they are referring to events of 1608: they speak of 'the third [private playhouse] neere St Pawles Church then beinge in the handes of one Mr Pierce But then unused for a playe house', and further refer to 'the . . . said howse neere St Paules Church' and 'playes at Paules' in the 'said howse neere Pawles'.[34] Clearly Paul's playhouse is under the control of the Master, Edward Pearce, and it appears to have been a 'private' house in two senses: firstly it is a 'private', as opposed to a 'public', playhouse and secondly it belongs to a 'private' individual; it is the house of Edward Pearce. It is also 'neere' St Paul's Church. In the *Visitation Report* of 1598 a complaint was lodged against John Pettley, carpenter, in that 'he greatly taketh awaie the lighte of St ffaithes Churche by laying his timber and bordes nere the windows on the south side of the same'; 'neere' is used in the sense of adjacent to, or against.[35]

The playhouse was, therefore, so much a part of the cathedral that it could be identified with it: plays were described simply as being performed 'at Paul's', both before 1590 and after 1599. In its second phase the Paul's company used a house specifically designed or adapted for the purpose of producing plays. Pearce disclaimed any responsibility for the dramatic side of their activities: in the same suit in which Woodford made his deposition, Pearce declares that he does not 'att any tyme disbourse anye money for buyeinge the playes which usually are acted by the Children of Powles, but his care is otherwyse ymployed for the Educacion of the . . . Childrene'.[36] Despite this disclaimer, the playhouse belonged to him and remained in his possession after the cessation of the dramatic activities of the company in 1608. The house was, then, probably already in Pearce's possession when playing resumed in 1599 and not acquired specially by him: Pearce may have had a simple monetary agreement with the managers of the second Paul's company, whereby he was guaranteed a fixed annual sum but had no direct responsibility, apart, probably, from teaching some songs and music used in the plays. We know that one specific house which was a perquisite of the Master (apart from the almonry house) was the house in the 'shrowdes' and in that area he had lost a substantial income owing to the prohibition against letting the cloisters for manufacturing purposes.

There exists a tradition as to the location of the Paul's playhouse – one which was strong enough in the Restoration for Richard Flecknoe to say, with a precision unusual for him, 'on

Week-dayes after Vespers, . . . the Children of . . . St. Pauls
Acted Playes, . . . behinde the Convocation-house in Pauls'.[37]
Flecknoe is by no means a wholly reliable witness, but this is the
most definite location he offers and it is in harmony with all the
other, rather more nearly contemporary evidence. It must not
be forgotten that no contemporary witness locates the playhouse in Paul's yard – a phrase constantly used in contemporary
documents in defining the location of the almonry house and
many other structures.

The conclusion is inescapable: Paul's playhouse was a private
house, in the hands of the Master, but by sufferance of the Dean
and Chapter, and it was within the liberty of the cathedral and
thus outside normal legal jurisdiction; the house was that built
by Mr Haydon, with the connivance of Thomas Benbowe, in the
decade of the 70s. It existed as early as the emergence of the
Paul's Boys as a commercial company and remained in the
hands of the Masters of the Choristers, during the tenure of
office of both Thomas Gyles and Edward Pearce. Since there is
no suggestion in the contemporary evidence, nor indeed in any
subsequent testimony, that there was more than one principal
location for the playing-place of the Children of Paul's, they
used the same place from the commercial beginnings under
Westcott in the 1570s until the final closure under Pearce in
1608. It was Haydon's house in the 'shrowdes' that was Paul's
private playhouse.

The Chapter House precinct may be associated with the
Master of the Choristers at Paul's even before the building of
Haydon's house. It is not improbable that it was the undercroft
itself which Redford used as his rehearsal area for his boys'
appearances before their sovereign, and Westcott simply inherited this habit from him. The undercroft was eminently suitable
for rehearsal since it was on the south side of the cathedral, the
same side as the almonry house, and it was protected from the
weather and easy of access. Casual spectators could watch the
plays without interfering. It may be that a simple process of
evolution then took place: in order to extend their range of
facilities the boys moved their plays back against the cloister
screen, for its openings (hung with curtains) provided ready-
made doors and houses – the 10 foot wide cloister behind this
facade would then afford a convenient tiring area. This concept

of a play performed with curtains across the cloister screen, at perhaps both upper and lower levels, is directly analogous to the performances known to have been presented before Tudor hall screens. One may, perhaps without undue improbability, suggest this evolution for the Paul's house: a beginning under the undercroft, a movement back to the cloister screen (under the influence of hall performance) and finally an enclosing of part of that screen (Haydon's house) to protect actors and spectators alike within the garth.

Under Westcott and Gyles, Paul's playhouse did not evolve very much further; they simply stabilised the basic facilities already made available by the physical structure of the cloisters and garth. The stage, now inside a house, was probably a simple raised platform (there was no trap) either placed diagonally across the north-west corner of the cloisters and projecting into the garth, or, more probably at this early stage, projecting from either the north or east cloister faces. It was arranged with a central door flanked by two side doors, all of which were used for entries – thus implying that the house included three of the cloister arches. There was an 'above' (the upper cloister) which helped create the illusion of a house or houses, and in one part of this above there was a window. This initial emphasis upon a facade which had a three door main stage entry, and suggested clearly defined house locations, remains the characteristic feature of Paul's theatre interior until the final closure in 1608.

One of the most attractive features of the Paul's playhouse to its promoters was that it was available free, since the whole cloister area was under the control of the Master. Apart from costumes and properties, the only expenses would have been for a certain amount of maintenance and for the wages of some auxiliary helpers. Sebastian Westcott left 10s 'To Shepard that kepeth the doore of playes' – this door may have been that of the playhouse itself or, more probably, the entry to the precinct from the nave – and a further 10s to 'Pole the keper of the gate', who presumably opened the churchyard gate to allow spectators in or out for the performances.[38] Since the churchyard gate was closed at dusk Pole's duties imply that the plays went on after dark, and indeed in December 1575 artificial light would almost certainly have been needed even in the afternoon. From the beginning, then, the Paul's audience were accustomed to

6 Compton Wynyates, the hall screen, early sixteenth century

seeing their plays lit by the often fitful glow of tapers, candles and torches.

In mid 1599 Reignold Chunnell and his family, who had been living in Haydon's house during the latter days of Gyles' mastership, were dispossessed and the building was renovated for re-use as a playhouse. The basic shape was not changed but it is possible that the orientation of the stage was altered to place it across the corner of the cloister facade, rather than flush against it. The *Antonio* plays of John Marston are the source of a detailed description of this renovated interior at this point in the evolution of Paul's playhouse. There is some probability that Marston himself was, at least partially, responsible for the improvements since he, in the persona of Crispinus, confesses to Horace (Jonson) in *Poetaster*:

By PHOEBUS, here's a most neate fine street, is't not? . . . I am enamour'd of this street . . . There's the front of a building now. I studie architecture too: if ever I should build, I'de have a house just of that *prospective*. (III.i.30–5)

The facade of the stage was certainly two storeys, there was an 'Above' (*A.R.*, Fᵛ) which seems to have extended the full width of the main stage; it was a gallery with a double role–it accommodated the musicians, and provided an upper acting area. The main stage, at ground-floor level, was a raised platform initially built without a trap–this was not added until 1600/1 for the performance of *Antonio's Revenge*, and it was made large enough to be used as a grave. The trap (when added) was located in 'Midde of the Stage' (*Aphrodysial*) and was easily accessible from below, so that entries could be made from it (*A.R.*, I3). This main acting area had a central double door, which was provided with a curtain and could be left open to be used as a discovery space. It was flanked by a narrower door on either side; adjacent to, or in, one of these doors was a grating used as a cell window (*A.R.*, D4ᵛ) and one of them had an operating lock and keyhole (*The Puritaine*, G2ᵛ–G3). Sometimes all three doors were used for entries, as in *The Maydes Metamorphosis* where Ioculo, Frisco and Mopso enter *'at three severall doores'* (D4ᵛ). The central wider door may have been used for processional entry two abreast. The stage itself was small: there was insufficient room for spectators to sit on it (*W.Y.W.*, Induction) but it could accommodate at least seventeen actors

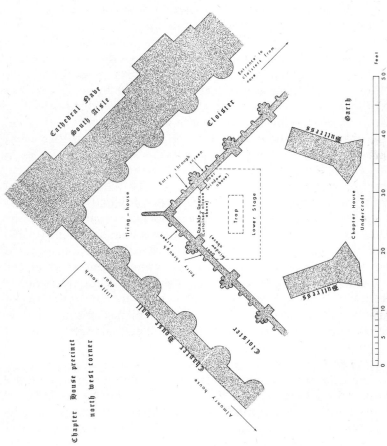

7 The site of Paul's playhouse and the arrangement of the stage at the time of *Antonio's Revenge*, 1600/1

and a coffin at the same time (*A.R.*, C3). The discovery space was large enough to hold a dining-table and eight actors (*W.Y.W.*, G3).

In conjunction with the main stage and its three doors, the 'above' completed the illusion of a street with three houses, as in Percy's *Forrest Tragaedye in Vacunium 'Tremellioes Castell, Affranioes Mannour, Sir Clodioes Desmene'*.[39] There was a central space (presumably with a railing, or built up to waist level like the Compton Wynyates screen), which was curtained and used as an upper acting area (*A.M.*, B3).[40] At one side of this opening there was an operating casement window, which could be closed to effect an exit. At the other side there was a trap window (*M.T.*, A4^v) – presumably one with a hinged or sliding cover. Access to the above was effected by means of a staircase, invisible to the audience, which required no more than eight lines of dialogue to descend and make an entry on the main stage (*J.D.Ent.*, C4–C4^v). There is some indication that a final modification was made to the stage *c.*1604 when an additional staircase, visible to the audience, was provided. In *A Trick to Catch the Old-one*, as Hoard and a gentleman enter a tavern, the Drawer, while pointing, says 'Up those stairs Gentlemen' (E2) and they ascend to an upper room. This visible staircase must have seriously decreased the already limited acting space on the main stage and made entry from at least one of the doors rather difficult; it would also necessitate alterations to the upper facade, for if it rose to the central area, which seems most likely, this would then have had its frontal shape changed so that it became an entry platform which gave access to the two side rooms with their windows.

The peak of development at Paul's playhouse may be localised in the period between the provision of the trap (1600/1) and the addition of the frontal staircase (*c.*1604). It had reached its evolutionary apogee in its representation of, simultaneously, a house or a street with houses. How complete the illusion remained, despite any later alterations, may be gauged from *The Woman Hater* where, at the beginning of the third scene of the fourth act, a Boy enters with Lazarello inquiring of him where they are. The Boy replies 'by all tokens this is the house' (G4) and he declares he can recognise it by its 'broken windowes'. As Jonson made Marston say, 'a house just of that *prospective*'.

The physical size and shape of the Paul's stage had a direct influence on the way in which at least some dramatists handled the disposition of their characters and the sequence of their dramatic action. In 1601 William Percy prepared a tragi-comedy, *Arabia Sitiens or A Dreame of a Drye Yeare*, for performance at the Paul's playhouse: it is custom-designed for this theatre, at the evolutionary peak of its development. The play at once reveals his familiarity with the staging practice at Paul's, for Mahomet as Prologue is described as carrying *'an Alcoran under his arme and sylver Crescent on his Turbant, and all in greene, vicegerent of Heaven, without Mustache if for Poules and bare faced'* (f. 32). This custom at Paul's—the boys did not affect facial hair for adult roles—is confirmed in the first scene of the first act. After Mahomet has declared his intention of punishing the sins of the Arabians by laying waste their lands, pronouncing sentence:

> From East to West, from West to East I will
> Destroye, by this now mortiferous drough [drought]
> From Arabia each Mothers offspring; (f. 33ᵛ)

his attendant angels, Haroth and Gabriel, attempt to intercede on man's behalf and Gabriel pleads:

> Deare Mahomet, graunt us this request.
> . . .
> I will not let goe my hold, Mahomet,
> Unles thou graunt mee this Petition.

At this point Percy directs:

Here he held him by the Bearde, or clawd him on the face, If for Powles this, Bearde for th'other.

Clearly, at least in the first years of the revival, the boys of Paul's did not use false beards or moustaches. This did not, of course, deter them from using wigs for the ladies, as in *Antonio and Mellida* where in the first scene of the third act Flamineo promises to look like a princess when he has changed his 'perewigge' (Fᵛ).

Percy's *Arabia Sitiens* was to be staged with a three house setting: *'At one doore Mecha'*, with a tomb downstage with *'Two burning Tapers'* upon it; *'At Midde doore a Canopie with a Tribunal and but a greene cushion for Mahomet to sit on'* and finally an alehouse as the Porter's lodge. Each of these house locations was to be identified by a name-board; as for Mahomet, *'over him*

61

Olympus' (f. 32ᵛ). Percy assumes that the stage is large enough to accommodate twenty-four actors as well as the tomb, with a *'chorus of spirits'* 'above'. The tomb was to be covered with green velvet and decorated with *'goodly Carbuncles'* and on it a *'Bason of sweet water and Tulips to sprinkle'*. The Porter's lodge was to be provided with tankards and glasses on shelves. All this stage furniture restricted the available acting area and Percy admits that the actors' costumes have to be narrow if there are a number on stage; his attendant angels must be *'without cumber of wings, if for Poules'*.[41] The plot concerns the wrath of Mahomet for the sins of men:

> one blown with Bellowes of Ambition
> Does reare ungratefully rebellious Armes
> Against his Sworne Lord and Anointed Prince,
> Another for durty lucre and Pelf
> Betrayes unto his foe his other Self,
> A Third tempts the Matrymonie bed. (f. 33ᵛ)

Percy was clearly orthodox in his politics, with Mahomet's conformity to the Tudor dogma against 'disobedience and wilful rebellion', but there is also more than a touch of Calvinist moral severity in the remaining injunctions. Mahomet sends two angelic messengers to investigate whether the sins of the Arabians are as grievous as is reported, but they, Haroth and Maroth, fall in love with the *femme fatale* of the piece, one Epimenide, described as *'Marquesse of the Deserts, wyld and savage'* (f. 32). She is besieged by a number of other suitors, including Caleb and Tubal, for whom she sets impossible-seeming tasks as a proof of their devotion. Epimenide has ambitions above her station, for in response to the suit of Haroth and Maroth, who are like 'young men', she haughtily insists that she will only marry an angel; at once they offer to carry her off to

> a Town of burnisht Gold,
> The Streetes be pavd with Pearle and Crysolite,
> With Turkeyes, Chalcedoins and Hyacinths,
> Whose people clad in sylks and Costly Tissewes,
> With heavenly notes and melting Harmony
> Carroll about the Carrfours of the Town. (f. 46ᵛ)

Once in heaven, Epimenide is taken to meet Mahomet who promptly falls in love with her, but she is at length rejected by him as she wants to humiliate him by making him clean her shoes. The judgement given by Mahomet is to condemn Epimenide to live as a 'slave to Amphipolis' (f. 58ᵛ), and the drought is remitted from Arabia to compensate those who have suffered from Epimenide's shrewishness.

It is clear that Percy felt this to be a suitable play for the Children of Paul's, provided certain modifications were made beyond the mere omission of beards and moustaches. The main tenor of the changes is to reduce the number of actors as in Act IV, Scene v where he directs:

Mahomet, Metraon, Epimenide Gabriel Adriel More Angells if for Actors; These for Powles. (f. 47)

and to simplify certain aspects of the action. In the first scene of the fourth act, Mahomet suggests a dance to 'passe the Tyme', while awaiting the return of their investigating angels. The dance is a complex logical and directional symbol; as they dance they sing a four part *'Logicall song'* (f. 45). The instructions for the dance require of the boys a pattern of exchange of corners and places in sequence with the spoken word, similar to a Morris or complicated folk dance. A special alternative is provided for adult actors, while the dance in the main text is intended for boys; the men are required to perform a much more complex pattern of diagonal exchange of places and sides and also of symbols – they represent not merely the characters of the play and the directions of the compass, but also the various winds. Indeed it is so involved that Percy feels it necessary to offer: *'if this shall not be so fitt for the understanding (It being uncouth to the Audience) The other Alteration . . . may well serve'* (f. 61). While he expects the Children of Paul's to be quite capable of performing new dances, he recognises the need to simplify the requirements. In 1601, then, they were expected to dance part of the dramatic entertainment but were not as skilled in that form as they were in singing. The Children were required to sing during the dance; the men were not.

Percy consistently uses entr'acte music and *Arabia Sitiens* contains seven songs as well as the dancing song. Essentially the action takes place on the main stage in front of the doors and tombs, but certain scenes require 'discoveries', as in the tenth scene of the fourth act where Percy directs, *'Here the Arras drawn*

by, Sergius appeared writing' (f. 50ᵛ); presumably the curtains
across a door (left open) were to be drawn for this effect.
Action frequently takes place above, as when Belpheghor
speaks from *'the Trap-windowe here let fall'*, but it was not *'to be
shutt to before the coming in of the Two Angells next'* (f. 47). The
trap over one of the windows in the 'above' is used to effect an
exit and the action there is to be visible from the main playing
area, as with the seventh song, *'A Miracle, All looking up to the
Trap window shut to'* (f. 55ᵛ).

There is some possibility that Percy had at least one specific
actor in mind when designing roles for the Children of Paul's:
one of the angels may have been played by Solomon Pavy, the
subject of Jonson's celebrated epitaph,

> Yeeres he numbred scarse thirteene
>   When *Fates* turn'd cruell,
> Yet three fill'd *Zodiackes* had he beene
>   The stages iewell;
> And did act (what now we mone)
>   Old men so duely,
> As, sooth, the *Parcae* thought him one.[42]

In 1600 he was 'apprentice to one Peerce' and in *The Faery
Pastorall* one of Percy's *dramatis personae* is 'Saloman A Schoole
Boy' (f. 62). During the course of the play he acts the part of a
'Philosopher without a Beard' (f. 69) and during the last two
acts disguises himself as a monster to frighten his schoolmaster: he may also have doubled in the role of Tiresias. In
addition his command of Latin is fluent and erudite and he is a
player on the 'getterne' (f. 75ᵛ). How did this accomplished
actor become one of the Chapel Children by 1601? The explanation may be that, since he was not a chorister, Pearce simply
sold his indentures to Henry Evans, having failed to estimate
his potential accurately. The Master of Choristers may have
had two sources of recruitment for the playhouse, the regular
press for the choir and the legal process of indenture of
apprentices as actors.

Percy has designed his play with a heavy reliance on music,
song and dance and the orchestra (playing from the side
galleries above, behind the casement and trap windows) probably consisted of only two families of instruments, the cornets
and the strings. The cornets, along with sackbuts, were used

for the band in royal processions and they entertained King
James and King Christian of Denmark in Paul's yard in 1606.[43]
Cornets were church instruments and probably players were
easily to be found in the cathedral; it is indeed possible that
theatrical demand, through increasing employment, acted as a
stimulus to encourage the expansion of cornet playing. They
are used for a wide range of purposes, particularly by Marston;
for signalling, when they were 'winded' like horns (*W.Y.W.*,
G4ᵛ), or 'sounded', played normally, as an introit (*W.Y.W.*,
E4). They can serve to announce a battle (*A.M.*, B2) or provide
music for a lavolta (*Blurt*, D2). Along with them, and played by
the same musicians, were the 'still flutes' (*A.R.*, G4), almost
certainly recorders, and viols, which are frequently used for
'sweet ayres' (*A.M.*, I4ᵛ). In addition, either in the band or
among the company, Paul's needed a player of the 'base Vyole'
(*A.R.*, F3), a harpist (*A.M.*, H3ᵛ), a lutenist for solo accompaniment, the provision of music from 'Taber and Pipe' (*J.D.Ent.*,
A2ᵛ) (but possibly the Morris brought their own pipe player),
and later they needed fiddlers (*W.Hoe*, H) and a player for the
regals (*Mad World*, C). Marston never employs the noisiest of
the instruments, hautboys or trumpets: in their place he uses
cornets for his 'lowdest musick' (*A.R.* H3ᵛ): if trumpets are
specified in a Paul's play it is normally because the play has
come from elsewhere, as in *Satiro-mastix*, '*whilst the Trumpets
sound the King is welcom'd*' (D4). Trumpets were used at The
Globe, but probably cornets were substituted at Paul's. The
loudest instruments were avoided for practical reasons; in a
small playhouse their volume was unnecessary and music that
was too loud might well disturb other cathedral functions; the
noise from the trunkmakers in the cloisters was the reason
Pearce had had to get rid of them. The theatre orchestra was
probably quite small, say a quintet of strings, some of whom
could have been choristers, and another quintet for cornet,
sackbut and recorder – but these latter would have had to be
fairly versatile players. These musicians would certainly have
been paid, but the wage scales are unknown. If they were
recruited from among the vicars choral, they would already
have a small annual stipend of about £12; if from lay musicians, their stipends ranged between £6 13s 4d and £10, unless
they were lucky enough to be paid at the same rate as the

musicians of the Chapel Royal, who received at least £40 per annum.[44] In all cases, however, the additional fees would have, no doubt, been welcome.

Whether or not Percy's *Arabia Sitiens* was actually performed on the stage of Paul's playhouse, his testimony is invaluable for he was a contemporary who knew the house in detail and wrote his play-script with specific conditions in mind. His conscious- ness was clearly dominated by the need to economise on space and movement, but the three house setting of the play and its use of music required virtually no change – these were notable features of the Paul's house.

The only space in the Chapter House precinct wide enough to accommodate the playhouse is a corner, for the width available between the extreme edge of the buttresses and the cloister screen is, apart from the corner, only some 6 feet at best. While the north-west corner is the most likely location, all corners are of the same dimensions. Since the stage was a raised platform with a three door entry (and the two side doors may have been set at an angle to the central door) the most likely placing for it is attached to the north-west corner of the outside cloister screen, projecting into the garth. I suggest that the extreme corner (at both upper and lower levels) was squared off by a wood screen, with below a 'discovery space' and above an equal-sized space with a curtain; the platform stage then extended into the garth up to, or slightly beyond, the level of the second rank of projecting cloister arches. This arrangement would offer door- ways at either side, which were entries through the cloister screen, and the cloister itself served as the tiring-house. This would give a 'discovery space' about 7 feet wide and the two side doors could have been up to the full width of the cloister arch (about 7 foot 6 inches). The thrust stage may then have extended some 10 feet or more into the garth (excluding the triangular discovery space). The area of the main stage could have been in the order of 170 square feet (including the discovery space), and this assumes a projection of only 10 feet with a 20 foot width at the front. It may, of course, have been larger than this for the width into the garth could easily have been increased. It leaves over 300 square feet for spectators in the garth area (but excluding any projection into the undercroft) and there would have been room for a gallery, although this may have obscured one or more of the windows of the Chapter House. The 'above' had a fixed width of 10 feet which afforded ample room for actors, musicians and the necessary stairway or stairways; the lower cloisters, used as the tiring-house proper, had over 550 square feet of usable space; the shape of the 'above' was, of course, an exact duplicate. As far as spectators were concerned – allowing a generous 4 square feet per person as this was a 'select house' – and even supposing the stage projected 15 and not 10 feet into the garth, this allows some 150 square feet or space for about forty spectators (without including those who could have been accommodated in a gallery). A reasonable (and probably conservative) estimate of the seating capacity at Paul's was fifty to one hundred spectators accommodated with ease and comfort. This is a small playhouse by contemporary standards, but not the smallest operating house.[45] Since the main framework of the cloister screen was easily adaptable to a three door or three house pattern, the playhouse could have been orientated at a different angle (with the stage thrusting from the north or west screen) but this would not alter the dimensions very significantly. It is improbable that the stage could have been built between the buttresses, as entry (apart from the rear, out of the undercroft) would have been extremely difficult without making the stage too narrow. Spectators could have been admitted to the playhouse by doors on either (or both of) the north or west junctures between the ends of the buttresses and the cloister screen: since the Master of Choristers controlled the whole precinct, it may have been the custom merely to charge for entry to the precinct at the doorway out of the nave.

In all there was over 1,000 square feet available at the ground-floor level for this house in the 'shrowdes' and at least another 550 at the second-storey level: surely ample room for a private playhouse. The cloister and garth had originally been built in the fourteenth century and the paving was 'composed of squares and lozenges of Purbeck marble'.[46] The cloister columns themselves were also built of Purbeck marble, but the shafts of the Chapter House were of Caen stone. While the paving in the tiring-house may have been left alone, that in the auditorium-garth may have been replaced by a wooden floor. The structure of the house, pinned to the existing Chapter House and cloisters

8 A sermon at Paul's Cross, 1620

(and no doubt one of the causes of their serious decay) would, presumably, have been the traditional timber pattern with wattle and daub fill and a slate roof.

In 1573 Claudius Holyband in his *French Schoole-maister*, printed for 'Abraham Weale, dwelling in Paules Church-yarde at the signe of the Lambe', takes his French visitor to hear a sermon at Paul's Cross, 'for there preacheth no body, but is of choyce, and of great learning' (p. 72). His guest agrees, declaring 'I doo think that they be ye best sermons that men may heare in all the rest of the Realme of England' (p. 72). The sermons were popular, 'for men doo see all Sundayes and holy dayes a greate and a noble company in Paul's churchyard'. They find space to sit on one of the 'formes' with difficulty, but manage to be close to the preacher and, while waiting for him to begin, look around at the lords and ladies in the galleries. As a surviving illustration of 1620 makes clear, the arrangements for the sermons were as Holyband describes them – benches (and separate stools) in an arc in front of the cross, additional spectators standing behind them and the more distinguished auditors in roofed galleries (built between the buttresses on the exterior of the north wall of the choir): this gallery had an upper and a lower level. This setting is significantly like the interior arrangement of the Paul's playhouse after 1599; it is possible, therefore, since the 'shrowdes' were sometimes used for these sermons before 1598, that some existing seating arrangements may have been taken over and incorporated into the playhouse. As Millar Maclure points out:

If we look at the scene as a whole, it reminds us of the Elizabethan theatre; groundlings and notables, pit and galleries, and, in the midst, the pulpit as stage. Indeed it was a theatre.[47]

It is to be hoped, however, that the playhouse in the shrouds was more pleasant a setting than the theatre of the cross, where 'the sheddes before the Crosse doe much anoye the Churche inso muche that one of them doth smell verie mutch and at one tyme a Chimney was a fyer in the sermon tyme'.[48]

Paul's playhouse was situated in the parish of St Gregory, which also incorporated almost the whole area of the church-yard with its innumerable tenants. Outside the yard, the parish was known for the mercers who lived in Bowyer Row, as the top of Ludgate Hill was named; for the stationers who lived in

Paternoster Row (formerly the place of business of the makers of rosary beads); the spurriers of Creed (or Spurrier) Lane; the Doctors of the Civil Law and the Arches (like Gabriel Harvey) who kept their commons in Paul's Chain and for the various ecclesiastical dignitaries who lived in the churchyard or in the neighbouring streets. As might be expected in such a commercial area as Paul's yard there were a large number of lodging-houses and inns, including the King's Head, the Golden Lion (twelve houses short of Amen Corner in Paternoster Row), the Bell and the Mermaid in Carter Lane and the Powle Head in Paul's Chain. St Gregory's parish, since it included the churchyard and the middle aisles, was often a place of theft and violence, for among the transient crowds there were pickpockets, whores and thieves. In the three decades from 1576 to 1608, during most of which the Paul's Boys operated as a commercial venture, this parish was the most populous in the immediate area of the cathedral and its numbers progressively increased during the period, until in the first decade of the seventeenth century it was substantially greater than its attained size in the 70s. It may have doubled in size between 1575 and 1605.[49] In contrast the parishes to the east of the churchyard (Paul's School side), St Augustine's and St Vedast's, were less than half the size of St Gregory's and, while there was a certain amount of immigration into them, their total size remained more or less static. St Anne Blackfriars to the south-west of the churchyard (which, of course, included the playhouse of Paul's major rival, the Chapel Children) was initially a very small parish like St Augustine's and St Vedast's, but in the mid-90s it experienced a period of phenomenal growth until its size, at the turn of the seventeenth century, was comparable to St Gregory's. Adjacent to it was St Andrew Wardrobe, a parish not dissimilar in size to St Gregory's; it too grew greatly during the period but its rate of increase was more steady and less dramatic than that of St Anne's. The parish adjacent to St Gregory's, St Martin's Ludgate on the west side of the churchyard, was akin to St Andrew Wardrobe, with a steady rate of population growth, significantly increasing itself within three decades, without any sudden surges. It appears to have been a relatively peaceful and law-abiding locality, illegitimate births are virtually non-existent, and there are no burials of unfortunates found in the street; it did, however, know its own mute tragedies. On 19 July 1600 there was buried a still-born child of George Corless, merchant tailor; on the following 25 November he was himself interred; then, on 9 January 1601, 'was buryed Dorothy Corlesse widow, sometime the wife of George Corless merchant tailor whoe killed her selfe with a kniffe'.[50]

The overall baptism-to-marriage ratio for these six parishes was only 2.75, a percentage well below the needed level for stabilising the population, let alone increasing it.[51] An exception is St Augustine's where the relationship of births to marriages was almost 4, a somewhat more healthy, but not yet stable situation. Nevertheless the surviving baptism, marriage and burial statistics suggest a distinct increase in population and certainly reflect a positive and often steep increase in the baptismal rate (co-extensive with a rise in the marriage rate). Immigration into the parishes from outside the area must have been taking place to account for this growth. Those who came in appear to have been, in the main, unmarried men who subsequently married and had families within the parish. This would, of course, increase the number of families at their economically most productive and vigorous peaks. This is particularly true in the decade of the 90s.

The picture that emerges is of a population constantly changing. This is especially so in St Gregory's and St Anne Blackfriars, where, in the plague year of 1603, the death rate was $4\frac{1}{2}$ times the thirty year average: servants, journeymen and apprentices would constantly have flowed in to replace the losses from the bubonic epidemic. An exception may be St Augustine's where the marriage rate has a slight downward trend – perhaps here the population was more stable and it is possible that the average age was higher. But St Augustine's, like the other parishes adjacent to the cathedral, was affected by that proximity: towards Paul's yard gravitated the destitute, like 'Philippe Latham a poore man, who dyed in the street, as he passed throught the parishe' on 30 December 1605 and the desperate, like 'Henry Barnes, [who] sioarning [sojourning] in the house of Thomas Wattzone, was buried the 3d of September [1601] by nighte. He caste himselfe headlong out of a wyndowe'.[52]

In an age when the overall life expectancy was perhaps as low as 30 (that is, when the expectancy takes into account the very high infant mortality up to the age of 10),[53] to live in the parishes of St Gregory, St Martin, St Andrew, St Anne, St Augustine or St Vedast was to exist in a society of the young. To be able, as John Howe claims he was,[54] to recall events of the 'fiftie yeres last past' was clearly exceptional, and whenever an 'old' man is buried, it is a matter for comment by the parish clerk. The people who inhabited the churchyard and the surrounding area of St Paul's playhouse were a group who had short memories (many were immigrants from elsewhere in London and the countryside) and they were in a parish situation which was constantly unstable. But a growing birth rate and a continuously changing population with an increasing number of families at their productivity peaks, make sound commercial sense for the location of a playhouse. To a certain extent too, the growth of the parishes of St Gregory and St Anne may have been partially due to the stimulus provided by the theatre to service industries, like 'comfit makers', 'bakers' and, perhaps, 'spektacle makers'. Not merely were the liberties of Paul's and the Blackfriars suitable sites for private playhouses in terms of safety from the jurisdiction of the City Magistrates (and even the law as a whole) but also because these locations offered, ready made, a potential audience which was continuously growing. In the case of St Gregory's and, even more marked, in the case of St Anne, the population had begun to increase very significantly before the second phase in the operation of the theatres of both Paul's and the Chapel Children.

As far as audience was concerned, Paul's playhouse was not usually a wholly exclusive preserve, for in 1589 James More, servant to William Darrell of Littlecote, who was lodging in Warwick Lane (at the corner of Paternoster Row and Ave Maria (or Ave Mary) Lane) went casually to a play (perhaps *Midas* or *Mother Bombie*) at a cost of 6d.[55] Again in 1603 two tradesmen, John Flaskett and John Howe, the former a bookbinder, the latter a barber-surgeon, as well as Edward Brompton, servant to John Milward, preacher at Christ Church in Newgate Street, all of whom lived locally, visited the theatre.[56] Paul's playhouse served as a place of entertainment for the inhabitants of the adjacent streets. While no doubt many would travel from afar to The Globe or Fortune, it was easier if one lived near St Paul's, or was shopping there, to go to the local playhouse for 2d or even

6d, rather than spend 2d on entry to a covered seat at The Globe and pay the boatmen a fee for a trip out and back across the Thames. Certainly going to Paul's playhouse was a great deal more convenient than the effort of the journey to the South Bank. If the evidence of the plays is to be trusted, for the surviving examples are sparse, the audience during the first phase of Paul's under Westcott was, while interested in courtly forms of entertainment, desirous of a form of amusement both modern, fashionable and yet reasonably broadly based, for when Lyly tried to narrow the frame of reference to the court alone it caused an adverse reaction. The proximity of the middle aisle of Paul's would, from the beginning, cause pressure to be exerted upon the playhouse, to allow the admission of a cross-section of that various and mixed group who congregated there: the multitude of shopkeepers and lawyers who used Paul's as their place of business would have little difficulty in finding the modest fees (2d, 4d, 6d) demanded.[57]

Between 14 April and 16 July 1589, William Darrell spent an average of £1 11s per day at his lodgings on food and household expenses. The 6d which he paid for James More to see a play at Paul's was only just over $1\frac{1}{2}$% of this daily outlay and thus no more than a small fraction of 1% of his weekly expenditure of some £10 17s. That 6d could have been used instead to go by boat from the Temple steps to the court at Westminster and back; to pay for a servant's shoes to be repaired; to have two shirts laundered; to buy 'silk to make button holes', or a book, or four ounces of dates, or a quart of claret or white wine or a tobacco pipe – but tobacco itself was very expensive at 5s or more per ounce. Darrell was a courtier and given to extravagance, but it has been calculated that the average weekly household expenses of a London baker in 1618 were £6 10s 1d. Thus, even allowing for inflation in the decade after the closure of Paul's playhouse, 6d would still amount to less than half of 1% of a tradesman's disposable weekly income.[58]

In the parish of St Martin Ludgate between 1602 and 1606 – it lies directly to the west of Paul's yard – there were at least two hundred and seventy families permanently resident and active in the sense of being professionally employed or employing others and bearing children. The heads of these households, normally men between the ages of 25 and 45, may be divided into a small fraction of 'gentlemen', 9% who did not work with their hands, and over 36% who were haberdashers; the remainder were mainly other professionals, merchant tailors, barber-surgeons, innkeepers, scriveners, weavers, goldsmiths and stationers. There were, then, a significant number of households of sufficient affluence (for Flaskett, the bookbinder, was by no means an outstandingly successful member of his profession) to have fairly easily afforded a visit, at least by the head of the household and a friend or servant (like Flaskett and Howe) to Paul's playhouse. In fact Woodford may have been able to raise the regular charge to 6d (*Michaelmas Terme*, A3) because there were so many relatively affluent households for his local journalistic drama.[59]

In St Martin's parish an impression of general affluence is reinforced by the fact that seventy-five of its households had occasion to bear the expense of and preside over the funeral of one or more servants in the early 1600s. In St Gregory's parish there were at least three hundred and ninety-one active families during the Woodford/Kirkham period at Paul's and this excludes tenants and businessmen from the churchyard itself. Sixty-five of these families were headed by a 'householder' and seventy-nine overall were involved in the burial expenses of servants: 10% of the whole parish were 'gentlemen'. In all there were at least one hundred and fifty-five households which were probably of sufficient affluence to have afforded a visit of two persons to the Paul's playhouse on at least an occasional basis.

There were, then, in only two of the surrounding parishes of St Paul's, St Gregory's and St Martin's, over five hundred households where potential spectators resided: since the capacity of the playhouse was less than one fifth of this total, the Paul's management were making a commercially sound decision when they sought to appeal directly to it. These local spectators, moreover, represented only a small fraction of the audience available merely by advertising in the middle aisle.

3

The business of theatre
in court and city

The first favourable review received by the Children of Paul's for a dramatic performance was delivered not by one of their compatriots, but by an Italian. Gasparo Spinelli, secretary to the Venetian Ambassador in London, attended a banquet given by Cardinal Wolsey on 7 January 1528. As usual with the Cardinal's entertainments, the dinner was sumptuous; when the feasting was ended and the guests sated, 'the scholars of St Paul's, all children, recited the *Phormio* of Terence, with so much spirit and good acting that [Spinelli] was astounded'.[1] This was a compliment worth having, for Spinelli was an accomplished and well read diplomat: the boys pleased him more by their elocution than their actual embodying in movement of the plot, but some attempt had obviously been made to make this more than merely an animated, memorised play-reading. The hall was arranged with 'a garland of box' in the front, on the middle of which was inscribed in gilt letters, '*Terentii Phormio*'. Then, on one side, was inscribed on paper, in Gothic letters, '*Cedant arma togae*', and on the other, '*Foedus pacis non movebitur*'. Beneath the garland was written '*Honori et laudi Pacifici*'; this latter motto was an allusion to Wolsey's title '*Cardinalis Pacificus*'. Additional mottos were hung in various places to make flattering allusion to the occasion being celebrated, which was the Pope's escape from his confinement in the Castle of St Angelo.[2] The play was followed by an allegorical show in which three girls, Religion, Peace and Justice, amplified the foregoing theme and 'When the girls had finished, a little boy, who had already recited with great applause the prologue of the comedy, delivered a Latin oration . . . The grace with which this little fellow delivered [it] could not be imagined.'

This entertainment was, in a sense, as much for the furtherance of the children's education as it was for the amusement of the onlookers. The boys were practising their skills in memorisation, pronunciation and enunciation, their command of voice projection and delivery as well as showing their grasp of the grace and decorum demanded of their behaviour in exalted and powerful company. The children were a credit to Wolsey, as Spinelli testifies, and their dramatic rendition of the *Phormio*, probably a recitation with gestures and some localised action, while sub-dramatic, nonetheless marks their degree of accomplishment in theatricals at this early date. It cannot, of course, be claimed that these 'children of Paul's' were the choirboys of the cathedral, for they may well have been composed of a group from Paul's grammar school. Conversely there is no reason why choristers were not included, for they were grammar school boys too.

After the mid-point of the century, however, the Paul's choir alone takes over the dramatic function which had previously been a responsibility and an accomplishment of the choristers and grammar school boys together. A celebrated instance was Elizabeth's progress to the Earl of Arundel's Nonsuch estates in 1559, where 'the Queen had great entertainment with banquets, especially on Sunday night . . . together with a mask; and the warlike sounds of drums, and flutes, and all kinds of music, till midnight. On Monday [7 August] was a great supper made for her; but before night she stood at her standing in the further park, and there she saw a course [a passage at arms, a joust]. At night was a play of the children of Paul's, and their master Sebastian. After that, a costly banquet, accompanied with drums and flutes; the dishes were extraordinary rich, gilt. This entertainment lasted till three in the morning.'[3] The boys simply provided one of a sequence of spectacles, much as they had done for Wolsey. The reason for the gradual separation between choir and grammar school, which had already occurred by this time, was the desire of John Redford, who was choir master in the decades of the 30s and 40s, to make his boys pre-eminent in the entertainment of the sovereign. In 1559 Westcott was merely following suit in a, by then, clearly established tradition.

John Redford was a strict but compassionate teacher; Thomas Tusser, whom Redford pressed, speaks of him with affection[4] and Redford collected around himself at Paul's a group of sympathetic friends with literary and musical interests. Members of the circle included John Heywood, a staunch Roman Catholic, player of virginals for Henry VIII and dramatist, and Miles Huggard, poet and anti-Protestant polemicist.[5] There survives a manuscript which probably represents some part of the literary and musical production of this group; much of it was intended for performance by the Paul's choir.[6] The most important surviving work in it is Redford's play fragment *Wit and Science*: this play marks the beginning of the future pre-eminence of the Children of Paul's. The drama, which was written sometime during Redford's tenure of the Mastership of Choristers (*c*.1534–*c*.1547), while still a Morality, concerning the desire of Wit (or Intelligence) to marry Science (or Knowledge), is modern in some of its usages, as when Redford directs:

Confydence . . . now wyll ye see a goodly pycture [of] of wyt hym
cuth in wt   sealfe hys owne image sure face/bodye/armes/legge/both
a pycture   lym & ioynt as lyke hym as can be in every poynt yt lakth
of wyt   but lyfe . . . (51–5)

During the sixteenth century there was, throughout Europe, a marked increase in the frequence of individualised and exact portraiture with names and dates of birth:[7] this picture of Wyt is 'Masterly done! / The very life seemes warm upon [his] lip' (*Winter's Tale*, V.iii. 65–6). Despite the excellence of its execution, however, the portrait is not accepted as being a wholly good likeness, for later in the action Science argues that the picture is 'nothyng lyke in myne eie' (790) to Wyt, and Experience explains that the portrait is 'fayer plesant & goodlye' and 'ye [Wyt] are fowle dysplesant & [good] uglye' (795–6). The painting was a flattering and smiling version of Wyt who is required, until he is converted by Instruction and Experience, to play his part with an 'ugly' look. The transition from innocence to experience was then effected in part by a visual change and presumably make-up, but prefigured allegorically by the portrait introduced at the beginning.[8] The fact that the picture was full length may also indicate that the change in Wyt was to be marked by a change of costume, so that the actor and his image agreed at the end of the play. The living painting was a symbol of the goal of Wyt's search for knowledge.

This use of a portrait as a dramatic property established the first identifiable feature of the Paul's repertoire. Its use was copied, as indeed was the whole plot and form of Redford's play, when Sebastian Westcott presented the boys in *The Marriage of Wit and Science*: it was played sometime after Redford's death and before 1569. It is a modern sophistication of Redford's earlier version but in it the significance of the portrait and its allegory is eroded; it has become merely a 'picture of mine [Wit's] to be seene' by his beloved (262). But pictures are to figure again in the repertoire at Paul's: in c.1589 in *Campaspe*, Apelles, a painter, falls in love with Campaspe's portrait and in 1599 two portraits, one of the patron and the other of the author, are presented in Marston's *Antonio and Mellida*. In *The Wisdome of Doctor Dodypoll* (c.1600), the action begins with '*A Curtaine drawne, Earle* Lassingbergh *is discovered (like a Painter) painting* Lucilia, *who sits working on a piece of Cushion worke*' (A3). In all these cases the presentation of portraits, which are specific likenessses, bears witness to the authors' sensitivity to the growing concern with the preservation of individual identity, especially for the affluent who could afford to commission a painter.

Redford's *Wit and Science* is clearly intended as a bid for the royal favour and is written as a compliment to Henry VIII and his queen of the day, or perhaps the woman who is about to be queen, for the play is a marriage celebration. At the end Reson declares,

> fyrst in this lyfe wysh I here to fall
> to our most noble kyng & quene in especiall
> to ther honorable cowncell / & then to all the rest
> such Ioy as long may reioyse them all best. (1120–3)

The play concludes with a four part song, sung to viols played by the singers – and this tradition of teaching the boys to play the viol was continued by Westcott and his successors.[9] The implication of this concluding musical entertainment, which requires the 'fowre with violes' to sing an unknown song called 'Remembrance' and, after 'all make cursye', they 'goe forth syngyng' (1124–6), is that the accompaniment here for the singers, and elsewhere for the other incidental music, was a group of four string players. Certainly the songs were integral to the action, for when the suit of Wyt to Science is beginning to succeed he welcomes her musically, 'here wyt / Instruccion / studye / & digigence syng wellcū my nowne [own] / & syence / experience / [&] reson / & confidence cū in at / As & answer evre second verse' (1032–5). The song was organised either as two quartets with a line to each of the four singers, with two chorus lines, or more simply as a chorus with 'Wyt and his cūpanye' singing

O ladye deere be ye so neare }	to be knowne
my hart yow cheere yoᵣ voyce to here }	welcū myne owne

Science and 'hir cūpanye' responded with

As ye reioyse to here my voyce }	fro me thus blowne
so in my choyce I show my voyce }	to be yoᵣ owne

This singing display involved almost the whole official choir; since eight singers are needed here, the implication may be that the parts were played by the principal choristers, but it is possible that deeper notes were intermingled with the boys' sopranos by the inclusion of older superannuated choristers with 'broken' voices. The musical style involved is, of course, unknown but perhaps it followed the advice offered in 1597 by an authority who was trained by Sebastian Westcott. Thomas Morley in his *Plaine and Easie Introduction to Practicall Musicke* insists on the fitting of the pitch to the voice for, 'take a voice being never so good, and cause it sing above the naturall reach it will make an unpleasing and sweete noise, displeasing both the singer because of the straining, and the hearer because of the wildenes of the sound'. But he goes on to admit that while 'above all thinges' one must 'keepe the ayre of your key' sometimes the ditty 'will compell the author . . . to admit great absurdities in his musicke' (p. 166). Morley, who was a chorister both before and during 1574,[10] was taught under a tradition inherited from John Redford and it could well be the Paul's musical tradition which is reflected in his counsel, 'if the subiect be light, you must cause your musicke go in motions, which carrie with them a celeritie or quicknesse of time, as minimes, crotchets and quavers: if it be lamentable, the note must goe in slow and heavie motions, as semibreves, breves and such like . . . you must have a care that when your matter signifieth ascending, high heaven, and such like, you make your musicke ascend: and by the contrarie where your dittie speaketh of descending lowenes, depth, hell, and others such, you must make your musicke descend' (p. 178).

Morley's urging to blend the music to the context of the words was Redford's doctrine, in the sense that he began by establishing at Paul's a tradition in plays of songs being part of the action of the plot: they are not purely extraneous amusements, but variations and arpeggios on the themes, with the words suiting the stage reached in the development of the action.

Redford's efforts to make the choir pre-eminent in courtly entertainment were clearly successful, for from the mid-sixteenth century it is always the choir and not the grammar school who provide the entertainment for the court, and this is particularly marked in the reign of Elizabeth. The Children of Paul's were the company most frequently invited to her court during the 60s, 70s and 80s, making over three dozen appearances, commencing before her accession with a performance at Hatfield House during the winter of 1551/2. Payments were made to 'the Kinges Maiesties drommer & phiphe the xijth Februarie, XX.s. Mr Heywood, XXX[s]. and to Sebastian, towardes the charge of the children with the carriage of the plaiers garmentes, iiij[li]. XIX[s]'.[11] This pre-accession visit to Elizabeth probably marks the beginning of a long and close association between Westcott and his sovereign: he was so much in favour that Elizabeth's intervention, through Leicester, was the principal reason why he avoided the harsher consequences of his obstinate romanism.[12]

The success of Redford, and of Westcott after him, as purveyor of courtly revel was not an unmixed blessing for the choir: they had to put up with the whims of Elizabeth. During the Shrovetide entertainments of 1573/4 a group of children were boarded out while 'they Learned their partes and Jestures meete for the Mask in which ix of them did serve at hampton court'.[13] They were then conveyed from Paul's wharf in a barge which 'caryed The Masking geare, and Children with their tutors and An Italian Woman etc. to dresse their heades as also the Taylors property makers and haberdashers'. On Shrove Monday the whole company kicked their heels 'whiles they wayted to know whether her Maiestie wolde have the Mask that nighte': the masque was not called for, and they lodged that night at Kingston-on-Thames. The next day the barber was sent to trim their hair and that night they stayed again with Mother

Sparrow in Kingston 'whiles they staied for botes'. The masque was not, apparently, presented at all. They did not make their way back to London until late on the Wednesday and Thomas Totnall was paid 6s 6d 'for ffyer and vittells for the Children when they Landed sum of them being sick and colde and hungry'. Their experience was not untypical of service in the office of the Revels.

Apart from Redford's *Wit and Science,* few of the names of the plays presented by Paul's at court have survived, and fewer still of the plays themselves. The demand was, however, great. On one occasion in the Christmas–Shrovetide season of 1567/8, payment of £13 6s 8d was made to Sebastian Westcott:

for seven playes, the firste namede as playne as Canne be, The second the paynfull plillgrimage; The tthirde Iacke and Iyll, The forthe six fooles, The fyvethe callede witte and will, The sixte called prodigallitie, The sevoenth of Orestes and a Tragedie of the kinge of Scottes, to yᵉ whiche belonged divers howses, for the settinge forthe of the same as Stratoes howse, Gobbyns howse, Orestioes howse Rome, the Pallace of prosperitie Scotlande and a gret Castell one the othere side Likewise.[14]

Some types may be identified: morality (*Wit and Will*; *Prodigality,* or *The Contention betweene Liberalitie and Prodigalitie; The Paynfull Pillgrimage*); classical tragedy (*Orestes*); comedy (*Jack and Jill* and *Six Fooles*) and tragical-historical (*King of Scots*). In addition, from other performances, the choir may be credited with plays entitled *Effiginia* (28 Dec. or 1 Jan. 1571/2), *Alkmeon* (27 Dec. 1573), *The History of Error* (1 Jan. 1577/8), *The History of Titus and Gesippus* (19 Feb. 1577/8), *A Morall of the marryage of Mynde and Measure* (1 Jan. 1579/80), *Scipio Africanus* (3 Jan. 1580/1), and a *Story of Pompey* (6 Jan. 1581/2); but no new types present themselves. Most, at least of the classical plays, required 'howses of peynted Canvas', and for the *Story of Pompey,* acted at Whitehall, no expense was spared, for on it 'was ymploied newe one great citty, a senate howse and eight ells of dobble sarcenet for curtens and xviij paire of gloves . . . The duble sarcenett maid into Curtyns and Implowid about Storie of pompey plad by the Childring of powles.'[15] These orange double silk curtains, costing over £4 and 10 yards long, may conceivably have been used either to enclose the Senate house or perhaps the tents of Caesar and Pompey before the battle of Pharsalia, which is likely to have figured largely in any account of Pompeius Magnus.

81

There does survive one outline of the argument of a classical play, either performed by or proposed to the Paul's company during their period of consolidation and metamorphosis into a group of city entertainers from their more restricted educational and courtly role. *Publii Ovidii Nasonis Meleager*[16] belongs sometime after 1572 and before 1590, but in my view it is highly likely, given the very similar circumstances of the Percy plays, to date from *c.*1575 when Paul's had successfully founded commercial theatre and were in the market for new plays. The story of Meleager is basically simple: when he was seven days old the Moerae declared he would die as soon as a brand of wood burning on the hearth was consumed. Althea, his mother, extinguished the brand and hid it. Meleager, however, was in later life responsible for the death of his uncles; his mother, to revenge her brothers, cast the brand upon the fire and Meleager died.

The Paul's version begins with a dumb show of the three fates, Clotho, Lachesis and Atropos, who mime Meleager's destiny. This show involves 'consuming a bronde wth ffier'. Later in the fourth act Althea 'puttes the Bronde in . . . a flamyng Alter'. The author, then, presumed that the children were able to cope with an open fire on stage – perhaps in a metal brazier. In addition, the author also makes the interesting assumption that there is no problem in the direction 'The Lordes standing in doubte of the infortunate sequell, of so unhappie a beginning, are appoynted by *Melpomene* to sitt as *Chorus* over the stage to vewe the ende of everie accident, & to explaine the some of euie [every] Acte.' So the boys had facilities for an upper acting area by the date of the creation of this proposal. Some confirmation of this assumption is to be found in *The Marriage of Wit and Science* where Wit suggests to Science:

> Here in my sight, good Maddam, sitte and viewe,
> That, when I list, I may loke uppe on you. (1436–7).[17]

Both plays require an 'above' upon which characters are visible and can view the action on the main stage. They could have been presented in a great hall with a screen like that at Compton Wynyates, or in Paul's playhouse which was similarly designed.

The second act of *Meleager* opens with the entry of '*Oeneus* and *Althe* the Queene . . . w^t *Phlexippus* & *Toxeus*, her Brethren, *Meleager*, *Athalanta* wth her virgens, *Thesius*, *Pirythous*, *Acastus*, *Ancaeus*, & their companye'. Ten principals are required and sundry extras: ten was the fixed number of the choir and their ages are indicated in *The Marriage of Wit and Science*. In Act II Scene ii Science and Will conduct a short dialogue:

Science . . . What age art thou of, my good sonne?
Will   Betwene eleven and twelve, Madame, more or less.
             . . .
Science How old is the gentilman thy maister [Wit], canst thou tell?
Will   Seventene or there aboute, I wote not verye well. (465–73)

There is no reason to doubt the general authenticity of these ages and while eleven or twelve is typical of a chorister, seventeen is surely too old. The casting demands for *Meleager*, with its ten main actors and extras, are not unreasonable and, if Will is to be credited, the senior actors at Paul's in the mid-70s were in their late teens and the junior parts were taken by choristers proper (Will is Wit's page), who were about eleven.

Meleager culminates in a scene of physical agony followed by a short concluding episode which is the entire fifth act; it focuses on the spiritual grief of Oeneus, father of Meleager. After Althea has cast the brand into the fire, '*Meleager* entreth w[th] *Attalanta* [his beloved], *Theseus*, and y[e] virgins crying owte for helpe affirming his burning heate was so intollerable that y[t] surpassed the invenomed shirte w[ch] confounded *Hercules* . . . the unhappie *Meleager* dieth in the Armes of his beloved . . . *Oeneus*, the adged Kinge, lamenteth over the deade Bodie of h[is] sonne . . . wisheth all miseries to confounde him.' The final episode, which is apparently intended as a soliloquy by Oeneus, was seen on the Paul's stage: in the fifth scene of the fourth act of Marston's *Antonio's Revenge*, Pandulpho, Alberto and a page keen their sorrow over the dead body of Pandulpho's son Feliche:

> Death, exile, plaints, and woe
> Are but man's lackies, not his foe.
> No mortall scapes from fortunes warre,
> Without a wound, at least a scarre.
> Many have led these to the grave:
> But all shall followe, none shall save
> Bloode of my youth, rot and consume,
> Virtue, in dirt, doth life assume.   (I[v])

These sentiments, which are derived from Whyttynton's *Seneca*,[18] provide as fitting an epitaph for Meleager as they do for Feliche.

Apart from displays of classical erudition in stories derived from Ovid or Roman history, the boys also presented updated versions of older successes. *The Marriage of Wit and Science* is a modernisation, completed under Westcott's mastership, of Redford's original *Wit and Science*. Its sophistication is immediately apparent in the wooing scenes even though, as Will points out, the actor who played the suitor Wit was thin-legged and suffered from acne:

> . . . what if she finde fault with these spindle shankes,
> Or els with these blacke spottes on your nose? (271–2)

But Wit, whose page Will is short, thin and much younger, is not deterred for he avows, at the opening of the play,

> nowe . . . of late I kyndle in desire,
> And pleasure pricketh fourth my youth to feele a greater fyre,
> What though I be too young to shewe her sport in bed,
> Yet are there many in thys lande that at my yeares doe wedde,
> And though I wed not yet, yet am I olde inowe
> To serve my Lady to my power and to begynne to woo. (43–8)

The adapter has skilfully utilised the physical characteristics of his teenage actor to suit the requirements of the play: Wit desires to embrace learning, and the boy, experiencing the onset of puberty, is falling in love for the first time. As the chorister-scholar develops his education, and his thirst for knowledge, so the actor-chorister portrays young love, for he is just that, a young lover of learning and girls. Elsewhere the youthful inexperience of the actors is deliberately highlighted – just as happens in the later repertoire – for the author directs that Wit should *'practise in daunsing al things to make himselfe brethles'* (1121–2). This is, in a sense, an extra-dramatic incident, for Wit, the actor-chorister, is here showing the audience the way in which the children were taught dancing; yet it is also integral to the action, for the dance is therapeutic, designed to assist Wit in his search for a balanced education (IV.iii). The audience were thus given a glimpse of an actor's training, just as, in a sense, the whole performance was a rehearsal for presentation at court.[19]

In Act IV Scene iii first occurs a situation which the Children of Paul's were to make a hallmark of their repertoire in the first decade of the seventeenth century. Wit is apparently dead and

Will, directed to *'Rub'* and *'chafe him'* (983) cries out, 'For godde's love, hast! See, loe, where he doth lye!' (984) Eventually Wit is recovered by a two part song, sung by Will and Recreation:

> Give a legge, geve an arme, aryse, aryse!
> Hould up thy head, lift us thy eyes! (987–8)
> . . .
> Awake ye drowned powers! (993)

Wit's death was caused by Tedium and 'toyle' and he is resurrected by Recreation – a cure effected by the power of music. Apart from this instance of a song used medicinally with the words integral to the action, there is only one other song in the play. Sung by Idlenes, it is also incorporated in the plot, for Wit is lulled by it while he rests in her lap and a fool's coat is put upon him (IV.iv). There is less emphasis here in fact on singing than on dancing for, apart from Wit's display of their dance training, the boys put on a special show, again as part of the action of the play. In Act IV Scene iii Recreation calls upon Wit to dance (as part of his recovery from tedium) and he cries out, 'Pype us up a Galiard, mynstral, to begynne' (1090). Wit and Recreation both dance and go on with their display for some time, for the author directs, *'Let* Will *call for daunces, one after an other'* (1093). Will acts as 'dance caller' with the sequence of dances left to his discretion, presumably agreed beforehand with the musicians. Finally they offer an encore when Wit declares:

> This exercise hath done me good, even to the very hart.
> Let us be bould with you, more acquaintance to take,
> And dance a round yet once more for my sake. (1097–9)

Recreation, however, refuses; 'Enoughe is enoughe' (1101). The implication surely is that at the time of the public presentation of this play, Paul's had at least two outstanding dancers in their number, of whom the best was the teenage actor who played the part of Wit. While the galliard is taken over from Redford's version of the play, much more is made of it, and only in *The Marriage of Wit and Science* is there the display of dance training by Wit. The adapter was associated closely enough with the choir to be aware of the special talents of individual boys. In this sense his work is custom-designed for the Children of Paul's. The company, then, is already developing an embryonic awareness of the public value of the star system and actors of special talent also star in their later repertoire.

At least one other morality has survived from the decades of the 60s and 70s; it is *The Contention betweene Liberalitie and Prodigalitie*,[20] performed on 2 February 1574/5 at Hampton Court. For it the Revels Office provided 'A Cote, A hatt, & Buskins all over covered with ffethers of cullers for vanytie . . . skynnes to furr the hoode . . . [&] ffor making of ij sarcenet hooddes for Cyttyzens . . . a ffelt yt was covered with mony . . . cownters to cast awaye by players . . . a cote and a payer of Buskyns with a hatt made all over with sylver coyne and . . . sylk for the same . . . corde and a halter for an asse . . . a planck and Beeche for a ladder . . . sylver paper to make mony'.[21] The ladder was used for perhaps the most dangerous scene the company ever had to stage. Prodigalitie is required to scale a ladder, at which point '*Fortune claps a halter about his neck, he breaketh the halter and falles*'. Prodigalitie at once cries 'Swounds, helpe, Dick: Helpe quickly, or I am choakt' (906). One hopes the halter was completely severed before the boy was 'turned off', although Vanitie laments that the rope was 'so brittle' (929).

This play, while undoubtedly performed by the Children of Paul's, was later either stolen by the Chapel Children, who performed it in February 1601[22] when they were hastening to capitalise on the successful revival at Paul's of late 1599, or planned as a revival by Paul's but not produced. Its text may well be modified for the Blackfriars but it does imply the need for an 'above' as do *Meleager* and *The Marriage of Wit and Science*. *Liberalitie and Prodigalitie* makes much more liberal use of song than *The Marriage of Wit and Science*; it has seven songs, including one which sets the moral of the piece to music:

> *The passage first seemes hard:*
> *To vertues traine: but then most sweet,*
> *At length is their reward.*
>
> *To those againe that follow vice,*
> *The way is faire and plaine:*
> *But fading pleasures in the end,*
> *Are bought with fasting paine.* (1127–33)

This play was successful enough to be brought before Elizabeth twice by the Children of Paul's, in 1567/8 and 1574/5: its success at court may be an indication of its popular appeal. Certainly it was still felt to be good enough for a revival in 1601: if she saw it for this third time, Elizabeth might well have found the occasion highly nostalgic, for the play had first been presented before her some three decades earlier.

In Redford's *Wit and Science* the staging demands no more than an open hall floor, for it tends to be a static argument play rather than one filled with movement and action. Sometimes stage business is indicated in the manuscript, as when Idleness remarks, 'wher is my whystell to call my boye' (443) and Redford directs, '*here she whystleth and ingnorance cūth in*' (444–6). The whistle was obviously worn as part of the costume. In addition the actors needed a whip and a sword, and probably a whole group of devil's accoutrements for Tediousnes when he performs a war dance before his encounter with Wyt. It is also possible that the action was designed for use with an 'above', if one were available. Confidens informs Wyt that

> upon yonder mowntayne on hye
> she [Science] saw ye strike that hed from the bodye. (1012–13)

The mountain could well have been imagined 'off', but if an upper area were available in a hall screen, Science could have viewed the battlefield from that elevation. The impression created by the play is that the staging requirements are intentionally permissive, so that the performance may be fitted to the physical properties of the location. In the same way the demand on actors is not great: only eight players are vital to the action and all the other parts may be doubled. Only Wyt, Instruccion, Studye, Dyligence, Science, Experience, Reson and Confidens are together on stage at the same time and this group may well have included the four who played the viols.

In *The Marriage of Wit and Science* the requirements are greater: two house locations, one for Reason, Science, and Experience and a den for the monster Tediousness. Entries are often made from these houses (395, 589) and exits can also be effected in this way (1204); at the close of the play, Science invites 'all five' to 'come after me . . . and I will lead you in' (1555). Science's house is more substantial than a mere silk-hung lath frame, for she tells Wit, 'Here in this Closet our selfe wil sitte and see / Your manly feates and your successe in fyght' (1428–9), and as Lennam points out we must suppose that the closet or small inner room is situated in a raised place, perhaps an upper storey of her house, and that Science's viewpoint is a window large enough for her not only to see the combat below, but also large enough for her to be seen by the audience. (p. 108)

When staged in the Paul's playhouse, Science would be seated at the front of the upper acting area, leaning on the rail either in the centre or at the open casement window. The 'deadly denne' of the 'monstrous Giant' (702) Tediousness can also be used for entry and exit (701); the Giant is defeated in combat by Wit who promptly beheads him (1520) and, at Study's suggestion, mounts 'his head' upon his 'speare' (1524).

A choral chant follows this triumph when Wit, Will, Instruction, Study and Diligence cry in unison 'Tediousness is slaine!' (1536) a conclusion similar to the choral rendering of 'Mellida is dead' at the end of *Antonio's Revenge*. Tediousness was beheaded on stage and the false head was a special device of the monster's costume. In the original version the decapitation takes place 'off' and Wyt re-enters with 'the hed upon his swoorde' (1002–3) – sophistication has developed to allow the gory spectacle in full view of the audience. The scenic arrangement before which this ritual was carried out probably had the 'house' of Science at one side of the main acting area and at the other, in opposition, the den of Tediousness. The other characters probably entered centrally between the two.[23] The stage was thus arranged in three sections, just as the Paul's playhouse interior had three identifiable house locations upon it.

Only simple properties are needed: a picture of Wit (262); a 'glasse of Christal cleare' (838); a fool's coat (1175–7); a whip and a knife (1331); and various weapons including a sword, buckler, dagger and spear. Some indication of what it cost the general public to see the play may be gleaned from a remark by Ignorance. Idelnes, Ignorance's mother, offers to show a spectacle of Wit's humiliation, which is the ensuing action of the play, and Ignorance declares:

Choulde geve twaye pence to see it and tway pence moore. (1169)

This offers some evidence for the prices at Paul's in the mid-70s and early 80s: possibly Shepard collected 2d at the door from the cathedral nave[24] and better seats could be had for an additional 2d. Lyly remarks in *Pappe with a Hatchet* (1589) that a Marprelate play 'If it be shewed at Paules . . . will cost you foure pence.'[25] But one could pay more than this, for in mid-1589 William Darrell of Littlecote paid 6d for his personal secretary, James More, to see a play at 'Powles'.[26] The price range, then, was 2d to 6d.

Like the domain of Science in *The Marriage of Wit and Science*, *The Contention betweene Liberalitie and Prodigalitie* requires a substantial 'house'. This is an impressive structure, a palace, and Tenacity applauds it, 'Ah goodly Lord, how gay it is!' (184). It has an upper storey where Fortune can sit upon a 'stately throne' (290) to view the action and she descends from this upper level to make her exit. Some part of this upper area had an operating window that might plausibly be entered, for Dick advises Prodigalitie that to get his money back he must

Scale the walles, in at the window. (897)

He then uses the ladder and is almost hanged. The 'homely bowre' (132) of Virtue is adjacent to Fortune's splendid palace and there is also an inn. This inn probably had an upper storey, for the Host speaks wearing a 'nightcap' (70) apparently from an upper bedroom window, when Prodigalitie demands entrance by banging on the door below. This three house arrangement, two of which seem to have had upper storeys with windows, and the third, the palace, which may have afforded Fortune a central viewing position 'above', is a very close depiction of the physical characteristics known to exist at Paul's after 1599: the text may, therefore, betray late modifications.

The surviving elements from the repertoire of the Children of Paul's under Redford and Westcott are few and scattered, and generalisation is hazardous, but it is possible to be reasonably confident that one type of play, at least, remained popular and successful from the 1540s to the early seventeenth century. This was the story of the Prodigal, in its various guises, for *Wit and Science*, *The Marriage of Wit and Science*, *Liberalitie and Prodigalitie* and probably also *The Paynfull Piltgrimage, A Morall of the Marryage of Mynde and Measure, Wit and Will* and perhaps *The History of Error*, were all studies on this theme.

In its first presentation by Redford the story of the Prodigal Son is at its simplest and most explicit. When Wyt appears to woo Science, unaware that he is wearing the fool's coat of Ignorance, which his own waywardness has earned him, Science reprimands him for his folly:

> I take ye for no naturall foole
> browght up a mong the innocente scoole
> but for a nawgty vycious foole
> browght up . . .
>   wyth Idellness in her scoole
> of all arrogant fooles thow art one. (806–11)

Wyt's initial reaction is that of the prodigal, for he dismisses the accusation as coming from 'a drab that . . . doth dysdayne him' (819); but then he looks in a glass and sees 'a foole . . . deckt by goge bones lyke a very asse / Ingnorance cote hoode eares' (835–7) and this change in his appearance brings about the beginnings of his moral regeneration, 'nay verely I knowe / now it is so the stark foole I playe / before all people . . . / evrye man I se lawhe me to scorne' (845–8). From his self-disgust, he progresses to an awareness of how he has slandered others, 'alas ladye science . . . / how have I rayld on her' (852–3) and he deeply regrets his folly; in place of her hand he has won only 'hatred beggry and open [shame]' (863). At this point Wyt is whipped by Shame, but this punishment is interrupted by Reson when Wyt cries, 'oh syr forgeve me I beseech you' (887), and when Reson asks Wyt if he will still honour his betrothal to Science, Wyt's response reflects the progress of his repentance, 'oh syr I am not woorthye to carye / the dust out where your dowghter shoold syt' (891–2). Reson's action in forgiving Wyt and re-admitting him to his former status is directly analogous to the behaviour of the Prodigal's father in Luke 15; the variance is merely that Wyt returns to the paths of scholarship from the ways of idleness, and the suitor returns to his true love. Wyt, thus redeemed, slays the monster Tediousnes and is embraced by Science: the espousal is conceived as an actual marriage to a woman of some spirit and independence, for his bride warns him:

> yf ye use me well in a good sorte
> then shall I be youre Ioy & comfort
> but yf ye use me [w]not well then dowt me
> for sure ye were better then wyth out me. (1061–4)

Wyt hastens to assure her that he will follow her father Reson's advice. The union of Wyt and Science is concluded on a carefully articulated religious note, for Wyt assures his auditors that he will never so love Science as to forget God, but together the couple will trust in His grace.

This allegory of man's proper use of knowledge may well have been reinforced by Wyt's dress – he and his portrait agree at the close, and perhaps both were represented in a Master's gown, suitable for a wedding and also for Wyt, the graduate. Indeed coats play a very significant part in this play, for Wyt, at the outset in a scholar's gown, loses it to Ignorance who is, however, unable to keep it on; Wyt's repentance allows him to regain it from Reson and his final reward is Science's wedding gift of the 'gowne of knoledge' (1016).

In *The Marriage of Wit and Science* the clear-cut allegory of Redford's work has been muted to allow the amplification of a lyric, romantic note: the prime interest of the play is in the love affair between Wit and Science, conceived largely as human lovers and not abstract qualities. A continuous ribald commentary upon this love affair is supplied by Will, Wit's impudent page, and he is in no doubt how to cure Wit's lovesickness:

> Care for no more, but once to come within her,
> And when you have done, then let another win her. (561–2)

Will's scorn for the antics of lovers is persistent; his eye is always on the practical effects once the suit is won and the sickness cured. His initial advice to Wit is not to give up the freedom of his bachelorhood, when they may both enjoy good fellowship and 'may laugh and be mery at bord and at bedde' (306). This is an ironic commendation of the life of lechery, for Will's phrase is designed to recall the bride's promise in the old Sarum marriage rite of pre-Reformation Catholicism:

[She promises] to have and to holde fro this day for warde for better: for wors: for richer: for povere: in sykenesse et in hele: to be bonere and buxom in bedde and at te borde tyll dethe us departhe if holy chyrche it wol ordeyne.

Will's pragmatic attitude to the love affair of Wit and Science is a good-natured parody of the absurdities of lovers and it looks forward to that master of comic lovesickness, Launce of *The Two Gentlemen of Verona*.

Will is the most sophisticated human character of the play and yet he also represents temptation and waywardness in Wit. It is through too unthinking a reliance on undirected Will that Wit falls foul of the monster Tediousness and unjustly blames Science for this mishap:

> The matche was over much for me . . .
> How did I give her cause to shewe me this despyght.
> Accursed be the time and hower, which first I did her see.
>
> (1031, 1032, 1036)

This is more of a lover's tiff, however, than a true crisis of awareness and we are conscious that Redford's Prodigal is gradually being metamorphosed into a wayward lover; his redemption is contingent upon the continued love of his virtuous paramour. This is certainly the tone of his reaction to the discovery that he is wearing a fool's coat:

> . . . O rufull chaunce to me!
> O Idleness, woe worth the time that I was ruled by thee!
> Why did I lay my head within thy lappe to rest?
>
> (1291–3)

This is closer to a bad conscience in a suitor who has spent a night in another's bed, than a developing awareness of unrighteousness. When Shame threatens to whip him, Wit reacts with all the hyperbole of the ascetic lover who has suddenly discovered his own sensual weakness:

> O spare mee with the whippe, and sley me with the knife.
> Ten thousand times more deare to me were present death then lyfe.
>
> (1331–2)

Reason reminds him of his betrothal and, to escape the censure of the world (Wit remains wholly egocentric), he determines to tackle Tediousness again. The defeat of the monster in itself redeems Wit:

> Thy hed this day shall mee prefer unto my harte's desyre. (1519)

Science's reaction is to accept Wit for he is purged by this evidence of manly courage: in a sense the Prodigal's story has become an allegory of the gradual growth from youth to adulthood. Wit, who began unable to show his lady 'sport in bed', has by defeating Tediousness become a fit partner for Science and the couple are now 'one soule in bodyes twayne' (1562). While the structure of the Prodigal story is still apparent here, it is evolving into the basic romance plot of the later comic drama, where lovers overcome the vicissitudes of their own characters as well as the opposition of other people to achieve a lasting bliss.

In *The Contention betweene Liberalitie and Prodigalitie*, the prodigal is at once identifiable: from his first entrance, creating an uproar at an inn late at night, Prodigalitie is a loud, arrogant spendthrift. His rake's progress is a gradually deepening involvement in sin and crime; he attempts forcible entry to regain his squandered gold, then commits highway robbery and finally becomes an assassin, as the Constable reports:

A plaine simple man ryding on his Asse,
Meaning home to his Country in Gods peace to passe,
By certaine Roysters most furious and mad,
Is spoyled and robbed of all that he had.
And yet not contented, when they had his money,
But the villaynes have also murderd him most cruelly. (1059–64)

The gratuitous violence of this murder is in marked contrast to Prodigalitie's attitude at his ensuing trial. He pleads guilty and throws himself on the mercy of the court and, although the Judge passes the death sentence, Prodigalitie is allowed to make a plea:

I confesse, I have runne a wanton wicked race,
Which now hath brought me to this wofull wretched case:
I am heartily sorrie, and with teares doe lament
My former lewd, and vile misgovernment.
I finde the brittle stay of trustlesse Fortunes state.
My heart now thirsteth after Vertue, all too late. (1298–1303)

The court is impressed by these signs of penitence and the Judge himself promises to intercede with the Prince in the hope that 'though your punishment be not fully remitted, / Yet in some part, it may be qualified' (1311–12). This reclaiming of the Prodigal is more nearly akin to Redford's plot, than to the ending of the redaction of his work. It implies the availability of grace even after sentence is passed, and offers the same kind of unexpected and wholly unmerited salvation which the Prodigal's father offers in the parable. It was a popular version of the story, without the subtlety of Redford, but more easily and obviously a compliment to the sovereign who is the Prince to whom the appeal is made.

In this play the emphasis is upon the incidents of Prodigalitie's excesses and they give rise to much splendour of action, with money being flung by the players among the audience; the gorgeousness of the costume was a distinctive feature with Vanity in a coat decorated with multi-coloured feathers to suggest frivolity, and Money in a coat with coins stitched upon it. There were also some grand processions, as in the opening of the sixth scene:

Enter Fortune in her Chariot drawne with Kings. (242)

Fortune, who was probably carrying her wheel, advanced in state as a prefigurement of Tamburlaine's entry, '*drawen in his chariot by Trebizon and Soria with bittes in their mouthes, reines in his left hand, in his right hand a whip, with which he scourgeth them*' (II,IV.iii.l): it was Marlowe's hero who usurped her place. Fortune's costume was as magnificent as her entrance; she appears in 'pompous shew', in 'vestures wrought with gold so gorgeously' (261–2) and her attendant Kings would, no doubt, have been arrayed with equal dignity. This pomp and circumstance is in deliberate contrast with the simple sobriety of Virtue. *Liberalitie and Prodigalitie* in a sense made up in display both for what it lacked of Redford's analytic allegory and for where it was deficient in human interest.

By 1574/5 the fee for play performances at court had increased from £6 13s 4d to £10 and this increase is coincident with the flocking of the public to the Paul's house. In the same way the children became suddenly valuable properties in themselves: one of Westcott's boys was either kidnapped or perhaps bribed to transfer his allegiance elsewhere.[27] The children had become fictional amateurs: the convenient notion was preserved that they were rehearsing for court performance before the general public, but this was merely a legal evasion like the retainer status of the adult actors. If the evident popularity of the Children of Paul's may be trusted, their metamorphosis into a fixed-base theatre company which charged spectators, may have been forced upon them by public demand: 'fees' to see their rehearsals were perhaps a way of limiting, rather than increasing audiences.

For some seven years after the complaint was lodged against him for profiteering, Westcott and his amateur-professional actor-choristers (and ex-choristers) enjoyed considerable and continued success. His company between February 1575 and December 1581 appeared at court ten times, with the Master being paid, in total, £129 0s 4d with an additional bonus of 10 marks in 1575.[28] An additional £20 per annum for court appearances as well as profits, between 2d and 6d per head, for 'rehearsals' before the general public was a significant addition to the emoluments of the Master of Choristers. Westcott was successful as a theatrical entrepreneur, but his personal life was not without its trials. He had long been a source of concern to the ecclesiastical establishment; as Grindal put it, he had been guilty of misinforming his charges in 'corrupte lessons of false Religion [which he] instilled into the eares and myndes of those children committed unto him'.[29] Tolerance by Grindal, at Leicester's urging, had been long but Grindal's successor John Aylmer had Westcott brought before the Privy Council as a recusant at Hampton Court on 20 December 1577. He was ordered to be confined in the Marshalsea the following day, but pleasure prevailed before 'false Religion', for his imprisonment was postponed until December, so that his children could still appear before the Queen at Hampton Court.[30] From December to the following 19 March Westcott was in jail: this, presumably, caused a cessation in the public performance of plays by the children, so at least his profits were reduced.

On 3 April 1582, 'beinge greved withe sicknes', Sebastian Westcott made his will. It reflects a wide range of fraternal involvement with the other members of the cathedral establishment: he left £5 to the minor canons, £4 to his fellow vicars choral and £10 to the choristers (presumably £1 each); there are also smaller legacies to the minor officers of the church such as the vergers and bellringers. In addition he left substantial furnishings to the almonry house for the use of future choristers and almoners. He does not forget seven ex-choristers, 'Bromehame, Richard Huse, Robert knight, Nicolas Carleton . . . Bayle . . . Nasion, and Gregorye Bowringe', to whom he leaves £1 each, just as he had done to the choristers. In the choir list drawn up for Bishop Sandys in 1574, Henry Nation, George Bowring and Robert Knight appear, and in the list for 1554 is a Richard Hewse. Westcott also leaves £6 14s 4d to 'Peter Phillipe' who, like the others, was still maintained by the cathedral establishment as an ex-chorister.[31] Peter Phillipp appears in the 1574 list of choristers. The ages of these superannuated boys, ranged from the extreme of about thirty (if Hewse and Huse are the same) to the late teens (like Wit). In all probability these are the names of Westcott's senior actors who both stiffened the action by providing a greater maturity for certain parts, and could strengthen the singing with a bass sound alongside the boy sopranos.

Westcott's will further prescribes 'to my loving frende Mr henerye Evans six poundes thirtene shillinges fouwer pence, and a little cuppe of silver and a cover withe twoe litle winges on the cover'. Evans, later called my 'deere friende', is made assistant executor and Westcott asks Evans to care for Elizabeth Westcote, his widowed sister. It was this Henry Evans who was to become closely involved with the theatrical activity of the boys.

The settled and ordered affairs of the choir with their regular court and city acting were seriously confused by Westcott's death. The new Almoner was Thomas Gyles: he presumably moved into the almonry house, to which Westcott had left so much of value, as soon as Westcott was buried, and remained there until his own death some eighteen years later. Gyles seems to have had a quite different personality. It is clear from the extra conditions pertaining to the appointment of his successor, Edward Pearce,[32] that after his confirmation as Master of Choristers in 1584, Gyles was guilty of a very liberal interpretation of the rules governing the conduct of his office. Westcott was allowed to appoint a deputy or deputies to exercise his functions after his 1559 reappointment;[33] Gyles was similarly privileged, and there is every reason to believe that John Lyly acted semi-officially in this capacity, for Gabriel Harvey remarked that Lyly 'hath not played the Vice master of Poules and the Foolemaster of the Theater for naughtes.'[34] This substitution was hardly in conformity with the terms of his appointment, where Gyles was allowed a deputy only 'by reason of sickenesse or other causes' – the 'other causes' being intended to be akin to 'reason of sickenesse'. Secondly Gyles was strictly commanded 'neyther to sett nor lette any parte or parcell of the house belonging to the Almner'. He did contrive to have William Creek allowed to rent at least one room at ground level and two additional ones as a loft conversion. He seems to have taken on additional paid work, for Pearce was warned not to 'depart or searve elsewhere under payne of forfeyture'. He may also have been selling star boys and collecting transfer fees, for Pearce is instructed not 'at anie tyme . . . to consent to the selling or shifting awaye of anie Chorister . . . for money or for anie other reward or consideration'. Later in his tenure of office, Gyles sublet the cloisters to trunkmakers, thus denying their use both for plays and as an alternative site for the Paul's Cross sermons. Finally from April 1598 he grew more and more remiss in the performance of his duties, and failed to appoint a deputy to act for him, probably because he was unwilling to pay the necessary fees. As a result the choir was in a dishevelled and ragged state. The impression created is of a careless man, more interested in his own comforts and profits than in the welfare of the choristers. Westcott, on the other hand, with his careful provision for the physical comforts of the boys, gives a much more positive impression. Gyles was idle, negligent and only barely acceptable in terms of basic performance – the choir was 'well instructed' and had sufficient 'food and drink', but that was all.[35] With a man of this kind now in charge, it is hardly surprising that the dramatic activities of the choir should take quite a new turn.

After 1582 there is a reversion to the amalgamated status of the choir in its acting role, such as had prevailed before Redford's mastership; it was not now a group composed of choir and grammar school, but a joint company, variously mixed, created by the temporary amalgamation of the Children of Paul's and the Children of the Chapel at the Blackfriars.

Between 26 December 1581 when Westcott presented his last play before the Queen at Whitehall and 1 January 1583/4 when there was played John Lyly's *Campaspe* 'before the Queenes Maiestie . . . by her Maiesties Children, and the Children of Paules', the Paul's company did not entertain their sovereign. Their new image, on the resumption, was declared in the Prologue to *Campaspe*:

Whatsoever we present, we wish it may be thought the dauncing of *Agrippa* his shadowes, who in the moment they were seene, were of any shape one woulde conceive: or *Lynces* [the most keen sighted of the Argonauts], who having a quicke sight to discerne, have a short memorie to forget. With us it is like to fare, as with these torches, which giving light to others, consume themselves, and wee shewing delight to others shame our selves.

97

This stress on the transitory nature of dramatic performances, on the insubstantiality and fickleness of actors and spectators, on the dreamlike quality of the whole experience is so distinctive a change from the more robust and positive repertoire under Westcott, that a significant shift in direction and policy has taken place.

From April 1582 to May 1584 Gyles was on probation, concentrating on proving himself suitable for advancement to the Mastership. His main emphasis was undoubtedly the singing of the boys in the choir, for this was his primary function. For this short period the history of the Children of Paul's and the Chapel Children at the Blackfriars merges, for on several occasions – 1 January 1583/4 when *Campaspe* was played, 3 March 1583/4 when the play was *Sapho and Phao*, and 27 December 1584 when the play was the (lost) *History of Agamemnon and Ulysses* – the companies performed as a composite group with the Earl of Oxford giving the dignity of his title to the amalgamated company. On the first two occasions the £10 fee was paid to John Lyly.[36] Why did Gyles permit the pre-eminent Paul's choir to be at least temporarily swallowed by their chief rivals? The explanation is surely that Gyles lacked either Redford's or Westcott's personal ambition or commitment to the cause of the choir as a whole. He was much more self-centred and it was convenient for the dramatic side of the choir's activities to be continued, with little personal involvement from himself, while he consolidated his own position as Master of the music. Under Westcott's mastership the choir had been very much dominated by him and while for a period in the 60s he may have had the assistance of John Heywood,[37] essentially it was he alone who controlled their acting. Gyles had no apparent dramatic experience: he was merely a vicar choral and, unlike Westcott who is named as successor in Redford's will, there is no mention of Gyles in Westcott's.

Henry Evans, Westcott's 'dear friend', had the same function as Westcott in Redford's will:[38] in a sense he is the main legatee of Westcott's achievements. He acquired the lease of the Blackfriars theatre from William Hunnis, probably before November 1583, possibly with the intention of trying to move the Children of Paul's to these larger premises and set up a monopoly: Paul's were the most successful company, whereas William Hunnis

had had difficulty in paying his rent. Evans bought his lease
from Hunnis and a John Newman partly because they were
being pressured by Sir William More, the owner of the Blackfriars buildings, who objected to the use of his rooms as a
playhouse and, this pressure continuing, Evans sold his lease to
the Earl of Oxford, about June 1583. Oxford gave it to John Lyly.
By Easter Term 1584 the lease had reverted to Sir William
More.[39] For a short period, then, Evans along with Lyly and
Oxford (who had a company of boys of his own) were involved
in an attempt to formulate the best possible combination of
young acting and singing talent in London. The Children of
Paul's, supplemented by the Chapel Children, may well have
performed not only in their own house in the 'shrowdes' but
also in the Blackfriars theatre. Certainly they were successful
enough to be presented twice at court in plays by Lyly. Gyles
appears to have taken little or no part in these proceedings,
contenting himself with teaching music and probably receiving
a fee from Lyly and Evans for the loan of his choristers.

Campaspe, which is almost certainly Lyly's first play, reveals
the influence of the established repertoire of the company for
whom he is writing. In the first scene of the fifth act, three star
turns are offered one after the other: the first is a dance display
by Perim (E3^v), the second an acrobatic act, '*Milo tumbleth*' (E3^v),
and finally Sylus offers 'Now shall you heare the third, who
signes like a Nightingall' (E4), and '*Trico singeth*' – the latter was,
probably, a principal choir soloist with, like Marston's Forobo-
sco and Castilio, a 'high stretch minikin voice' (*A.M.*, H3^v).
Peter Saccio argues that this scene is a demonstration of 'courtly
accomplishments that Diogenes explicitly condemns as sub-
human'[40] and while it may well be true that the scene is integral
to the various anecdotal themes of the play, it is hard to see
acrobatics or the ability to sing like a soprano as a 'courtly grace'.
Lyly is, I suggest, aware of the special abilities of the boys and
the habit of using outstanding choristers for special 'star' turns,
but he is also attempting to make them integral to the action. He
partially succeeds.

Campaspe is a play with an important unifying device of
portraiture. Like Wyt in Redford's *Wit and Science*, Campaspe is
portrayed throughout the play by means of a painting. The
painter, Apelles, falls in love with his creation and eventually is

allowed by Alexander to wed the real Campaspe, thus uniting art and nature or, as Redford would have it, bringing together the image and the reality. From the first scene of the second act the stage is largely taken over by Apelles' workshop and its paintings. Apart from the 'sweete face of *Campaspe*' (B3ᵛ), there are paintings of Laeda (C3ᵛ), Alcmena (C3ᵛ), Antiopa (C3ᵛ), Danae (C3ᵛ), Europa (C3ᵛ) and Venus (C4) – all of which are pointed out by Campaspe and commented on by Apelles (III.iii), which makes it clear that the audience could see them and thus they were of substantial size. A gallery of portraits was hung on stage, for as Apelles remarks, 'It were pittie, but that so absolute a face [as Campaspe's] should furnish Venus temple amongst these pictures' (C3ᵛ). All the paintings are of the erotic delights of Jupiter who ravished all the women portrayed and, as Saccio points out, the paintings continue the play's theme of the relationship of love to power.[41] Similarly the guide to decorum which the play is embodying suggests later that Alexander, the monarch, is unfitted to be a painter for, after a lesson in charcoal drawing from Apelles (III.iv), Alexander ruefully remarks if 'ones hand, ones eie, ones minde, must all draw together, I had rather be setting of a battell, then blotting of a bourd. But how have I done heere?' Apelles replies, truthfully, 'Like a king' (D2). The lesson in drawing is not extra-dramatic, but integral to the phases of the plot; yet it is like the demonstration of dancing, acrobatics and singing in being a special accomplishment. Like Westcott's Wit, who was an exceptional dancer, so now Lyly has an Apelles who is an outstanding artist. Lyly's set may also have been similar to that used for *The Marriage of Wit and Science*, for in the first scene of the third act Apelles commands Psyllus to stay at the 'window' of his house (C2ᵛ).

Sapho and Phao, almost certainly Lyly's second play for the joint company, possibly following within weeks of his first, was presented at court on 3 March 1584: *Campaspe* had been presented the previous 1 January. This second play shows no signs of the influence of the Paul's repertoire or special talents in the company. It is more consciously Lyly's own style. It is episodic and anecdotal in the extreme, so that continuous attention is not required. It could be sampled as noise, conversation and other distractions allowed. The absence of any star turns or any demands upon the audience's powers of concentration suggests that its form is not teleological but rather accretive. It presents itself as a conscious circumlocution,

We fear we have lead you all this while in a Labyrinth of conceites, diverse times hearing one device, & have now brought you to an end, where we first beganne. (Epilogue, G2).

It is a play about the social decorum to be shown in one's emotional involvements. It seeks to entertain without intruding on other activities which may be coincident with it.

In both *Campaspe* and *Sapho and Phao* the organisation of the dramatic action and the arrangement of the characters is concentric rather than linear: the purpose is not so much to reach any predetermined end as to weave variations on the basis of a given theme. In *Campaspe* the action turns on the relationship between Alexander, the monarch, Campaspe, whom he loves, and Apelles, the painter, who also loves Campaspe; but this triangular relation is overlaid by the more significant issue of the decorum which must govern a king's conduct in a mere commonplace emotional affair. Alexander must love as a man, without losing the dignity of being a king; and at the same time, since Campaspe's real affection develops for Apelles, the change of the direction of this love must be conducted without slighting Alexander's greatness as a ruler. Campaspe's soliloquy at the beginning of the second scene of the fourth act reveals her change of heart:

Campaspe, It is hard to iudge whether thy choice be more unwise, or thy chaunce unfortunate. Doest thou preferre, but stay, utter not that in woordes, which maketh thine eares to glow with thoughts. Tush better thy tongue wagge, then thy heart break. Hath a painter crept further into thy mind then a prince? *Apelles* then *Alexander*? Fond wench, the basenes of thy mind bewraies the meannesse of thy birth. But alas, affection is a fyre which kindleth as well in the bramble as in the oake, & catcheth hold where it first lighteth, not where it may best burne. Larkes that mount aloft in the ayre, build their neastes below in the earth, and women that cast their eyes upon kinges, may place their hearts upon vassals. A needle will become thy fingers better then a Lute, and a distaffe is fitter for thy hand then a Scepter. Ants live safely, til they have gotten wings, and Iuniper is not blowne up, till it hath gotten an hie top. The meane estate is without care as long as it continueth without pride. (E)

101

The disclosure begins by shifting the emphasis away from a personal anguish to a philosophical debate – is it human will or divine will that has caused the change? It reverts briefly to a personal dimension with 'thy heart break', but at once steadies into a resolution in terms of the decorum of the issue; Campaspe argues convincingly to herself that the estates should remain distinct; her lowly birth and Apelles' meanness of station are a fit unity, whereas Alexander's royalty is a station to which decorum could not permit her to aspire. Essentially in place of the gradual self-discovery which both Redford's and Westcott's Wit found as a result of their departure from their true paths, Campaspe reveals to us not her self, but the mode in which human emotions ought to channel themselves. Since Campaspe recognises that she violates decorum with her affection for Alexander, his kingship is untarnished: a discovery not of self, but of propriety. She is not a fit mate and Alexander remains the unwed king: a compliment to the Virgin Queen. Campaspe is largely depersonalised; she represents ideas and philosophies rather than embodying them. Lyly's characters are not so much persons as intellectual vehicles, a movement into rather than away from symbol, whereas the opposite tendency was beginning to be prevalent in the Paul's plays under Westcott, where Wit and Science, at least, were emerging from allegory into humanity and Will had already become a man.

To the audience who had earlier patronised the Children of Paul's and who had shown its appreciation of the Prodigal plays, which had a clear teleological design, this change must have been very surprising. There is some indication that their initial reaction to *Campaspe* was distinctly unfavourable, for *The Prologue at the Black fryers* to *Sapho and Phao* begins with an apology and a wistful lament:

Where the Bee can suck no honney, she leaveth her stinge behinde, and where the Beare cannot finde *Origanum* to heale his griefe, he blasteth all other leaves with his breath. Wee feare it is like to fare so with us, that seeing you cannot draw from our labours sweete content, you leave behinde you a sowre mislike, and with open reproach blame our good meaninges: because you cannot reap your wonted mirthes. Our intēt was at this time to move inward delight, not outward lightnesse, and to breede, (if it might bee) soft smiling, not loude laughing: knowing it to the wise to be as great pleasure to heare counsell mixed with witte, as to the foolish to have sporte mingled with rudenesse.

As has been pointed out by a number of critics, Lyly is, in this argument, seeking to achieve Sidney's notional 'comedy of delight', which is to be distinguished from an 'extreame show of doltishnesse . . . fit to lift up a loude laughter and nothing else', for 'though laughter may come with delight, yet commeth it not of delight . . . Delight hath a joy in it . . . wee are ravished with delight to see a faire woman . . . We delight in good chaunces . . . We delight to hear the happinesse of our friendes . . . [and he concludes] the ende of the Comicall part bee not uppon suche scornfull matters as stirre laughter onlie but mixe with it, that delightfull teaching whiche is thee end of Poesie.'[42] Sidney's argument is designed to produce a comedy where thought and reflection on the pleasing instances of successful human endeavour and the happy chances of fate should not be annihilated by the overwhelming emotion of laughter. Lyly certainly seems to have striven to attain this end, but his audience, at least in the semi-public arena of the Blackfriars and Paul's playhouses, did not find the new style and tone desirable. There was not enough laughter in it and his allusive, allegorical style was probably too complex.

In *Campaspe* the dramatic situation is centred and made coherent around a group of similar questions: what is true magnanimity? What is the true quality of kingship? How far is a monarch merely a man when in love? The examination of these questions is further governed by an overriding determination to display instances of conduct which may instruct the Prince, whether Alexander or Elizabeth, in the true arts of peace, as Hephastion argues:

it resteth now that we have as great care to governe in peace, as conquer in war: that whilest armes cease, Artes may flourish, and ioyning letters with launces we endevor to be as good Philosophers as soldiers, knowing it no lesse praise to be wise, thē commendable to be valiant. (A2)

Peace and war are brought into contrast, just as are love and duty, but the love theme of the piece is essentially incidental: Alexander's relationship with Campaspe is never more than a flirtation. The real business of the Prince, and therefore of the play, is self-knowledge, for at the close Alexander admits:

It were a shame *Alexander* should desire to commaund the world, if he could not commaund himself. (F4)

103

This is not, however, a conclusion anticipated as a purpose of the dramatic action; nor is it a deduction emergent from the experience of that action. There is no sense of growth in spirit, rather the end is an inductive realisation provoked by the changing situations and groupings of persons within the course of the play. Lyly is seeking less to entertain than to instruct. Despite the fact that many of the plays of the Children of Paul's under Westcott were moralities, they offered less in the way of overt lessons in conduct. Lyly is providing a drama much more, rather than less, specifically related to a special context. His eye is on the court and the sophistication of only a relatively small group of influential members of that court. His plays for the Children of Paul's are deliberately circumscribed in their appeal. It is clear from later Prologues, and perhaps from the plot of *Mother Bombie* itself, that Lyly was not a successful dramatist in the playhouse whatever his success at court might have been.

On 22 May 1584 Thomas Gyles, Almoner, was confirmed in the appointment of Master of Choristers: at once he reasserted control over the Children of Paul's in their dramatic role. He displaced both Evans and Lyly as court payee, but Lyly remained purveyor of plays. Gyles' confirmation as Master also marks the separation of the Paul's children from the Children of the Chapel. The joint company broke up, never to be re-formed. In the following year, on 27 April 1585, Gyles' confidence was further boosted when he received a royal commission of impressment – like Westcott he could now take up boys anywhere in the kingdom. Gyles may have been encouraged to take over the plays at Paul's by support from the group of friends who were associates of Nicholas Yonge, one of the vicars choral, for Yonge describes how, 'since I first began to keepe house in this Citie, it hath been no small comfort unto me that a great number of Gentlemen and Merchants of good accompt (as well of this realme as of forreine nations) have taken in good part such entertainment of pleasure, as my poore abilitie was able to afford them, both by the exercise of Musicke daily used in my house, and by furnishing them with Bookes of that kinde yeerly sent me out of Italy and other places'.[43] Although the music may well have been modern, with the inclusion of the latest Italian madrigals, the style remained courtly: Lyly's plays were court literature in their preoccupation with courtly manners, compliments to the sovereign and simplicity of staging based on the facilities available in the Tudor great hall.

Gallathea begins with a Prologue which is an apotheosis of courtly hyperbole, 'Your Maiesties iudgement and favour, are our Sunne and shadowe, the one comming of your deepe wisedome, the other of your wonted grace. Wee in all humilitie desire, that by the former, receiving our first breath, we may in the latter, take our last rest . . . Your highnesse hath so perfit a iudgement, that whatsoever we offer, we are enforced to blush' (Aij). Years of experience of such terminology would no doubt moderate the effect of the flattery; indeed the praises had to be lavish to be heard at all, in an atmosphere of competition for favour through praise. The play is a pastoral; its opening words indicate its mood and the visual setting of the piece:

The Sunne dooth beate uppon the playne fieldes, wherefore let us sit downe Gallathea, under this faire Oake, by whose broade leaves, beeing defended from the warme beames, we may enioy the fresh ayre, which softly breathes from Humber floodes. (B)

It is a setting which is at once recognisably English (oak and Humber) and also Arcadian ('the Sunne dooth beate') and the staging involves a consciousness of these two elements.

The main acting area is dominated by this oak, which had golden leaves (E4), and probably other trees ('these woods are to me . . . wel known', B2^v); it seems to have been secure enough to bind Hebe to it (V.ii). Greater use is, however, made of costume and make-up than of set: in the main plot Gallathea is disguised as a boy from the beginning – her costume is distinguished by a white coat ('I sawe Eurota howe amorouslie you glaunced your eye on the faire boy in the white coate', D2^v)[44]; Phillida's coat is coloured and distinctive by its shortness (B3^v). Costume, then, offers a means of differentiating between the two lovesick boy/girls. In contrast the Alchemist's boy, Peter, is either a blackamoor or made up like one: 'What blacke boy is this?'(C3). Lyly uses coats again as a distinguishing and disguising device in *Mother Bombie* where the two lovers, Livia and Candius, contrive to be married in full view of their disapproving parents, who think they are witnessing the wedding of two neighbours' children, for the two pairs of lovers have exchanged 'coates' (H3^v).

Transvestism is a major theme of the play, with Gallathea and Phillida (both boys acting girls' parts) disguised as boys, each wishing to be a boy, or at least of a sex other than what they are. At the last a promise is made that one of them will become a changeling, at the very inception of the marriage ceremony. There are clear hints that Gallathea is to be this changeling. There is a delicate punning on the transvestite/transformation theme: Gallathea and Phillida, distinguished by their white and coloured coats, spar with ironic deceit that each is pretending to be of a sex they are not:

Phil. . . . I say it is a pitty you are not a woman.
Galla. I would not wish to be a woman, unlesse it were because thou art a man.
Phil. Nay I doe not wish to be a woman, for then I should not love thee, for I have sworne never to love a woman.
Galla. A strange humor in so prettie a youth. (D4)

The plot demands this confusion and longing and hinges on the final metamorphosis of one into the other sex, but the means was an established tradition in the repertoire of the Children of Paul's. In *The Marriage of Wit and Science* Wit had deliberately used the fact of his actual youth and inexperience to heighten the realism of his falling in love with Science: so here Lyly uses the fact of the boy's masculinity ironically, for Phillida is played by a boy with a voice still soprano, whereas Gallathea is a superannuated chorister, with a broken voice (or one breaking): Phillida remarks, 'I feare me he is as I am, a mayden . . . Tush it cannot be, his voice shewes the contrarie' (D4^v).

In terms of staging no emphasis is placed on location; it is pastoral, in a forest, with entry from side or rear: the themes of the play are highlighted not by a contrast of opposing entries or houses but by visual (coats) and verbal (voices breaking and unbroken) clues. It is eminently suitable for performance in any open area with the minimum of facilities, but its mood is directed not merely to the court, but primarily to one section of that court, as the Epilogue, spoken by Gallathea, makes clear:

You Ladies may see, that Venus can make constancie ficklenes, courage cowardice, modestie lightnesse, working things impossible in your Sexe, and tempering hardest harts like softest wooll. Yeelde Ladies, yeeld to love Ladies, which lurketh under your eye-lids whilst you sleepe, and plaieth with your hart strings whilst you wake. (H2)

In a sense Lyly has intentionally not merely limited the appeal of his play by the dominant courtliness of his theme, lessons in love's mysteries, but also consciously subdivided his potential courtly audience still further. His appeal is to the ladies of the court alone: men benefit only incidentally. As far as the dramatic provenance and vitality of the Paul's company were concerned this was a dangerous narrowing; their appeal was being deliberately restricted. It is to Lyly, then, that the Children of Paul's owe their traditional image as courtly entertainers; but in terms of their repertoire and history as a whole, this was only a phase.

Gallathea required only a small cast: in Act V Scene iii eleven principals were needed as well as Diana's nymphs (G2^v); in *Mother Bombie* the number is even smaller, nine speaking parts and some non-speaking extras could perform it (with extensive doubling). Its set and locale are more specifically defined than in Lyly's previous plays. It was staged using multiple-function houses. These houses, of which the principal is Mother Bombie's (E4), give the impression of being placed in opposition to each other on the main acting area. They served variously as 'Stellios house' (C4^v), which may have had a visible upper storey, for Stellio speaks of having 'penned [up his daughter] in a chamber, having onely a windowe to looke out' (A4^v), or that of Sperantus, Priscus, Memphis or the Scrivener. Probably one of the houses served as this multiple and flexible location. Opposite was a tavern, which is a frequent point of exit, 'All friendes, and so let us sing 'tis a pleasant thing to goe into the taverne, cleering the throate' (C3^v) – the song which follows is singularly appropriate to the location, 'Io Bacchus! To thy Table / Thou call'st every drunken Rabble'.[45] If organised in this way, the staging would locate the house of Mother Bombie in the centre, separating the other two locales.

This play is not dominated by courtly preoccupations; its theme is neither the propriety of love nor honour: 'It is without opportunities for spectacle; it is without the beauties of mythology; there is no hint of allegory; pastoral grace is absent.'[46] The theme is more domestic than courtly, concerned with the scandals of the marriage market: 'many a match is broken off for a penie more or less, as though they could not afford their children at such a price, when none should cheapen such ware, but affection, and none buy it but love' (B2^v). Its appeal, as Hunter has suggested, is less to the courtier than to the general public.

In general Lyly's dramatic productions for the Children of Paul's caused a narrowing in the size of the audience they might reasonably expect, but conversely, in another sense, he expanded the potential implications of his plays beyond the immediate impact of the spectacle in the theatre. *Midas* is a case in point: the story is derived from Ovid, both of Midas' golden touch, which he at first desired, repented of and wished removed, and also of his choosing Pan before Apollo in a contest of music and song and thus earning himself the ears of an ass. But the play is also an attack on tyranny and bad kingship, demonstrated through the lust for gold and power: the Alexander of *Campaspe* is the direct obverse of the kind of kingship Midas represents. Midas is at once a weak king with his lust for gold, and a foolish man who is unable to tell good music from bad.

In the contest between Apollo and Pan, Apollo is the first to perform and he sings '*A song of Daphne to the Lute*'; the Nymph Erato exclaims 'O divine *Apollo*, ô sweete consent'. Pan is unable to play his pipe and sing at the same time, so he does each in turn; this time the Nymph's reaction is that he has kept neither 'measure, nor time; his piping as farre out of tune, as his bodie out of form' (E^v). Pan is costumed as a Satyr and his music is equally grotesque. There can, surely, be no doubt that the scene was played just as the Nymph describes it, with Apollo clearly the finest solo performer among the children. But Midas, perversely, chooses Pan and thus Midas, the gold-lover, becomes an ass: he is also a parable of the King of Spain, for Philip II was equally, in English eyes, an insatiable lover of the gold of the Indies, and an ass. Midas eventually repents when he agrees that

Though my souldiers be valiant, I must not therefore thinke my quarrels iust. There is no way to nayle the crowne of Phrygia fast to my daughters head, but in letting the crownes of others sitte in quiet on theirs. (G4)

This conversion of the tyrant Midas is a fairy tale of a change of heart in a real enemy, Philip. The Midas/Philip equation is a simple and probable parable, which is easily comprehensible to an audience who would perhaps be unable to grasp the complexities of the debate on love and honour which predominates in Lyly's other, earlier plays.

In the latter part of the decade of the 80s, then, Thomas Gyles and the Children of Paul's seem to have allowed themselves to rely, almost exclusively, upon John Lyly for their texts. Lyly's consciously affected, mannered style with its focal centre on the court and its amusements was a dangerously narrow base for a commercial theatrical operation, and already by 1589 the dangers inherent in this choice were apparent. The *Prologue in Paules* with which *Midas* begins laments:

Come to the Tayler, hee is gone to the Paynters, to learne howe more cunning may lurke in the fashion, then can bee expressed in the making. Aske the Musicians, they will say their heads ake with devising notes beyonde Ela. Enquire at Ordinaries, there must be sallets for the Italian; picktooths for the Spaniard; pots for the German; porridge for the Englishman. At our exercises, Souldiers call for Tragedies, their obiect is bloud; Courtiers for Commedies, their subiect is love: Countriemen for Pastoralles, Shepheards are their Saintes. Trafficke and travell hath woven the nature of all Nations into ours, and made this land like Arras, full of devise, which was Broade-cloth, full of workemanshippe. (A2)

He goes on to declare that, as a result, the present play is a 'Gallimaufrey', a 'Hodge-podge' (A2^v). Variety is what the public demanded but Lyly could not supply. There was a restlessness among Paul's playhouse audience over the limited courtiers' diet they were being served.

The search for novelty and variety in Lyly's plays partly accounts for the prevailing desire to read them as acrostics, with various characters personating courtly figures of the day. *Endimion* is a famous case, where Cynthia is fairly clearly a flattering portrait of Elizabeth herself. Later critics have found further allusions, with Endimion himself being Leicester, or Oxford, according to which theory one favours.[47] If our contemporaries find Lyly's plays irresistible as courtly allegories, so did his, for Gabriel Harvey remarks, 'all you, that tender the preservation of your good names, were best to please Pap-hatchet, and see Euphues betimes, for feare lesse he be mooved, or some One of his Apes hired, to make a Playe of you; and then is your credit quite un-done for ever and ever: Such is the publique reputation of their Playes'.[48] Others corroborate this view, for in an *Ironicall Letter* of 1585 Jack Roberts warns Sir Roger Williams to 'take heed and beware of my lord of Oxenfordes man called Lyllie, for if he sees this letter, he will put it in print, or make the boyes in Poules play it uppon a stage'.[49] Paul's, then, perhaps largely as a result of the public demand for greater variety, developed a reputation under

Lyly, and because of Lyly, for personal satiric allusions and contemporary allegory in their plays, and while this added spice to the audience's enjoyment of a performance, it led the Children into serious trouble, for their association with Lyly drew them into a grave quarrel between church and state.

On 9 February 1589 Richard Bancroft (later Bishop of London) delivered a sermon at Paul's Cross which was an eloquent defence of the Tudor orthodoxy of the validity of episcopacy:

I am fully of this opinion, that the hope which manie men have conceived of the spoile of the Bishops livings, of the subversion of cathedrall churches, and of a havocke to be made of al the churches revenues, is the cheefest and most principall cause of the greatest schismes that we have at this day in our church.[50]

From the point of view of the establishment this devaluing of motive was the answer to the attacks being made upon the Elizabethan settlement by the Martinist schismatics, for a campaign was being waged by advocates of religious devolution, using the pseudonym Martin Marprelate. They wished to bring about the democratisation of the hierarchical structure of Anglicanism. The authorities, recognising that prelates and scholars were often at a disadvantage in skirmishes which required less learned eloquence than a readiness to adapt the truth to the argument, used the services of some professional writers to produce pro-episcopal copy. Thomas Nashe was so employed and so was John Lyly.[51]

In polemic accuracy is no necessary virtue, and when pamphlets are weapons and words crafted as spiralling invective, truth and fiction are not easily separable; the very eloquence of the writer carries his pen away from the facts. In *Pappe with a Hatchet*, produced in mid-October 1589, Lyly attacks the central problem of Martin's identity:

Would those Comedies might be allowed to be plaid that are pend, and then I am sure he would be decyphered, and so perhaps discouraged.[52]

Whether or not this was an idle boast, it was a dangerous exaggeration, for his known association with the Paul's theatre incriminated the children in the pamphlet war. Lyly goes on to assert that Martin 'shall not bee brought in as whilom he was . . . but in a cap'de cloake', with the implication that costume will be, and has been, used to identify Martin. This was not a new technique for Lyly; he distinguished Gallathea and Phillida in this

110

way. Lyly goes on to make this association between the play of Martin's unmasking and the Children of Paul's even closer,

If it be	Would it not bee a fine Tragedie, when *Mardocheus*
shewed at	shall play a Bishoppe in a Play, and *Martin Hamman*,
Paules, it	and that he that seekes to pull downe those that
will cost	are set in authoritie above him, should be hoysted
fowre	upon a tree [the gallows] above all other.[53]
pence . . .	

Nashe supplies further details of this Martin unmasking in the *Returne of Pasquill* (20 October 1589), 'Methought *Vetus Comoedia* began to pricke him at London in the right vaine, when shee brought forth *Divinitie* wyth a scratcht face, holding of her hart as if she were sicke, because *Martin* would have forced her; but myssing of his purpose, he left the print of his nayles uppon her cheekes, and poysoned her with a vomit, which he ministred unto her to make her cast uppe her dignities and promotions.'[54] This vomiting forth objectionable words and titles makes an effective scene: Jonson deployed it upon Marston and Dekker in *Poetaster* and then Dekker responded similarly upon Jonson in *Satiro-mastix*, 'played at Paul's'.

Did a play or plays exist, written against the Martinists, and were they performed at The Theatre or at Paul's playhouse with a focal purging scene? Bond thinks that at least one play was performed at The Theatre and perhaps another (in October/November 1589) elsewhere in London, in which Lyly was involved.[55] The threat that they might exist was apparently enough, for this vulgarisation of the serious political and religious issue of the status of episcopacy, which was the very heart of the hierarchical state, could not be tolerated. The official position was ably demonstrated by Archbishop Whitgift in a letter to Burghley of 24 August 1589:

for my owne parte, in respect of my self (the greatest moate in there [the Martinists'] Eye) I make smale account of there mallice, nether Dyd I ever break slepe for the care thereof: yet in respect of my calling and profession, and of the scandall that may, by such Lewde Libles, be ministred to men apt to beleave anie thing, I could wish them delt with acording to there Desertes, and the qualitie of there offens . . . that the world may know that wee are men not cast off on all sydes, as abiects of the world, but that Justice shal as well take place in owre causes, as yt Doth in all other mens. the rather by cause wee susteane iniuries by Martynistes, for Doing of owre Duties in suppressing sectes and wicked opinions, and in manteyning the state and government by lawe established.[56]

In this climate, once the Martinist press was captured (August 1589), the Privy Council wished to suppress all aspects of the controversy as quickly as possible.

The Printer's Preface to the 1591 Quarto of *Endimion* bluntly announces:

Since the Plaies in Paules were dissolved, there are certaine Commedies come to my handes by chaunce, which were presented before her Maiestie at severall times by the children of Paules. (A2)

The Epilogue of the play had made an unavailing appeal to avoid this dissolution:

Dread Soveraigne, the malicious that seeke to overthrowe us with threats, do but stiffen our thoughts, and make them sturdier in stormes: but if your Highnes vouchsafe with your favorable beames to glaunce upon us, we shall not onlie stoope, but with all humilitie, lay both our handes and hearts, at your Maiesties feete. (K3ᵛ)

Elizabeth ignored this request and playing at Paul's ceased sometime between 6 January 1589/90 (when the children performed at Richmond)[57] and 4 October 1591 when *Endimion* was entered in the Stationers' Register. The reason for this inhibition, which was to last until 1599, was essentially political.

4

Interregnum and new departures

The Children of Paul's were suppressed as a theatre company after Lyly's Marprelate indiscretions in 1590/1 and no children's drama was available to the general public in London until the very last weeks of the sixteenth century. There is some likelihood, however, that on occasion private performances were still given with access restricted to invited guests. In 1592 Thomas Nashe's *Summer's Last Will and Testament* was performed in Whitgift's household, and the Prologue announces that 'we, afraid to looke on the imaginary servant of Envy, paynted in mens affections, have ceased to tune any musike of mirth to your eares this twelvemonth, thinking that, as it is the nature of the serpent to hisse, so childhood and ignorance would play the goslings, contemning and condemning what they understood not' (B^v). This reference to a year's inhibition and the children's indiscreet meddling in affairs beyond their competence sounds much like the kind of apology that the Children of Paul's would have felt it desirable to make at this time. An entertainment for a leading ecclesiastical dignitary may have been the swan song of the Children of Paul's in their first period: they ended, as they had begun in 1528 with the *Phormio* for Wolsey.

Within the cathedral, conditions during the period of the cessation of playing remained as dire, and the rapacity of its governors remained as severe as before. Alexander Nowell continued as Dean; having been originally appointed in 1560, he was to remain in that office for forty-two years. The Sub-Dean was Hugh Andrews and his appointment to that office is more or less coincident with the suppression of the theatre. The second minor canon, who was Senior Cardinal, was Ambrose Goulding who was appointed at the beginning of the last decade of the sixteenth century, in December 1591. Goulding had been advanced from the post of third minor canon or Junior Cardinal but no successor was appointed to that latter post until

10 December 1597, a gap of some six years. This delay was not for the lack of a candidate; William Maicocke was very anxious to be appointed to the office, but Ambrose Goulding opposed him. Goulding, from 1585, was rector of St Gregory's, the parish church of the cathedral, to which the Master and the choristers all belonged.[1] He, along with the Junior Cardinal, was responsible jointly with the Master for the spiritual welfare of the choir; he was their father confessor.

Goulding was a contentious and turbulent man and his opposition to Maicocke provoked physical and verbal abuse on both sides.[2] He could be violent – on one occasion he slipped out of a sermon by Dean Nowell and 'beate one George Hopkins very sore at Mr Sleggs doore', and then, apparently, crept in again without Nowell having noticed his absence; he was contumacious, paying no heed to Nowell's repeated commands that he and Maicocke should be reconciled; he was slanderous, accusing Maicocke, unjustly, to Bishop Bancroft of having the French Pox and he was rich in insult, calling Maicocke a 'Barkinge Curr', a 'Beggarlie Jacke' and 'Goodman red scabbe'. His allies were Hugh Andrews, the Sub-Dean, and his wife, but they were not often sober for with them there was 'Continuall runninge to the taverne wth wine potts untill ten of the Clocke' and, to finance their tippling, Andrews was embezzling the minor canons' plate. Although Sub-Dean, Andrews 'hath not tarried a sermon in Powles, for many yeres togeither . . . butt spendeth that time often in drinking & playing at tables'.

Maicocke's allies were the family of a certain Edward Slegg. Slegg had trained his daughters to shout insults, including 'preests chitts, preests bastardes . . . preests dingdongs', at the children of the minor canons. Slegg, who clearly had Roman Catholic leanings, was rumoured to be giving refuge to John Harrison, servant to Robert Barnes, 'the Recusante'[3] and he had secret bolt-holes and escape routes within his house to evade the authorities.

Both Jane Goulding and Mary Maicocke were active participants in the quarrel, and on one occasion, in the minor canons' garden, Jane 'offered to thrust a knyfe at' Mary and 'Mrs Andrew strock Mrs Maicocke divers blowes'. On 8 February 1597/8 the Maicockes 'sett their schollers to abuse Gouldings wife wth nicknames, and so hadd they don before time and threw stones'.

Similarly Mistress Maicocke was 'sene to sett a boye to write libells against Gouldinge and his wife, aboute Easter 1597'. Thus the chorister-actors of Paul's were given on-the-spot training in slander by their erstwhile spiritual advisers. Throwing stones and inventing nicknames is typical schoolboy behaviour, but the Maicockes manipulated it as part of their personal dispute with the Gouldings: excellent dramatic training for mocking and abusing other contemporaries in stage plays. It was reported, also, that William Maicocke 'eavesdroppeth, and watcheth secretlie in the darke to heare mens talke, setteth it downe in writinge what daie & tyme and place and y^t reserveth for his opportunitie'. The choristers were accustomed, then, to raillery and their junior spiritual adviser was a practised informer.

The Goulding–Maicocke quarrel was a notorious scandal, 'Manifestlie knowen throughe out all London and . . . all men speaketh shame of them'.[4] It is known to us because of the appointment of Richard Bancroft as Bishop of London in 1596, for he ordered a Visitation to be conducted in all churches in his diocese and the questions he put to the clergy and officers of St Paul's were especially searching. All the respondents to those questions – and there are replies from all the minor canons, the vicars choral, the bellringers, the vergers and others – speak of the affair and they all agree in condemning its excesses. Only one man failed to make any report to the Bishop, and this was Thomas Gyles, Master of Choristers; he submitted that he was too ill to do it. There is no doubt, by 1598 at any rate, that Gyles was no longer performing his duties and in consequence the strongest determining influence upon the choristers may well have been the Cardinals. The general dishevelled and unruly state of the choir in 1598/9 may well have been due not only to the decline of Gyles, but to the rise of the influence of Goulding and Maicocke.

Alexander Nowell and the Chapter were eventually stirred to take extraordinary action to protect the choir, and the impetus for this action is likely to have originated with Richard Bancroft. On 11 May 1599 the irregular step of appointing a new Master without dismissing the old was taken. They appointed 'Edward Pearce of the cytie of London gent . . . to be Almener and Maister of the Choristers of the Cathedrall Church of St Paule . . . with such stipend as to the sayd Almener and Maister is of right apperteyning or belonging, when and as soone as the sayd Almenershipp either by death, surrender, forfeyture, or by anie other lawfull meanes whatsoever shall become voyde'.[5] The phrasing of the appointment suggests that Nowell and the Chapter were very anxious to find a solution to Gyles' delin-quency: one may wonder whether his illness was not, in some respects, 'convenient' to avoid possible dismissal, for Pearce's Document of Appointment does not indicate that Gyles' life is despaired of. This extraordinary appointment may, in fact, have been a device to avoid another scandal while the Goulding–Maicocke affair was still in full flood.

Pearce's indenture made two substantial reservations. Firstly he received no stipend until his predecessor, Thomas Gyles, died or resigned: Gyles lingered in his last illness until July 1600. Secondly Pearce was not allowed to find an alternative source of income either by permitting 'anie Trunkmaker or anie man of anie other trade or occupation to use the cloysters or Shrowdes of the Chapiter howse of the . . . Cathedrall Churche or anie part or pcell [parcel] thereof as a shoppe or warehouse to put or sett Trunckes, bordes Chests or anie other kynde of wares or Lumber in, or to give anie private dore or entrie into the . . . Cloysters or Shrowdes' or by consenting to the 'selling or shifting awaye of anie Chorister of the . . . Cathedrall Church for money'.[6] Pearce was even denied his rights in the almonry house, for Gyles continued to live there, so that Pearce re-mained the responsible Master but was essentially unrewarded. He had obvious motives for seeking an alternative way to obtain an income from Paul's, that would not violate the terms of his indenture.

Coincident with the decline of Gyles and the appointment of Pearce were the developing literary aspirations of two residents of the Inns of Court. William Stanley, sixth Earl of Derby, was living in Lincoln's Inn in the late 1590s, and on 30 June 1599 George Fenner reported to Humphrey Galdelli that 'The Earl of Derby is busy penning comedies for the common players'.[7] John Marston, who was residing in the Middle Temple, was a playwright and satirist: as a dramatist he had produced *Histrio-mastix* for the Christmas Revels at his inn in 1598,[8] and as a satirist he was notorious. Two of his best known satires, *Pygmalion* and *The Scourge of Villanie*, were burnt by the common hangman on 1 June 1599, after being condemned as offensive by Archbishop Whitgift of Canterbury and Bishop Bancroft of London. Richard Bancroft was simultaneously involved in another inquiry into corruption as his Visitation of St Paul's attests. Marston's literary aspirations were temporarily arrested by the Bishops' action; he turned, however, to the professional stage and on 28 September 1599 was paid £2, as a loan, by Henslowe of the Admiral's Men, 'in earneste of a Boocke'.[9] Later in the year his father died, leaving him a substantial inheritance.[10]

Ambrose Goulding, notorious as Senior Cardinal of Paul's for his 'flyting' of his Junior partner, William Maicocke, was also an Inns of Court man, for in *c*.1596 he had become curate of Serjeant's Inn in Fleet Street.[11] Serjeant's Inn is, of course, immediately adjacent to both the Inner and Middle Temple. With his drunken friend, Hugh Andrews, Goulding kept open house at Paul's, for as William Maicocke and Thomas Langley complained, they 'doe table, and lodge, & entertaine gentlemen, & captains by meanes whereof, the colledge gates are often kept open all night, & when they are shutt, there is many times such knockinge and wrappinge at the gates, that all the petticannons & inhabitants there are very much disquieted [?] with all'.[12] Perhaps their guests may have included William Stanley and John Marston: certainly Goulding was in a position to influence Pearce over the use to which his appointment might be put. Goulding was a man of some substance, more than might have been expected from a minor ecclesiastic, and when he died in November 1606, although he left only a derisory one mark to the minor canons 'for or towards a spoone', he was able to provide amply for his widow to whom he left the residue of his estate, after giving £80 to his daughters Elizabeth and Marjery. He left only £10 to his daughter Joan as a punishment.[13] He may have made a rich match with his second wife, but these are substantial sums and perhaps represent, if not a share of the profits from the playhouse, then at least the kind of extra income a not over-scrupulous cleric could make from his involvement in the bartering of locations in the churchyard. Maicocke, who was described as a poor man in 1598, was not as fortunate in his investments as Goulding, although he was responsible for adding to the smell and

117

unwholesomeness of the churchyard, for 'the Auncient pissinge place was built upon by one Mr Waller deceased who had a lease graunited of the howse ioyinnge upon the same Alley', from the Junior Cardinal.[14]

On 13 November 1599 Rowland Whyte reported to Sir Robert Sidney that 'My Lord Darby hath put up the playes of the children in Pawles to his great paines and charge'.[15] The economic motives of Pearce and the hint of profits for Goulding had combined with the literary aspirations of Stanley and Marston to revive the Paul's plays. Before the sixteenth century came to its close, they were once more the talk of London.

Stanley's 'paines' may have been considerable, but his 'charges' were perhaps not so great, for the location of the playhouse was available free: both the upper and lower cloisters, and the undercroft and garth of the Chapter House precinct, were all under the control of Edward Pearce. The house, built by Haydon under Benbowe, was similarly available merely by turning out the bellringer Chunnell and his family. As far as modifications were concerned, Marston was the architect (or there is no point to Jonson's gibe against Crispinus)[16] and some of the materials may have been acquired from the yet remaining contributions for the restoration of the cathedral after the fire of 1561.[17] In addition St Faith's Chapel was in the possession of 'Erken ffessor a ioyner whoe useth the same for his dwellinge howse and for his shopp to worke in'[18] and John Pettley, carpenter, was the lessee of the Green Yard at the east end of the cathedral on the south side.[19] The cloisters, also, had recently been used for timber storage. Surely all this material and expertise would have reduced the 'charges', and perhaps also the 'paines'?

The new season and the new Paul's opened with a play specially written for the occasion by the architect of the playhouse renovations; it was John Marston's *Antonio and Mellida*.[20] It was presented in October 1599 with the audience arriving about 4 p.m. and expecting to remain until 6 p.m. or shortly after; they would have found themselves in a building always in need of artificial light, whatever the time of day. The show began with a non-dramatic illusion, as if it were still in rehearsal. Eight boys enter *'with parts in their hands: having cloakes cast over their apparell'* (A3)—these are the male principals in the play. At once they discuss the difficulties they have encountered in preparing the production; they can 'say' their 'parts' (A3) but they are 'ignorant in what mould we must cast our Actors' (A3). All of these choristers lack experience on the stage: Paul's has not operated as a dramatic company for some nine years, so there is no reserve of theatrical experience to draw upon. They must double some parts (the same boy plays Alberto and Andrugio) and each coaches the other in his role, with Marston seizing the opportunity to establish the basic outlines of his characters, as with Alberto, who defines his own part as a '*Venetian* gentleman, enamoured on the Ladie *Rossaline*: whose fortunes being too weake to sustaine the port of her, he prov'd alwaies desastrous in love' (A3). The boy who plays Antonio seems to have been one of the choristers whose voice was almost (if not completely) broken, for he is doubtful if he can plausibly play his designed role as Florizell, an Amazon. Alberto, however, assures him that an Amazon should have a '*virago*-like' voice (A4). Antonio's voice was man-like. The boys conclude that they have so much to offer and so many roles to personate that one play is insufficient, and a sequel is promised, provided that this first one finds 'gracious acceptance' (B).

The effect of this Induction played without properties, costume or scenic effect and conducted before the introductory music begins, is at once apologetic (with an implied request for the tolerance of inexperience) and invitational (soliciting response from the audience in guiding the future development of this theatrical enterprise). Marston is genuinely inviting audience reaction and promising, where necessary, to adapt his style to conform to this criticism; as the Epilogue insists, '*What imperfection you have seene in us, leave with us, & weele amend it . . . You shall not be more ready to embrace any thing cōmendable, then we will endeavour to amend all things reproveable*' (I4ᵛ).

After a Prologue almost unctuous in its flattery of the audience—'this faire troope', 'Select, and most respected Auditours', 'your authentick censure', 'attentive eares', 'your health of wit', 'your fertile spirits', 'such eares', 'most ingenious' (and all these compliments are concentrated within twenty lines)—the first act opens with a military parade of the principals in the company. Two ranks are formed on the lower stage of soldiers armed with petronels (large cavalry carbines), with

Piero, in armour, passing through this guard. This formation is maintained while the audience's attention is directed to the other available acting areas: Mellida, Rossaline and Maria '*Enter above*' (B3ᵛ) and watch while Galeatzo (a suitor to Mellida) passes through Piero's guard to be greeted by him (B3ᵛ). The action continues to take place on the lower stage, while the dialogue is reserved for the occupants of the upper stage[21] who discuss the implications of the arrival, first of Galeatzo and then of Matzagente (another suitor). These processions and the prominent use of the upper and lower stages involve a total of three characters above and ten named characters below (one of whom, Antonio, disguised as an Amazon, is invisible to the others) and an unspecified number of attendants. Marston has presented, in pageant form, the whole of the new Paul's company to the audience at the earliest possible moment in the action, and the audience has also been shown a novel use of the 'above' for an eavesdropping scene, for Marston uses the ladies as commentators to interpret the mime below for the spectators.[22] To stress the point he concludes this sequence with the direction '*a peale of shot is given*' (B4ᵛ). The ladies then descend to speak to Florizell/Antonio, taking only a ten line speech from exit above to entry below (C). This descent by Mellida to Antonio/Florizell shows her acceptance of him and her rejection of Matzagente and Galeatzo.

The Induction, Prologue and first act introduce the actors to the audience, reveal the extent of the company and exploit the architectural improvements to the playhouse's interior facade. In addition Marston offers extensive linguistic innovations. He either creates, or at least uses for the first recorded time on stage, a new word or phrase on average every fourteen lines – including terms like 'Iuicelesse' (A3ᵛ), 'strenuous' (A3ᵛ), 'impregnably' (A4ᵛ), 'acceptance' (B), 'abstruse' (Bᵛ), 'abhorred' (B2), 'Canon proofe' (B4), 'glibbery' (B4), 'monkish' (i.e. monkeyish, B4ᵛ). In case his select auditors have been slow to relish his linguistic innovations, Marston deliberately draws attention to them when, in the first scene of the second act, he causes Balurdo to savour one of these new-coined words, 'my legge is not altogether unpropitiously shap't. There's a word: unpropitiously? I thinke I shall speake unpropitiously as well as any courtier in *Italy*' (C4ᵛ).[23]

The second act is used to display, and draw attention to, additional skills among the company, for Castilio enters '*singing fantastically*', Rossaline runs a '*caranto pase*' (C3ᵛ) and a formal measure is performed by three sets of three (Mellida, with Galeatzo and Matzagente; Rossaline, with Alberto and Balurdo; and Flavia, with Feliche and Castilio). The music for this dance is played as a counterpoint to the dialogue, which is in turn contradicted by the sound, as Mellida remarks:

> O musicke thou distill'st
> More sweetness in us then this iarring world:
> Both time and measure from thy straines doe breath,
> Whilst from the channell of this durt doth flowe
> Nothing but timelesse griefe, unmeasured woe. (D2ᵛ)

Marston is consciously and deliberately using the special talents of his chorister-actors to extend the dramatic context with a musical dimension: a first tentative and hesitant step towards a pseudo-operatic form. In this musical mime Mellida is forcibly taken to dance by her parentally approved, but personally rejected, suitors Galeatzo and Matzagente. The visible gaiety reinforces the emotional irony and her turmoil of heart is abruptly stressed when she faints (D2ᵛ).

In the three central acts of the play Marston offers further intimate glimpses of his chorister protégés: Dildo is 'diminutive' (C2ᵛ), Catzo while 'peart' (C3ᵛ) is a musician (C3ᵛ), and Castilio, while a 'most sweete youth' (E3), is also a 'minikin' with a 'trebble' squeak (E3ᵛ). These are the younger and shorter members of the company, in contrast to Robert Coles and John Norwood and the other older boys who take the major parts.[24] Sometimes effects peculiar to choristers are utilised, as when Antonio is lamenting his supposed loss of Mellida, for Marston directs: '*The boy* [Antonio's page] *runnes a note, Antonio breaks it*' (G2ᵛ) – the sudden rupturing of a held tone, perhaps a high C, to act as an emotional shock to reinforce the lamentation.[25]

At the mid-point of the play, in the third act, Marston reminds us of the tentative nature of this first production of the revival by an apparently extra-dramatic scene which recalls the Induction, but which, like it, is integral to the action. Balurdo enters '*backward; Dildo following him with a looking glasse in one hand, & a candle in the other hand: Flavia following him backward, with a looking glasse in one hand, and a candle in the other; Rossaline following her. Balurdo and Rossaline stand setting of faces'* (F). On the one hand this is a child's amusement, making faces before mirrors; on the other it is an opportunity for the chorister-actor to demonstrate his skill at make-up, for Rossaline says of her reflection 'you looke as like the princesse, now I, but her lip is lip is [she hesitates as she applies the rouge] is a little redder, a very little redder: but by the helpe of Art, or Nature, ere I châge my perewigge, mine shall be as red' (Fᵛ). Mellida, the princess, is wearing a red wig and distinctive red lipstick and Rossaline makes herself/himself up to look like her/him. She achieves the effect by using a mixture of red and white colours (just as the modern actor does) and is consciously demonstrating her skill to the audience: these boy/girls are still a novelty sufficient to inspire curiosity as to how they were created. While this episode is largely extra-dramatic, the scene is part of the general satire against courtly excess which preoccupies the playwright, as in Balurdo's self-preening, 'By my golden teeth, hold up; that I may put in: hold up, I say [to Dildo with the mirror] that I may see to put on my gloves' (F). Marston seems to have provided Balurdo with a false dental plate set with teeth of gold, or at least gold tooth caps.

Apart from his conscious attempts to exploit the special talents of his actors, and to demonstrate his awareness of contemporary fashions, Marston brings a strong personal note to the play. Antonio and Mellida exchange lovers' confidences in Italian (for some twenty lines) and while the page apologises for this 'confusion of *Babell*' (G4), the author's excuse is that 'some private respect may rebate the edge of the keener censure' (G4). Marston is speaking directly to those in the audience who know him and reminding them of his origins: his mother was Marie Guarsi, daughter of an Italian surgeon. This personal element culminates in the final act. A painter enters with two pictures, and Balurdo describes them:

. . . whose picture is this? *Anno Domini 1599*. Beleeve mee, master *Anno Domini* was of a good settled age when you lymn'd him. 1599 yeares old? Lets see the other. *Etatis suae 24*. Bir Ladie he is somewhat younger. Belike master *Etatis suae* was *Anno Dominies sonne* (H2)

It has been generally agreed, by most critics, that the second of these portraits is of Marston, who was in his twenty-fourth year in 1599. The first portrait is 'of a good settled age' and thus

Marston is distinctly the younger of the two. In 1599 William Stanley, the financier of the revival, was thirty-eight or thereabouts; just old enough for Marston to be '*Anno Dominies sonne*'. As part of his intensive campaign to familiarise his audience with the new theatre, the new company and its talents, Marston does not hesitate to include himself and his Italian background: to show the audience a portrait of the patron of Paul's is a natural extension of this policy. In the same way Marston makes tentative steps to exploit his indoor environment. Act I takes place in daylight; Act II occurs in early evening, when torches are needed (C3^v); Act III is at dawn, 'the shuddering morn . . . flakes,/With silver tinctur, the east vierge of heaven' (D4^v); and Acts IV and V progress during the morning of that day. It may be that the conscious stress on changes of light reflects a habit of lighting and extinguishing some of the candles used during performances and perhaps opening or closing the window shutters in the sides of the playhouse. All this business would, of course, be the responsibility of the tireman and be done mainly between the acts.

It is in the fifth act that the focal display of the choristers' talents is found: they dance a masquerade (although Piero apologises that 'the roome's too scant', I) and take part in a singing contest, for the prize of a golden harp. There are three competitors: the first has a 'high stretcht minikin voice' (H3^v), one of the younger and more shrill sopranos; the second has 'a good strong meane' (H4), perhaps his voice had broken and he sang a mixture of baritone and tenor; but it is the third competitor, Balurdo, who unanimously carries away the prize for he sings 'above line' (H4), reaching a note above upper E in the treble (I^v). Balurdo's voice may already have broken too and he may have become a counter-tenor: his age was perhaps similar to Flavia's, whom he speaks of as 'an Iantlewoman of foureteene yeares of age' (I2). The Paul's company at this time can boast at least three soloists, six accomplished dancers, a harpist, and a painter.

Antonio and Mellida concludes with a daring and surprising spectacle: two deaths in reverse. Andrugio has a price of '*twentie thousand double Pistolets*' (I2^v) on his head and Piero expects to receive the decapitated skull, but in its place Andrugio presents himself with his own head still on his shoulders, 'Royally casked in a helme of steele' (I2^v) and immediately, after a '*mournfull Cynet*' (I3) on the recorders, a coffin is brought on. This contains

Antonio's corpse, but he promptly resurrects with the almost blasphemous assertion, 'I rise from death, that never liv'd till now' (I3^v).

The first night at second Paul's in October 1599, then, began with a discussion before the opening music, offered seven songs, background music to counterpoint dialogue and concluded with a consort of 'sweet ayres' (I4). The last word of the armed Epilogue (probably Andrugio/Coles) recalls the obsequious and humble tone of the Prologue, reminding the audience that this is a new beginning, *'What we are, is by your favour'*; and for the future *'What we shall be, rests all in your applausive incouragements'* (I4^v). It was this innovative, dramatic and musical spectacular, part pageant, part romance, which launched the 1599 season. There were a number of unfavourable reactions.

Jonson objected to certain aspects of Marston's eccentric linguistic style, 'three years [from *c*.1598] / They did provoke me with their petulant stiles / On every stage' (*Poetaster*, Apologeticall Dialogue, 96–8) and his anger pre-dated Marston's involvement with the Children of Paul's, which did not begin until September 1599. Clove, of *Every Man Out of His Humour* (1599), makes sarcastic reference to Marston's verbal phraseology in *Histriomastix* (a play for the Middle Temple) and his satire, *The Scourge of Villanie*:

Now, sir, whereas the *Ingenuitie* of the time, and the soules *Synderisis* are but *Embrions* in nature, added to the panch of *Esquiline*, and the *Inter-vallum* of the *Zodiack*, besides the *Eclipticke line* being *opticke*, and not *mentall*, but by the *contemplative & theoricke* part thereof, doth demonstrate to us the *vegetable circumference*, and the *ventositie* of the *Tropicks*, and whereas our *intellectual*, or *mincing capreall* (according to the *Metaphisicks*) as you may read in PLATO'S *Histriomastix*. (III.iv.21–9)

Jonson is attacking jargon, but doing so by using Marston's style as an example: his diction is beset by affectation, 'panch of *Esquiline*', '*Zodiack*', '*Eclipticke line*', 'demonstrate' and '*Tropicks*' all occur in *Histriomastix* and 'soules *Synderisis*', '*mincing capreall*' and '*circumference*' in *The Scourge of Villanie*. These words and phrases were original enough to be easily recognised. As far as Jonson was concerned, Marston's vocabulary was précieux and uselessly ornamented: it was an outward sign of an inner vacuity of mind.

For his part, Marston was irritated by Jonson's autocratic manner of electing himself as supreme judge of literary quality. In *Jacke Drums Entertainment*, his second play for Paul's, about Whitsuntide 1600, Marston makes allusion to his first play for them, *Antonio and Mellida*:

Brabant Junior	Brother how like you of our moderne witts? How like you the new Poet *Mellidus*?
Brabant Senior	A slight bubling spirit, a Corke, a Huske.
Planet	How like you *Musus* fashion in his carriage?
Brabant Senior	O filthily, he is as blunt as *Pawles*. (F4–F4^v)

The title of the play is a colloquial expression meaning 'a rough reception', or 'the turning-out of an unwelcome guest'. Brabant Senior, who is so derogatory about the new poet, is given this treatment and it is clear that his opinions, like his view of the Paul's plays as 'mustie fopperies of antiquitie' (H3^v), are as absurd as his crowning in the last act, with a 'Cap of Maintenance, the Coronet / Of cuckolds' and music sounds to 'solemnize' his 'Coronation' (I3^v).

Was Brabant Senior merely a typical envious and malicious critical opponent of the newly revived Paul's playhouse or was he specifically Jonson? If the Paul's company used the technique of disclosure by costume with which Lyly had threatened Martin Marprelate, both aims would be achieved, and certainly identification by costume was an established theatrical practice. On 24 June 1598 Count Maurice of Nassau, with the aid of an English contingent, captured the city of Turnholt from the Spaniards. On 26 October 1599 Rowland Whyte reported to Sir Robert Sidney that 'Two daies agoe, the overthrow of Turnholt was acted upon a Stage, and all your names used that were at yt; especially Sir Fra. Veres, and he that plaid that Part gott a Beard resembling his, and a Watchett Sattin Doublett, with Hose trimmed with Silver Lace. You was also introduced, killing, Slaying, and overthrowing the Spaniards'.[26] No one was likely to object to this, obviously a flattering and jingoistic version of an English victory, but the use of costume to establish identity is reminiscent of Lyly's threat to Martin and his practice in *Gallathea*. The technique was used in the Poets' War, for on the stage in Paul's playhouse (and at The Globe) there appeared '*Horace* [Jonson] *in his true attyre*' (E2^v) – but this was in *Satiromastix* (1601).

Jacke Drums Entertainment, which is Marston's defence against his detractors, begins in the same way as *Antonio and Mellida*, with a non-dramatic illusion. The Tireman is sent on to apologise to the audience that the play will not take place, a degree worse than the rehearsal which began the former play. But then one of the children enters to explain that the author has judged them 'not perfect / To rush upon your eyes' (A2ᵛ): there has been insufficient rehearsal and neither play nor cast are good enough for this 'generous presence' (A2), 'this choice selected influence' (A2), and the boy concludes with the avowal,

> Weele studie till our cheekes looke wan with care,
> That you our pleasures, we your loves may share. (A2ᵛ)

A suggestion, surely, that the actors had rushed into performance with *Antonio and Mellida* without sufficient practice to counteract their long absence from public performance on stage, and also that their choice of plays, 'mouldy fopperies of stale Poetry, / Unpossible drie mustie Fictions' (A2ᵛ) had not suited their audience either.

To avoid further audience displeasure, Marston largely dispenses in this play with plot (it is a sequence of episodes), and in the first act actors are also reduced into the background, for it is dominated by the performance of a Morris troupe, the Holloway Morris who normally performed on Highgate Green (A3ᵛ). Unfortunately, or perhaps intentionally, they do not perform very well for their heels are tripped up by drink (B). One of the aspects of *Antonio and Mellida* which seems to have come in for adverse comment was Marston's verbal display, for by the end of the first act of *Jacke Drums Entertainment* the frequency of his coinages has dropped by two-thirds, to an average of one in thirty-seven lines, but, as in the former play, several of the words are still with us, like 'barmy' (A3), 'squeasd' (A4ᵛ), 'slopt' (B) and 'feathry' (B3ᵛ). Some of his dramatic effects, however, had been praised, for he re-uses two of them in a new combination. While Mammon is singing the song 'Lantara', Pasquil, who is supposed to be dead, *'riseth, and striketh him'* (D2): a replay of both the interruption of the held tone and the death-reversal or resurrection scene in *Antonio and Mellida*. The use of the upper stage is also continued with a new modification. In *Antonio and Mellida* Marston used the 'above' as merely a raised acting platform; now, however, the sides of the upper stage, the houses, are utilised, for at the beginning of the second act, after a song, *'The Casement opens, and Katherine appeares'* (C2ᵛ). This window entry is repeated later in the same act when *'Winifrede lookes from above'* and *'Camelia* [calls] *from her window'* (D3) and at this point Sir Edward Fortune enters to complain that they 'do wrong the quiet of my house' (D3). Marston is establishing the characteristic street scene pattern of the stage facade at the Paul's house in this, its revival period.

As in *Antonio and Mellida,* so here in *Jacke Drum,* the boys display their dancing agility with a galliard although they need 'more roome' (H4) to perform it effectively: the ten actors on the stage at the time make such a complaint hardly surprising. Generally Marston tones down his innovations, as with the reduction of the manipulation of light and dark to a single instance when Flawne enters with a candle (C3) to indicate the time of day. He does not, however, reduce the frequency of solo songs, eight in all, nor the use of instrumental music: the first act is full of 'Taber and Pipe' for the Morris; music is used to create a mood suiting a lover when it *'soundes, and Pasquils Eye is fixt upon Catherine'* (H4ᵛ) and the play concludes with a concert of 'Iocund mirth' (I3) to mock the cuckolding of Brabant Senior.

The large claims and enthusiasm of *Antonio and Mellida* are tempered in this play. There is more hesitation about the boys' abilities, a plea for patience; as Sir Edward Fortune says, 'The Apes *in time* will do it hansomely' (H3ᵛ; the italics are mine), and for the present, at least, the audience has a more savoury context in which to sit, for Planet boasts

> . . . I like the Audience that frequenteth there
> With much applause: A man shall not be choakte
> With the stench of Garlicke, nor be pasted
> To the barmy Iacket of a Beer-brewer. (H3ᵛ)

The real reason why Paul's playhouse was not tightly packed may have been that it was not yet sufficiently popular, and this failing is neatly turned into an attraction.

Jacke Drums Entertainment acknowledges that Paul's have not yet satisfied all their supporters and the most trenchant criticism was clearly directed at their choice of plays. One of those objected to was probably *The Wisdome of Doctor Dodypoll* 'sundrie times Acted by the Children of Powles' and performed during

1600, before October: it is likely to be one of the plays Brabant Senior is referring to. It is an old-fashioned tale of the comic crosses of true love among a group of courtiers, which issues in the happy resolution of 'royall nuptials' (H3ᵛ). It may have been adapted from the plot of an earlier play so as to give prominence to the Paul's painter who plays the part of Lassingbergh and he entertained the audience with a number of swift line drawings of the action, like his sketch of the Doctor done 'eene now / With his nose in an Urinall' (B4ᵛ). In conception it is strongly reminiscent of Lyly's *Campaspe* where Apelles, like Lassingbergh, falls in love with his own artistic creations. While it utilises music and song (there are five) no special children's qualities are apparent: it is episodic and only loosely linked by cross-infatuation. No sense of the stage as a physical property to be exploited is present, and while there is a suggestion that Hyanthe should be given 'musicke at her windowe' (E), it is not done. Indeed this kind of evasion is not uncommon in the action, as when Flores promises 'Musicke' and a 'large Carowse' to give entertainment 'after our best countrie fashion': Haunce, however, cannot provide it as 'One of . . . the Haultboyes . . . is out of tune / . . . Drunke' (B2). The action of the play, which is confined to the lower stage and the two opposing doors (E2ᵛ), makes promises which it does not fulfil: a great disappointment after the amazing variety of *Antonio and Mellida*.

The same criticisms apply to *The Maydes Metamorphosis* of 1600, also 'sundrie times Acted by the Children of Powles': it is a pastoral in a woodland setting, reminiscent of Lyly's *Gallathea*. While full of songs (seven in all) and dancing of fairies, and nostalgic in its double transformation of Eurydice from a girl to a boy and back again – thus intensifying the deliberate confusion of sexual identity at the end of *Gallathea* – it lacks the subtlety of Lyly's action. Both this play and *Doctor Dodypoll* were probably commissioned rather hurriedly for the early revival period of late 1599 and early 1600: in a sense Marston was to blame for the problems that the plays caused the company. Paul's playhouse was reopened very hastily; Pearce was appointed in May; Marston was still negotiating with the Admiral's Men in late September and yet, by mid-November, Stanley had financed the revival and the theatre was operating again. Marston ceased dealing with Henslowe, switched his allegiance to the Paul's company and produced their opening spectacle, *Antonio and Mellida*, all during October 1599, or, at the latest, early November. This haste could not have allowed for very extensive alterations to the playhouse buildings: in 1599 Paul's were probably using a facade very much the same as that used by Gyles and Westcott. It is hardly surprising that so sudden a refounding should have found the company embarrassed for want of other suitable texts, and their instinctive reaction was to revert to the style that had been characteristic of their offerings in the late 1580s. This was a failure; the audience saw it as 'patch-pannell stuffe, olde gally-mawfreies and cotten-candle eloquence'.[27] The problems may have been aggravated if William Percy's strange and wayward style was allowed on the Paul's boards; perhaps Stanley's comedies found a public showing here too, and none of them were good enough to survive. In one respect, however, they were immediately successful: Paul's revival re-kindled a dormant interest in the children's drama and Marston's 'first night' play was sensational, although linguistic aspects of it were criticised; but then, unfortunately, the company failed to fulfil expectations and produced only revivals of old-fashioned material. By the winter of 1600/1, however, the company had recovered from the initial setbacks and was substantially and successfully founded: there is a new note of confidence in the sequel to *Antonio and Mellida*, which Marston produced at this time.

Antonio's Revenge opens with an assurance that the Induction to *Antonio and Mellida* lacked. In place of obsequious flattery, Marston goes so far as to suggest that spectators, if they are 'Uncapable of waightie passion' (A2), should 'Hurrie amaine from our black visag'd showes' (A2v): only the committed are welcome. At the burial of Feliche, son of Pandulpho, who has been murdered by Piero, Antonio asks his page to 'sing a Dirge' (Iv) but Pandulpho, deliberately misunderstanding him, replies on Feliche's behalf,

> No, no song: twill be vile out of tune

and Alberto adds, 'Indeede he's hoarce: the poore boyes voice is crackt' (Iv). The interruption occurs here before the song is begun and we are also perhaps expected to be aware that the boy who played Feliche a year and a half previously – he appears in *Antonio's Revenge* only as a corpse, but is important in *Antonio and Mellida* – is now 'crackt' of voice; he is no longer a boy, but a man or at least a youth and not a child. So too in place of the death-reversals of the first part, we have the dominance in the second part, in plot and action, of the spectre of the murdered Andrugio.

Artificial light is exploited; each act, except the fourth, begins with a scene in torch-light; the fourth act has all its scenes in daylight, but it follows an act with all its scenes in semi-darkness. Time is strictly regulated into exactly two days, and the place never varies from the Venetian court. Extensive use is made of mime to create visual dramatic irony and, as in *Doctor Dodypoll*, Marston exploits the surprise effect of the sudden drawing of curtains. This is used to reveal (probably in the central curtained area of the upper stage) not Mellida, as Antonio expects, but *'the bodie of* Feliche, *stabd thick with wounds, appears hung up'* (B4), and later, on the lower stage, the curtains of a bed are drawn to display to Maria the *'ghost of Andrugio'* (F4ᵛ). These sudden revelations, particularly that of Feliche, which is modelled on the death of Horatio in *The Spanish Tragedy* (II.iv), were a success, for in Middleton's *Blurt Master Constable* (also played at Paul's in this early period of the revival) the incident in *Antonio's Revenge* is deliberately recalled:

Camillo. To the Strumpet *Imperiaes*.
Omnes. Agreed, what then?
Camillo. There to find Fontinell; found, to kill him.
Virgilio. And kill'd, to hang out his reeking bodie, at his Harlots window.

          . . .

The Tragedie is iust . . . (G2ᵛ)

Middleton is presuming here that his audience is familiar with earlier plays at the same house: an audience, then, who were regular patrons.

The audacity of the resurrection of Antonio is matched in *Antonio's Revenge* by a death with an equal frisson of horror. Antonio holds up the body of Julio, son of Piero, whom he has just stabbed, and allows the blood to drip upon Andrugio's tomb as a pagan sacrificial offering to the god of Vengeance (F3). During this invocation, there comes *'From under the stage a groane'* (F2ᵛ), the ghost of Andrugio is heard below: Paul's stage now has a trap and its existence is deliberately emphasised when Feliche is buried in it, '*They* [Antonio, Pandulpho and Alberto] *strike the stage with their daggers, and the grave openeth*' (I), and by Balurdo, who uses it quite unnecessarily as a dungeon and climbs out of it on to the lower stage (I2ᵛ). The hasty revival may have prevented the completion of all the building improvements: the trap was only available from the time of the performance of *Antonio's Revenge*. Stanley may have been a cautious financier, for to make improvements gradually as success warrants makes good commercial sense.

In the final two scenes of the play (V.v and vi), there is a concentration of all of the pageant and display effects of the early part of *Antonio and Mellida*. On the lower stage the three masked conspirators against Piero dance a measure (as with the Feliche incident, this is repeated in *Blurt Master Constable* where the Masquers dance a lavolta, D2); they are watched by eight named and five unnamed characters; at the rear of the stage, behind the curtained central doors, is set a table of sweetmeats. During the dance Andrugio's ghost is positioned behind the curtains in the centre of the upper stage; he is flanked by the musicians and extra singers behind the casement and trap windows. The symbol is now complete. Andrugio, triumphant in glory, looks down on the hell of Piero who is about to consume his own-begotten flesh. The scene (V.v) concludes with the curtains being drawn across the centre of the upper and lower stages to effect the removal of the ghost and of Piero, who is now dead. The play ends (V.vi) with a grand chorus, 'a solemne hymn' on the theme '*Mellida* is deade' (K4), sung by the company on stage and probably additional voices – as many as could be found – above.

At this time Paul's company is at least seventeen strong and thirteen of them have speaking parts in *Antonio's Revenge*: in the penultimate scene of the play there are sixteen on the lower stage and one (Andrugio's ghost) on the upper, and it would seem that the part of Mellida was doubled with that of Andrugio's ghost – perhaps a soprano was felt best for the ethereal tones of a spectre. If Robert Coles was the actor who played Andrugio and Alberto in Part I, he is unlikely to have played Andrugio and Mellida in Part II unless his voice was exceptionally versatile, for the play gives no indication that Mellida spoke '*virago*-like', as does the Amazon, Florizell. The boys who played the main roles in Part I were in their early teens and for Part II, when Feliche's voice is 'crackt', some eighteen months later, the company seniors are probably in their mid-teens. This is very similar to the age distribution pattern in the first period under Westcott. The children of Paul's, in their early revival period of 1599, give the impression of having begun with no reserve of older youths, their leading players were only just teenagers; but the original players remained with the company and by 1600/1 they were verging on manhood. This transition from child to adult is one of the features of the company which Marston incorporated as a developing theme into the relationship between *Antonio and Mellida* and *Antonio's Revenge*.[28] Under Westcott Paul's had used young singers, or choristers proper, and they continued to provide much of the solo singing, as with Antonio's page, but also there were superannuated choristers who took the more serious and mature parts. For second Paul's it seems that this mature element became available only when the boys grew older.

Just as in *Antonio and Mellida*, Marston makes a point in' *Antonio's Revenge* of feasting us with new words and phrases:[29] the incidence here by the end of the first act is almost back to its original density, a new word every sixteen lines, and Balurdo emphasises the verbal invention in every act save the second. Many of these words are part of our contemporary vocabulary; 'rawish', 'fluent', 'juiceless' (A2) all occur in the Prologue, and 'snoring', 'howling', 'unseasoned', 'conscious', 'honey', 'Stygian', 'incubus' are all introduced in the first scene of the first act, either as wholly new concepts, or in a sense still current and not before known in public usage. On this occasion, however, Marston's verbal dexterity was to have serious repercussions, for Jonson's irritation with him escalated into a determined assault, the Poetomachia.

In *Poetaster* (early 1601) Jonson presents a scene in which Tucca, a decayed Captain, accosts Histrio, a player, declaring:

. . . I would faine come with my cockatrice one day, and see a play; if I knew when there were a good bawdie one: but they say, you ha' nothing but *humours, revells*, and *satyres*, that girde, and fart at the time, you slave.   (III.iv.188–91)

Histrio, however, assures him that 'we have as much ribaldrie in our plaies, as can bee . . . All the sinners, i'the suburbs, come, and applaud our action, daily' (194–6). Clearly Histrio is an adult actor from a public playhouse. Tucca replies that he hears the players intend to represent him on the stage and thunders, 'life of PLUTO, and you stage me, stinkard; your mansions shall sweat for't, your tabernacles, varlets, your *Globes* and your *Triumphs*' (199–201). It takes no great leap of the imagination to see in Histrio one of the Chamberlain's Men. The identity is further clarified later in the same scene when Tucca espies someone lurking in the shadows. Histrio explains, 'O, sir, his dubblet's a little decaied; hee is otherwise a very simple honest fellow, sir, one DEMETRIUS [Dekker], a dresser of plaies about the towne, here; we have hir'd him to abuse HORACE [Jonson], and bring him in, in a play, with all his gallants' (320–4). The reason that this has been done is economic: '. . . it will get us a huge deale of money (Captaine) and wee have need on't; for this winter ha's made us all poorer, then so many starv'd snakes: No bodie comes at us; not a gentleman . . .' (327–30).

Jonson's explanation that the primary reason for the escalation of the dispute was economic is also advanced by Gilderstone who, in the 1603 Quarto of *Hamlet*, admits that 'noveltie carries it away, / For the principall publicke audience that / Came to them [the adults], are turned to private playes, / And to the humour of children' (II.ii).[30] Later Rosencrantz elaborates further by blaming 'an eyrie of children, little eyases, that cry out on the top of question, and are most tyrannically clapp'd for't. These are now the fashion . . .' (II.ii. 335–8, in the Folio of 1623).

Before 1575 when the Paul's choir began their commercial exploitation of the drama from a fixed base, they had no rivals apart from the more casual performances at various city inns, but their lead was immediately emulated by The Theatre (1576) and the (first) Blackfriars (1576). History repeated itself for, after their 1599 revival, their renewal of the fashion for children's plays was exploited once again by the (second) Blackfriars (1600). The capacity of this second Blackfriars theatre was sufficient to seat 'several hundred persons' and this was the 'eyrie' of Rosencrantz, for the plays took place in an upper room: it was this theatre, and not the small Paul's playhouse, which created 'damaging competition' for The Globe.[31]

Was the information leaked deliberately to Jonson that he was about to be pilloried on the Globe stage? Paul's had a practised informer available, William Maicocke. The plan may well have been to provoke Jonson to react on the Blackfriars stage, for at this time he was their principal dramatist, and the adult actors would be able to participate in the struggle to the benefit of their box-office returns. Some substance is given this explanation by the almost four month delay between the information reaching Jonson and his production of *Poetaster*; he declares in the Prologue by Envie that it is 'fifteene weekes / (So long as since the plot was but an *embrion*)' (14–15). Certainly The Globe co-operated with Paul's in the riposte to *Poetaster*, Dekker's *Satiro-mastix* – a play hurriedly adapted to the Roman situation of *Poetaster* – which was presented publicly by '. . . the Lord Chamberlaine his Servants; and privately, by the Children of Paules'. It was on sale, later, at Edward White's shop 'neere the little North doore of Paules Church at the sign of the Gun'. The sequence of events points to a deliberate conspiracy to provoke the easily angered Jonson to a declaration that he could be made to regret.

While Jonson may be exaggerating the mean monetary motives of his adversaries, Shakespeare confirms the basic situation, and there is a high probability that the Poetomachia was a purely contrived situation, a seventeenth-century version of a modern publicity campaign to control taste. The Globe and Paul's co-operated to resist the greater popularity of their joint chief rival, the Chapel Children at the Blackfriars. This co-operation may have extended further, for the two companies at this same time (1600/1) jointly produced plays built upon the same sources, but independently: one designed for younger players (*Antonio's Revenge*) and one designed for adults (*Hamlet*). These two plays, despite the habit of their authors in quoting and borrowing liberally from sources, use no details from each other, and in Marston's case, at least, the play meant departing from an earlier comic form established in the play's first part, *Antonio and Mellida*.[32] It may be dismissed as coincidence, but that coincidence has an air of contrivance about it and if it were not planned, it was certainly exploited.

In *Poetaster* the armed Prologue defends the play as a

   . . . forc't defence:
Whereof the *allegorie* and hid sence

Is, that a well erected confidence
Can fright their pride, and laugh their folly hence (11–14)

but this is poetic licence and it represents the arrogant certainty
which Marston had first objected to. While Jonson may claim,
'His mind is above their injuries', his whole intention is to strike
first. The weight of the arraignment is reserved for Crispinus
[Marston] with Demetrius [Dekker], 'a very simple honest
fellow', comparatively lightly treated. Jonson, indeed, had little
he could use against Dekker for he was not known to be in
disagreement with him: Dekker had simply been hired to
provoke Jonson, who clearly felt that Marston was ultimately
responsible for the threat. In his enthusiasm to crush his
opponents, however, Jonson overreached himself, for in the
course of a single scene (I.ii) he managed to insult half the social
groups in London: 'players are an idle generation, and doe
much harme in a state' (37–8); 'Name me a profest *poet*, that his
poetrie did ever afford him so much as a competencie' (78–9); 'the
law makes a man happy, without respecting any other merit: a
simple scholer, or none at all may be a lawyer' (120–2); 'Your
courtier cannot kisse his mistris slippers, in quiet, for 'hem [the
players]; nor your white innocent gallant pawne his revelling
sute, to make his punke a supper. An honest decayed comman-
der, cannot skelder, cheat, nor be seene in a bawdie house, but
he shall be straight in one of their wormewood *comoedies*'
(47–52). It is hardly surprising that an uproar followed the
performance and there was talk of an action in the Star Chamber. His friend, Richard Martin, had to intervene to save Jonson
from the Clink and he dedicates the play to his 'noble and
timely' intervention.

In *Poetaster* it is to be doubted whether the idealised tribunal
of Roman poets giving their judgement for Jonson is more than
a wish-fulfilment. Jonson may only suggest the analogy between his own position as he saw it, under attack by envious
Poetasters, and that of the Roman poets: to write a play
admonishing his opponents, as they were planning to do
against him, does not verify the analogy. The judgement of
posterity, which acknowledges the distinction of Vergil, Horace
and Ovid, was not yet Jonson's to claim. He did, however,
make a sensational hit with the climax of the purging-pill
administered to Crispinus, forcing him to 'belk up' his turgid

diction: 'retrograde', 'reciprocall', 'lubricall', 'defunct', 'inflate', 'turgidous', 'ventositous', 'oblatrant', 'foribund', 'fatuate', 'spurious', 'prorumpd', and 'obstupefact' – none of which occur in Marston's works, and from *Antonio and Mellida*, 'Glibbery' (B4); from *Antonio's Revenge*, 'incubus' (A4), 'clumzie' (A2), 'strenuous' (I2) and 'clutcht' (A2); and from *Jacke Drums Entertainment*, 'barmy froth' (A3) and 'chil-blain'd' (C4ᵛ). All these are plays performed at Paul's immediately prior to *Poetaster*'s presentation; other samples of Marston's diction are derived from the *Scourge of Villanie*. There is hyperbole here to make Crispinus' humiliation the more devastating and the words which do not actually occur are similar in tone to the others. Among Marston's innovative terms, only 'glibbery' and 'magnificate' are now totally defunct; his other coinages have survived, although modified from the sense he originally gave to them.

The riposte of the Globe/Paul's alliance was a hastily adapted history play set in the England of William Rufus. Onto this background were superimposed Horace [Jonson] and Tucca of *Poetaster* and Crispinus and Demetrius. The preface admits that this *'terrible* Poetomachia' was *'lately commenc'd betweene* Horace the second, *and a band of leane-witted* Poetasters' (A3). The only references to an earlier stage in the quarrel are when Horace is made to swear 'not to bumbast out a new Play with the olde lynings of Iestes, stolne from the Temples Revels' (M) – a reference to Jonson's attack on Marston's diction in the character of Clove in *Every Man Out of His Humour*, and when Horace speaks of Marston as a 'light voluptuous Reveller' (C2ᵛ), like Hedon of *Cynthia's Revels* (III.iii.25), and Dekker as 'a strange arrogating puffe', like Asotus in the same play (III.iii.26). *Satiro-mastix* is a scandal play mocking Jonson for his early struggles, as a 'Bricklayer' (C2) and for how he killed the player, Gabriel Spencer (H2ᵛ). The main criticism against Jonson is that he is supercilious, arrogant and derogatory about Marston's early plays for Paul's, for he '(to make the Muses beleeve, their subiects eares were starv'd, and that there was a dearth of Poesie) cut an Innocent Moore i'th'middle, to serve him in twice; & when he had done, made Poules worke of it' (E3). Clearly Jonson did not like the two part *Antonio and Mellida* and *Antonio's Revenge*; just like Brabant Senior, he had no time for the 'new poet Mellidus'. Dekker insists that he and Marston 'envy not to see, / Thy friends with Bayes to crowne thy Poesie' (I3ᵛ) and their anger is deserved only because Jonson made them 'Dance Antikes' on paper.

The play's climax in the untrussing of Horace is effected visually with deliberate consciousness of the effect of the painting scene at the end of *Antonio and Mellida*. In the last act, Tucca enters, *'his boy after him with two pictures under his cloake'* (L2ᵛ): one portrait is of Horatius Flaccus, the other is of Jonson – probably they were both painted by the Paul's artist who had depicted Marston and Stanley in 1599. Tucca compares the faces together, saying of the Jonson picture 'thou hast no part of Horace in thee but's name, and his damnable vices: thou hast such a terrible mouth, that thy beard's afraide to peepe out: but, looke heere you staring Leviathan, heere's the sweet visage of Horace' (L4). The portrait of Jonson was fairly clearly a caricature with a face 'puncht full of Oylet-holes, like the cover of a warming-pan . . . [a] leane [and] hollow-cheekt Scrag' (L4ᵛ). Finally, handing him the portrait, Tucca concludes 'heere's thee Coppy of thy countenance, by this will I learne to make a number of villanous faces more, and to looke scurvily upon'th world, as thou doest' (L4ᵛ). Horace was, then, untrussed by a long established Paul's device, the portrait disclosure. Jonson, like Redford's Wyt, failed to match up to his portrayal in art.

Dekker, in the Epilogue to *Satiro-mastix*, declares that the audience may provoke a continuation of the Poets' War, 'if you set your hands and Seales to this, Horace will write against it and you may have more sport' and promises that he 'will untrusse him agen, and agen, and agen' (M3). But public opinion was against it, as John Davies of Hereford pointed out in *Wittes Pilgrimage* (1605):

> That Poets should be made to vomit words,
> (As being so rawe Wittes Mawe could not digest)
> Hath to Wittes praise, bin as so many swords,
> To kill it quite in earnest, and in Iest:
> Then, to untrusse him (before Knights, and Lords)
> Whose Muse hath power, to untrusse what nott?
> Was a vaine cast, though cast to hitte a Blott,
>
> O Imps of Phoebus, whie, ô why doe yee
> Imploy the Pow'r of your Divinity
> (Which should but foyle vice from which we should flee!)
> Upon impeaching your owne Quality?[33]

Davies is complaining that the Children of Paul's had allowed themselves to take part in a vulgarisation of the drama and had then brought the acting profession into discredit. Hamlet also noticed how much harm the children were doing their own careers: 'Will they not say afterwards, if they should grow themselves to common Players (as it is most like, if their meanes are no better) their Writers do them wrong to make them exclaim against their owne Succession?' (I F. 1623, II.ii.343–7). This is indeed exactly what was happening to the children. They were already almost grown up, and to attack the adult companies and their dramatists was to persecute themselves. Attacks on personalities had closed down the Children of Paul's once before in 1590/1; there was some danger that it could happen again and the closure could become general. It was probably fortunate for the continuance of the Children of Paul's that the dispute died swiftly, for it had no roots in real anger and remained a short-lived, albeit notorious, if artificially induced phenomenon.

As far as Marston was concerned, Jonson's attack in *Poetaster* eventually destroyed his association with the Children of Paul's and his own *Antonio's Revenge* was eclipsed by the infinitely superior parallel at The Globe, *Hamlet*. His severe handling by Horace was traumatic for Marston: he failed to pay his dues for his Middle Temple rooms in 1601 and was expelled on 14 October and it may be that he moved to obscure lodgings to avoid his detractors. Jonson did not, however, succeed in silencing Marston, for he replied to *Poetaster* with *What You Will*. This play is much less specifically concerned with the Poetomachia than was Dekker's *Satiro-mastix*. It may have been performed at Paul's to coincide with the presentation of Dekker's play at The Globe, for the Children of Paul's and the Chamberlain's Men were co-operating against the Children of the Chapel at Blackfriars. *What You Will* is a riposte by Marston to his critics and an avowal of continued determination despite them. It begins with a new non-dramatic illusion, which is also a novel method of beginning a play. 'Before the Musicke sounds for the Acte' (A2) three gallants (Atticus, Doricus and Phylomuse) sit on the stage and talk; their conversation suddenly becomes audible and the Tireman enters to light the candles. The play has emerged from the social context of the auditorium, with this difference; Paul's stage was too small to accommodate spectators (A3) so the presence of the three gallants would have been recognised as a new departure. They discuss Marston and his critics, just as the children in the Induction to *Antonio and Mellida* had discussed their first tentative steps towards acting, and make oblique allusions to other Paul's plays: Doricus speaks of *'sineor Snuffe, Mounsieur Mew*, and *Cavaliero Blirt'* (A2), a reference to *Antonio's Revenge* (Balurdo is the snuff taker, B3 and F4), *Jacke Drums Entertainment* (in which Mounsieur John fo de King plays a prominent part) and Middleton's *Blurt Master Constable*. They dismiss the objections of the critics, the 'leaprous humor' that 'Breaks from ranke swelling of . . . bubbling wits' (A2ᵛ) and Doricus argues that *'Musike and Poetry* were first approv'd / By common sence' for 'rules of Art / Were shapt to pleasure, not pleasure to your rules' (A2ᵛ): the test of a good play is the approval of the audience. Later, making direct allusion to *Poetaster*, Quadratus dismisses the idea of taking revenge against detractors in a play, with his sneering riposte to Lampatho's threat to be revenged, 'How pree-thee in a play?' (F4).

The three gallants introduce *What You Will* in a deliberately disparaging way to disarm criticism: it is 'a slight toye, lightly composed, to swiftly finisht, ill plotted, worse written, I feare me worst acted' (A3). Marston feels safe with his audience here, no 'squinting *Criticks*, drunken *Censure*, splay-footed *Opinion*' (A3) dwells among 'these ingenous breasts' (A3). At this point in the revival, Marston at least sees the Paul's audience as an educated, tolerant, elite enclave which insulates him from the intolerance and injustice of the world. Doricus and Atticus retire within the curtain at the rear of the lower stage and Phylomuse remains as Prologue vowing to expend *'industrious sweat'* (A3ᵛ) to please these *'gentle mindes'*, asserting that the author *'nor once dreads or care's* / *What envious hand his guiltles* Muse *hath struck'*. The audience would be aware of the reference to Horace/Jonson and perhaps Marston is telling the truth – he had made no overt attack on Jonson.

What You Will proper begins in a way defiantly similar to *Antonio's Revenge*. The latter play commenced with the entry of Piero *'unbrac't'* carrying a torch and followed by Strotzo with a *'corde'* (A2ᵛ); *What You Will* begins with Quadratus' entry, preceded by a page with a torch and followed by Phylus with a lute (A4); twenty-one lines later Iacomo enters '*unbraced and careles drest*' (A4). Visual recognition is expected. At once we are offered a replay of Marston's successful interruption technique; Phylus sings to the lute and '*is answered, from above a Willow garland is floung downe and the songe ceaseth*' (Bᵛ). The song is designed to 'bring *Celias* head out of the window', as Orpheus brought '*Euridice* out of hell with his lute' (B); it is interrupted by a garland of mourning. Heaven answers his complaint and Celia rejects his love.

The most interesting aspects of this highly episodic entertainment are the devices at the beginning of the acts. Act I played on visual memory as it recalled *Antonio's Revenge*; Act II reminds us of Marston's revelations behind curtains for, as with Andrugio's ghost, '*One knockes*, Laverdure *drawes the Curtaines sitting on his bed apparalling himselfe*'; Act III presents a dumb show, which takes place while the music is playing; in it Franciscus is dressed by Iacomo, Andrea and Randolpho while Bydet looks on. As when Balurdo and Rossaline practised faces before mirrors and completed their toilet, this scene merges into the action. The actors here are dressing themselves for the act, as they would normally do during the musical interlude, but this activity is part of the plot. In the same way Act V begins with a discovery scene, more elaborate than that in Act II. When the curtain is drawn four couples are revealed having dinner, and a song is sung to entertain them, both for their amusement and for that of the audience. This is at once a simple technique – beginning a scene with a discovery – and also directly analogous to the later theatrical practice of raising a proscenium curtain to reveal a scene-in-progress which is the play. Here we have a discovery that shows not a static surprise but an animated-talking-scene-in-progress which simply continues as the play. Here Marston has taken a familiar technique a stage further, just as he had done with the eavesdropping scene in *Antonio and Mellida*: despite *Poetaster* he was not afraid to continue to innovate.

As he had done in his previous plays for Paul's, Marston offers more intimate glimpses of the organisation, structure and operational pattern of the choristers. He presents in Act II a mock school lesson (C4–D) as a result of which some of the boys are recruited to become actors. Since the choristers were pupils of Colet's grammar school in Paul's yard, the obvious inference is that this is Mulcaster's school and indeed the citizen's wife in Beaumont and Fletcher's *The Knight of the Burning Pestle* (I.ii.22–7) assumes that this school was a recruiting ground for actors. But there were other boys available, for John Howe tells us that in 1598 there were boys taught in St Gregory's, St Catharine's Chapel, and in St John the Baptist Chapel[34] and Pearce had the right of impressment anywhere in the kingdom. In *What You Will* the school scene is essentially an audition and it takes place as an interruption of a regular Latin grammar lesson: Quadratus, Lampatho, Laverdure and Simplicus arrive and question the boys. One of them, Holifernes Pippo, when asked who gave him his name, replies 'My godfathers and god-mothers in my baptisme' (D). This is the reply expected of a chorister who had learnt his required response from Dean Nowell's Catechism. The schoolmaster declares he has been asked to allow Holifernes 'to play the Lady in commedies presented by Children', but the master refused on the grounds that the boy's voice was 'to smale and his stature to loe'. However he sings in a soprano and impresses the visitors and later, in the fifth act, these boys are recruited to play pages and they perform a play within the play (G4ᵛ), one of them '*attired like a Merchants wife*'. This certainly sounds very like a description of the normal method of recruiting new talent. It may also indicate that the senior and more experienced actors were involved in the assessment of new hopefuls.

In *What You Will* there is one aspect of his dramatic practice over which Marston completely capitulates to his critics. By the end of the first act of the play only six new words have appeared and four of them are doubtful: 'fan'd', 'coach'd', 'muff'd', and 'ladied' (B2ᵛ), which are used as terms to describe the fitting out of a gallant: technically these are new usages, but hardly startling. The incidence of verbal invention in *What You Will* has dropped to one in 68 lines; over 90% less frequently than in the *Antonio* plays. Ironically too, Iacomo, with whom most of the more extravagant language of the play is associated, is tolerated by the other characters as a harmless freak.

Marston was not, of course, the only dramatist writing for Paul's in the period up to the end of 1601; Middleton was certainly another. *Blurt Master Constable* was 'sundry times privately acted by the Children of Paules', but the influence of

141

Marston and his Paul's plays upon it is considerable. In the first act three couples dance a measure (just as in *Antonio and Mellida*) but it is abruptly interrupted by Violetta who *'on a sodaine breakes off'* (A4ᵛ), like Mellida who fainted during the enforced gaiety of her dance. Balurdo in *Antonio's Revenge* complains that he has 'taken a murre [a cold]' and asks Maria for snuff (F4) to cure it; Lazarello in Middleton's play argues that 'Tobacco is your only smoker away of rewme [a cold]' and later he refers to stretching a note 'above *Eela*' (E4) just as Balurdo did to win the singing contest (H4). Perhaps the same actor played both Balurdo and Lazarello. Again the play repeats another Marstonian feature with a masqued lavolta and offers a new and curious variation on the choristers' singing, for Middleton directs:

Musicke sodainly plaies, and Birds sing . . . (F2ᵛ).

Did some of the boys do imitations of bird calls? One of them certainly was, like Westcott's Wit, an exceptional dancer, for Middleton had him demonstrate 'The Spanish Pavin'; it is Lazarello/(?)Balurdo who is the star.

Until his humiliation in *Poetaster*, then, Marston's influence was paramount, but after *What You Will*, which is no stronger a riposte to Jonson than was Dekker's *Satiro-mastix*, his influence on the company declined. Despite the Poetomachia Marston gave Paul's a progressive and impressive image, rather than merely a negative and critical one. It has been argued, with some cogency, however, that all Marston was interested in was parody and that both his plays and the Children of Paul's were parasitic offshoots of the public professional stage.

Anthony Caputi has suggested that the children sought to burlesque their adult rivals and they caricatured men and manners; they were 'apes mimicking adult foibles and vices'.[35] In specific terms, as far at least as Balurdo of *Antonio and Mellida* is concerned, he is surely right. Balurdo is grossly exaggerated as a deliberate parody of the affected and foppish courtier; he is absurd in his aping of and admiration for unusual diction and taking it down in his notebook; his gold teeth and his costume are garish even by the extravagant standards of the day, for he wears a yellow doublet, blue breeches, orange silk stockings, a gilt rapier and a green hat with a red feather – the final touch is his shirt which hangs out of his breeches (H3). The caricature is completed by his arms which are 'a good fat legge of ewe mutton, swimming in stewde broth of plummes' (H2) and his motto, '*Holde my dish, whilst I spill my pottage*'.

Other critics, however, have sought to take the argument a stage further, in particular R. A. Foakes, who has characterised the *Antonio* plays as a whole in this way:

> The plays work from the beginning as vehicles for child-actors consciously ranting in oversize parts, and we are not allowed to take their passions or motives seriously. Their grand speeches are undermined by bathos or parody, and spring from no developed emotional situation, so that we are not moved by them, and do not take them seriously enough to demand justice at the end.[36]

This is, in fact, an exaggeration; it distorts Marston's actual intentions. Foakes has overstated the case, for the *Antonio* plays are, in the first place, tentative and provisional. In *Antonio and Mellida* the Prologue and Induction continually return to the theme of inexperience:

> For wits sake doe not dreame of miracles.
> Alas, we shall but falter, if you lay
> The least sad waight of an unused hope,
> Upon our weakenesse. (B^v)

In 1599 these Children of Paul's are acutely conscious of their own inadequacy.

The playhouse management took pains to avoid one of the more obvious means of establishing caricatures: they did not, at least between 1599 and 1602, use false beards or moustaches which, on a fourteen year old, are obviously comic. Percy makes this point clearly and it is reinforced by Marston in *Antonio's Revenge* where Balurdo enters to Piero '*with a beard half off, half on*' (C3^v). Piero exclaims 'What dost thou with a beard!' and Balurdo explains that it is to cover his 'bald' wit. Not merely are we to deduce that Balurdo's part was played barefaced, but also that to appear in a beard was a recognised incongruity on the Paul's stage. In *The Wisdome of Doctor Dodypoll* (1600), Alberdure, searching for his lost love Hyanthe, comes upon a peasant with a beard. He supposes it is Hyanthe in disguise, with the beard 'growne with griefe' and declares he will 'rip them out of thee' (E3). The Peasant is not amused. The beard which is assumed to be false, and Hyanthe's disguise therefore penetrable, is in fact real. This establishes the force of the custom at Paul's: the joke lies in the unexpected departure from the practice on other stages. At Paul's the only facial hair was real. This naturalism in make-up does not argue for deliberate caricature in characterisation as a guiding purpose. Similarly the hesitancy of *Antonio and Mellida* as a whole suggests a nervous uncertainty, rather than a bold satiric front.

Foakes goes still further, and argues that the grand passions of Antonio are false; but the rhetoric is as real as the beard of the Peasant. Marston was seeking to use the speeches of his characters as a pattern of rising and falling emotional tension, ranging from the grandiloquent to the humiliating: in a sense he tried to create a musical rhetorical score. In the fourth scene of the third act of *Antonio's Revenge*, Antonio delivers a soliloquy (H3v–H4). The scene is immediately preceded by the death of Mellida and Antonio commences his solo with a stoical, but Christian, acceptance of Heaven's decrees:

> I Heaven, thou maist, thou maist omnipotence
> What vermine bred of putrifacted slime,
> Shall dare to expostulate with thy decrees!

He accepts his loss and his own insignificance and then gives thanks for borrowing 'her of thee a little time'. At this point he lies on his back, in abject submission, crying as a child:

> I am a poore poore Orphant; a weake, weak childe,
> The wrack of splitted fortune, the very Ouze,
> The quick sand that devours all miserie.

But at once he contradicts this mood and tone by vowing bloody vengeance:

> For all this, I dare live, and I will live,
> Onely to numme some others cursed bloode,
> With the dead palsie of like misery.

This avowal contradicts all that has gone before, for it denies the Christian-Stoic fortitude of the soliloquy's opening, with its assertion of an active endeavour to avenge fate. The speech concludes with a blasphemous augmentation of this vow, for he declares 'My breast is *Golgotha*, grave for the dead': by implication he makes himself that contradiction in terms, a Christ-like avenger. In a sense too, a transition has occurred between the childish actor (the 'poore Orphant') and the manly courage of someone determined to live on for revenge: he lies down symbolically as a child and rises as a man. The speech began with the hyperbole of the agonised self-conscious suffering of childhood, but its concluding tone has nothing sentimental about it. Whatever one may feel about the handling of the diction, there can surely be little doubt that Marston was intending to show the hardening of resolution under the impact of misfortune and the concomitant maturing of the spirit. Antonio, the boy, finds the traditional teaching of the Christian-Stoic ethic inadequate and he casts it aside as his manhood seeks a more adequate philosophy.

There are other instances too where self-conscious sensitivity is used not to parody tragic action but to enhance it. Pandulpho, in the next scene which is concerned with the burial of Feliche, declares amid his grief:

> . . . all this while I ha but plaid a part,
> Like to some boy, that actes a Tragedie,
> Speakes burly words, and raves out passion:
> But, when he thinks upon his infant weaknesse,
> He droopes his eye. I spake more then a god;
> Yet am lesse then a man. (I)

Marston is suggesting that a youth, conscious of his limitations and weakness, is better able to project the realities of suffering and grief than the adult actor, whose vision is circumscribed by his own conceit in his maturity and power. Marston's method of inserting this extra-contextual remark suddenly widens the perspective of the action. The Induction to *Antonio and Mellida* was used in a similar way; it was an apologetical introit to the play which allowed the audience to participate in the creation of the dramatic performance and made them part of the ensuing action. Here, in Pandulpho's speech, we have a similar effect: the actor reaches out from his persona on stage to draw the auditor into an awareness of the grief the action demands. It is a technique, if skilfully used, likely to be extremely effective in a small theatre where there was little in the way of division between stage and auditorium.

Marston's actors are not attempting to create an illusion of reality by wholly becoming and always remaining the character they portray: they are seeking to stand apart from and comment upon those characters. This may have caused young actors to recite and symbolise, to posture rather than portray, and the musical dimension of the plays, both instrumental and rhetorical, would have enhanced this tendency towards an operatic style. The intent, however, was to create a new form in which the music of strings and words should combine to create a context where 'Never more woe in lesser plot was found' (K4).

5

New management: new methods

The first phase in the revival at Paul's ended in hostility and bitterness. After *What You Will*, owing to Jonson's antagonism, Marston withdrew from dramatic prominence there and his influence waned. In his place there came one Thomas Woodford, a theatrical *entrepreneur* of doubtful moral integrity. It was Woodford who was responsible for the acquisition by the Children of Paul's of George Chapman's play, *The Old Joiner of Aldgate*, for it was played by Woodford's 'meanes and appointment'.[1]

The principal actors in this play were a bookbinder in Paul's yard, one John Flaskett, who lived in Knightrider Street; John Howe, a barber-surgeon, who owned a house close to St Gregory's, and Dr John Milward, Preacher at Christchurch in Newgate Street, whose curate was William Maicocke. The female roles were performed by Mrs Margaret Sharles, a wealthy widow, and Agnes Howe, her niece, 'of a softe & bashfull nature of modest & shamefast behaviour'. There were a host of minor characters too, but the principals were translated onto the stage as Snipper Snapper the barber-surgeon (Howe), his daughter Ursula (Agnes), Touchbox, suitor to Agnes (Flaskett), a French doctor, also suitor to Agnes (Milward), and Mrs Glasbie, aunt to Ursula (Mrs Sharles).

The drama proper was initiated on 11 September 1600 when Mrs Sharles died, for she, being childless, left between £2,000 and £3,000 to her niece as a dowry. Agnes' father promptly began negotiations with a whole group of putative suitors for the best composition he could acquire for a share in this legacy: the fact that Agnes had been betrothed before her aunt's death did not deter him. This betrothal, which had taken place in August 1600, was between Agnes and John Flaskett and the ceremony, which took place in Flaskett's house in Knightrider Street, was conducted in very much the way of, and with similar words to, the betrothal of Canidius and Livia in Lyly's *Mother Bombie*:

Cand.   Here I do plight my faith, taking thee for the staffe of my age, and of my youth my solace.
Liv.   And I vow to thee affection which nothing can dissolve, neither the length of time, nor mallice of fortune, nor distance of place. (F2^v)

Unfortunately for Flaskett, Howe proceeded to auction Agnes to Thomas Field, Henry Jones, 'Humphrey of the Court', and a nefarious quartet, Povey, Wright, Cox and Leer. The three main suitors, Flaskett, Field and Jones, went to law and Jones, who had a flair for publicity, 'caused a Process to be executed and fixed upon a Sonday or Holliday at & upon the dore of . . . Christchurch . . . att which tyme . . . Dr. Milward was the . . . Preacher of the . . . Church'. This was, of course, Agnes' parish church. Howe, by now somewhat perturbed by the number of suits alleging pre-contract pending against him, sought Dr Milward's advice and explained the whole matter to him. Agnes was sent to see Milward: Milward promptly married her himself with the connivance of her mother but unbeknown to her father, and the marriage was conducted by Milward's brother, rector of the parish church in Barnet.

The wedding took place shortly after Easter 1601: Milward was at once sent to the Clink, but he appealed against the sentence and the legality of his marriage was upheld on 20 February 1602 by the Court of Delegates. On 28 February of the following year, however, another appeal reversed the judgement in favour of Flaskett and the court ordered Agnes to marry him. In order to influence this judgement in his favour, Flaskett had commissioned a play about the whole affair: this was *The Old Joiner of Aldgate* by George Chapman, who was paid £13 6s 8d for it by the manager of the Paul's playhouse. It was 'played by the children of powles' in their 'pryvate house' until a 'Requeste was made by doctor Whyte [Thomas White, a major canon] one of the Mrs of the churche of Powles . . . by the speciall procurement of . . . doctor Milwarde [who] through his Jelious consceynce erroniouslye pretendede yt to concerne him and his cause . . .' Pearce, however, affirms that Milward had had the text for two weeks before it was performed to satisfy himself that it was innocent of any slanderous intent.

148

Despite the obvious direct correlation between the Agnes Howe affair and *The Old Joiner*, even the principals themselves were able to argue plausibly that there was no intentional commentary. Flaskett and Howe went together to see the play, having no doubt heard of Snipper Snapper and Touchbox for it was a 'common report' in the city 'that the play played them'; but Flaskett refused to take it personally and did not 'make anie regarde or accounte of the same but as Toys & iests such as are acted in other Places'. He elaborated further, declaring 'he was at the first offended with the Play because [he] . . . was told . . . that he was meant by the name of Tuchboxe in the Play and [he] . . . sawe the same & then took the same to be but a iest perswading himself that he was not meant thereby but that the same was onely a meere Toye which had idle applications of names according to the Inventors disposicion thereof'. Flaskett, who probably 'plotted' the play, was supported by Howe, who declared 'he had no reason to take it to himself for that Kings had been presented on the stage & therefore Barbers might'. Despite the obvious similarities of the plot and the legal situation, nothing could be proved: Chapman, Woodford (Paul's manager), Pearce, Flaskett and Howe could not be convicted. The Children of Paul's managed to stage a dramatic version of a current scandalous affair of sufficient notoriety to eclipse, at least for a time, the domestic strife among the Cardinals.

In the end Flaskett was undone: during an interview with Bishop Bancroft he inadvertently admitted some doubt about the validity of his betrothal to Agnes and some of his witnesses were found to have committed perjury. Bancroft refused to allow Flaskett to act on the 1603 judgement, and by 12 November 1604 the marriage of Agnes and John Milward was finally declared legal.

The Old Joiner of Aldgate was intended to intimidate Agnes into marrying Flaskett, just as Jones had attempted to dominate her by his bill posted in her parish church. The Maicockes had attempted the same thing with the boy who wrote libels against the Gouldings. Chapman's play was acted right up to the date, 28 February 1603, on which judgement was given in Flaskett's favour. The text was already licensed before purchase and it was Thomas Woodford who bought it; Edward Pearce kept his hands clean of the actual transaction. There is some suggestion that the text may have been altered after Chapman had sold it: Woodford (or Pearce) made some of the situations in the plot more obviously directly applicable to the Howe affair. Certainly this was the intention and Edward Brompton, Milward's man-servant, saw the play and had no doubt at all what it implied; in fact, he declares Woodford told him that it had been written as a commentary on the Agnes auction. The price of the play, twenty marks, was higher than the fee Chapman usually received at this time: it is fairly clear that all the parties knew that it was a risky business, but excellent as a means of drawing spectators to the Paul's playhouse, which was the very focal point of the lives and dwellings of the characters involved. Anyone in the audience who lived in one of the surrounding parishes was a neighbour of the characters on the stage. The drama was successful enough to be performed on numerous occasions and its inhibition, for less than a week, no doubt served only to increase its popularity.

Howe, despite his disclaimers, knew perfectly well what the play portrayed and he sat side by side with Flaskett during a performance, with the other spectators making the allusions clear:

there was a stage Play plaied by the children of Powles concerning a barber & others & this defendant thinketh that the same Play was meant by this defendant & his daughter & Mris Sharles John fflaskett & others, att which Play he did once sitt together with fflaskett & sawe the same, being unawares unto him brought to sitt by fflaskett to see the Play And further he hath heard manie say that the Play was made of this defendant & his daughter & also of others.

During the Martin Marprelate affair there is a clear suggestion that Martin was visually identified on the Paul's stage by costume or mannerism or both, and the same was certainly done with Horace/Jonson in *Satiro-mastix*. In *The Old Joiner* this personal identity of the dramatic character was taken a stage further; now not merely were actual persons easily recognised on the stage, but the very dialogue demanded an influence on their legal affairs outside the playhouse confines. This was, undoubtedly, a dangerous practice and, while it may have been profitable, it led to searching inquiries and rigorous questioning by the authorities. Both Pearce and Woodford were asked 'whether . . . have yow threatened anie in this sorte, That yf they hindred the playinge thereof [*The Old Joiner*] there would be and was a plogue [prologue] made to the Spectato[rs] in excuse of the nott playinge ytt that woulde disgrace them [Howe and the others] muche more, and that they or some of them weare better give fortie pounds then ytt shoulde soe be'.[2] They vigorously denied it, but the suspicion remains that under Woodford's brief management of Paul's a stage play was used directly as a vehicle for extortion: Howe, Milward and Agnes were all, to some degree, blackmailed by *The Old Joiner*.

When one ascribes the blame for this prostitution of the theatre, both Woodford and Pearce must share the guilt and yet, perhaps, one may give the latter the benefit of some doubt, for on 2 December 1604 Edward Pearce caused Thomas Woodford 'grevious bodily harm' and in Easter Term 1606 he was sued and fined £13 6s 8d.[3] This may have been no more than the collapse of honour among thieves, or it may date Pearce's final impatience with a morally unscrupulous associate. Whatever the truth, it surely signifies the end of Woodford's notorious association with the Children of Paul's. Woodford was too dangerous a partner; his first venture had brought about a temporary official closure of the theatre and *The Old Joiner* seems to have come close to provoking a permanent inhibition like that of 1590/1.

While Marston was the dominant dramatic influence at Paul's in the first years of its revival, Middleton became the chief dramatist both during the later managerial period of Woodford and after his falling out with Pearce. Woodford was the main exploiter of the personalised abuse technique devised to attract audiences to Paul's and The Globe during their period of intense competition with the Blackfriars. His success with *The Old Joiner* cannot be questioned, but his methods were unscrupulous. Middleton, at first, was conscious of the special qualities that the Children of Paul's had achieved in their repertoire and he acknowledges Marston's contribution to them in *Blurt Master Constable*; he does so again in *The Phoenix*. This play was performed after the *Old Joiner* affair and may perhaps have been designed as the opening draw for the new season in the winter of 1603/4 after a period of closure because of the prevalence of the Black Death in 1603. It seeks to remind the audience of past successes. Tangle, like Marston in *Poetaster* or Horace in

Satiro-mastix, vomits the words of his legal disease, 'Oh an extent, a *Proclamation*, a *Summons*, a *Recognisance*, a *Tachment*, and *Iniunction*, a *Writ*, a *Seysure*, a *Writ of praisement*, an *Absolution*, a *Quietus Est'* (K2) and he is also designed to remind the audience of the notoriety surrounding the Cardinals in their quarrel. Tangle is involved in twenty-nine law suits, most of them wholly frivolous:

A stake puld out of my hedge, theres one: I was well beaten I remember, that's two: I tooke one a bed with my wife agen her will, that's three: I was cal'd Cuckold for my labour, that's foure: I tooke another a bed agen, that's five: the[n] one cald me wittal that's sixe: he kild my Dog for Barking, seaven: my Maide Servant was knockt at that time, eight: my wife miscarryed with a push, Nine, & *sic de coeteris*, I have so vext and beggerd the whole parish, with processe, Suppoenas, and such like molestations, they are not able to spare so much readie money from a Tearme, as woulde set up a new Weather-cocke: the Church-wardens are faine to goe to law with the Poores money (C–C^v).

This, with suitable satiric amplifications, reads like a case history of the Goulding–Maicocke affair, for they, like Tangle, had also lost their ability to discriminate between the trivial and the significant. Goulding was 'gyven uppon everie small occasion, to sue his neighbo^{rs} himself . . . having manie waies abused Mr Cowper, one of the Petticannons, yett not wthstandinge never lefte sueing of him, untill he made him quite forsake his dwellinge in the Petticannons, his wife quarreled wth a poore woman, in the markett, and he arrested the poore woman, to make her spend moneye, and the woman being arrested, he lett his Acton fall . . . there have byn tried and dooe depend eight or nyne accons, betwene [Goulding and Maicocke] . . . to the no small slaunder of the Churche'.[4] In addition there are two deliberate allusions in *The Phoenix* to the Howe affair, for an unhappily married Captain sells his wife for 500 angels, and Falso, a corrupt Justice, is conspiring to defraud his niece of some fraction of her £5,000 dowry by marrying her himself (E4).

Middleton reminds his audience of previous successes both in plot and stage business, for two of Falso's men come *'tumbling in'* and they are wearing *'False beards'* (F3^v). This is a visual joke like that in *Doctor Dodypoll* and *Antonio's Revenge*; beards, as the actors did not use them seriously, were a mark of comedy. Apart from this largely nostalgic play, Middleton contributed three or four others, *A Trick to Catch the Old-one*, *Michaelmas Terme*, *A Mad World, My Masters* and, possibly, *The Family of Love* – his dominance as chief dramatist seems to have endured from Marston's eclipse almost to the theatre's closure. Perhaps the most marked feature of these later Middleton plays is their toning down and eventual omission of any elements which make them specifically and recognisably individual to the Children of Paul's. It is true that Middleton localises his *Michaelmas Terme* in Paul's aisle with the discomfiture of Easy at the hands of the 'nips', Rearage and Salewood, but some features have changed. The price of admission has risen as Michaelmas Term announces, 'ours have but sixpenny fees all the yeare long, yet wee dispatch you in two howers, without demur' (A3). When the revival first began admission may have been free, with spectators however expected to donate rewards to the boys, as the Prologue to *The Maydes Metamorphosis* seems to imply,

> Drops not diminish, but encrease great floods:
> And mites impaire not, but augment our goods.

Perhaps the audience were expected to quoit coins on the stage, as Dekker advised the gallant to do in the choir. Later in 1601 'Twopence is the price for going in, to a newe Playe', as William Percy testifies in *The Cuckqueans' and Cuckolds' Errants* (I.ii) – but now, in 1604, it is 6d. This range is, however, identical to that under Westcott and Gyles at first Paul's.[5] But Paul's under the professional management of Woodford was moving more clearly towards the simple monetary base of the other theatres. In *Michaelmas Terme* Middleton is still aware of some special features, for a country wench enters with a '*Tyrewoman busie about her head*' (E^v); this boy/girl had his hair set by one of the women from the almonry house who looked after the choristers and were, apparently, also employed in the playhouse.

Middleton was impressed by the feigned deaths which had been so sensationally effective a feature earlier in the revival. At the close of Act IV of *Michaelmas Terme*, '*A counterfet Coarse brought in, Tomazin, and al the mourners equally counterfeit*' (H3); no doubt the spectators could remember the resurrection of Antonio. Music is, however, increasingly rare and song and dance have faded from the prominence they had into the kind of occasional occurrence that the public stage offered. Perhaps to make up for this lack, Middleton later in *A Mad World, My Masters* (c.1606) makes a feature of a novel instrument at Paul's, the regals or portable organ. Not merely is there a song sung to them by a 'consort of musicians' on stage, but while they play *'coverd dishes march over the Stage'*; a grand procession is staged to their music (C). In this play, however, there are already signs that actors are again facing difficulties, for Sir Bounteous Progress affirms that players 'were never more uncertaine in their lives, now up & now downe, they know not when to play, where to play, not what to play, not when to play for fearful fools, where to play for Puritaine fooles, nor what to play for criticall fooles' (G4ᵛ). Perhaps this is no more than a conventional complaint against prevailing conditions, but attacks against the players, especially Paul's, were soon to increase in acerbity at Paul's Cross.[6]

What has happened here to Paul's, however, is a crucial change: no longer are we conscious of individualised plays or playing – Middleton only spasmodically recognises any special features of this playhouse and indeed in *A Trick to Catch the Old-one*, also played about this time, there is little or nothing to distinguish it from any play at a public theatre. It is a commonplace Prodigal Son play with the outwitting of unscrupulous and tight-fisted usurers. The most significant effect, in fact, of Marston's disgrace at Paul's was to cause a change in the kind of entertainment offered. Under Marston the dramas were custom-designed and individualised; under Middleton/Woodford they are production-line plays suitable for any company or theatre of reasonable competence with more or less modern facilities. One additional visible reason for the change was that the boys were growing older. If the early teenagers of about fourteen who took the major parts in 1599 were still with the company in 1606, they would be over twenty by now. There is every likelihood that this indeed was happening, for contemporaries were aware of it.

On Wednesday 30 July 1606, King Christian IV of Denmark, who was on a state visit to England, spent the day at Greenwich in 'hunting, feasting and other private delights. On Wednesday at night, the Youthes of Paules, commonlye cald the Children of

Paules, plaide before the two Kings, a plaie called *Abuses*: containing both a Comedie and a Tragedie, at which the Kings seemed to take delight and be much pleased'.[7] While the term 'youth' is an elastic concept at this time, implying anything between seven and twenty-one, clearly the author is aware that these players are older than children proper, and 'youth' normally meant the period between puberty and manhood. Certainly Shakespeare used the word in the sense of young men of an age to be soldiers; 'Now all the youth of England are on fire' (*Henry V*, II Chorus 1). Some confirmation that the ageing of the 'children' was recognised is to be found in *The Family of Love*, where Glister asks Geraldine where they have come from, and she replies, from a play which was performed by 'youths' (I.iii); it is clear from the context that the children's theatre is being discussed.[8] Again in *The Woman Hater*, in 1607 'latelie Acted', Lazarello declares he is twenty-eight (D) and a doctor is spoken of as 'bout sixe and twentie' (D4ᵛ). This is not a play which reveals any signs of customised design for the Paul's company and it would not, therefore, be reasonable to take this as a literal and specific notion of number. The ages do, however, in a general sense coincide with the other evidence: it would also make sound commercial sense to continue to use your best-trained and experienced players as long as possible. Certainly there is an indication that Thomas Gyles did just this after Paul's suppression in 1590/1 for at that time in the City of Gloucester, there was paid 'to the Children of powles xxs'.[9] This was not the cathedral choir, for it was required in London daily to sing, but rather a group formed from the superannuated choristers who were by then a touring company, having been forbidden to play in the capital. The name Children of Paul's was, then, in both periods of its flourishing, something of a conventional title for an acting company consisting largely of young adults, accompanied by younger boy sopranos.

Woodford's influence at Paul's was, fortunately, short and his association with the company was over by December 1604, but his legacy, or at least a reaction to him, may be the explanation for the coherently and astringently moral tone of most of the plays in the 1604–6 period. Under Pearce and Middleton an almost defensive insistence on innocence is a recurrent feature of the repertoire and an assertive defence of the institutions of the state is common. The tone is first set in *The Phoenix*, which was perhaps consciously designed to restore and repair the public reputation of the children after the unsavoury legal tangles of *The Old Joiner*: here the sanctity of the law is rigorously upheld:

> Thou Angell sent amongst us, sober Law.
> Made with meeke Eyes, perswading Action,
> No lowd immodest Tongue, voic'd like a virgin,
> And as chaste from sale,
> Save onely to be heard, but not to raile. (C2)

This eulogy is paralleled later in the action, once again by Phoenix, with a similar hymn to 'Reverend, and honourable Matrimony' (D4ᵛ) and later he saves a maid from a 'foule den, / Of theft and purpos'd incest' (G3). He goes on to condemn Tangle's excesses and proves his fitness to reign by his strict and impartial upholding of the scriptural moral law and the legal framework of the state. This kind of strong moral theme is, of course, a commonplace in Middleton's plays, but the repertoire is consistent in that the two plays by Dekker and Webster of this period, *West-ward Hoe* and *North-ward Hoe*, also lay some stress on conventional moral attitudes.

In *West-ward Hoe* one of the climactic moments of the action is the humiliation of a licentious Earl for his unlawful desire for a virtuous merchant's wife. The discomfiture is effected visually:

Whilst the song is heard. The Earle drawes a Curten, and sets forth a Banquet: he then Exit, and Enters presently with Parenthesis attird like his wife maskt: leads him to the table, places him in a chaire, and in dumbe signes, Courts him, til the Song be done. (F3ᵛ)

The music which is the background to this attempted seduction may have been played, ironically, to accompany a song called *Vertue* and the Earl is exposed as a mean and foolish lover by the absurdity of his courtship to the disguised husband of his erstwhile mistress. Like the Prodigal, he repents and cries:

> Oh God thou hast undone thy selfe and me,
> None live to match this peece, thou art to bloudie,
> Yet for her sake, whom Ile embalme with teares,
> This Act with her I bury, and to quit
> Thy losse of such a Iewel, thou shalt share
> My living with me, Come [*to Parenthesis*] imbrace. (F4)

This act of magnanimity redeems him and it is clear that the play approves of such redemptive behaviour and expects the virtue of the woman who rejects him to be applauded. It is exactly similar in *North-ward Hoe*, which opens with the inflamed rhetoric of a falsely accused wife's denial of her infidelity to her husband;

> . . . if ever I had thought uncleane,
> In detestation of your nuptiall pillow:
> Let *Sulphur* drop from Heaven, and naile my body
> Dead to this earth. (B3)

At times the assertions of moral integrity, fidelity, honour and the attack on unworthy suspicion seem almost to amount to a moral crusade against 'false opinion' and the cynical, derogatory evaluations of human conduct and motive so usual in common parlance. The apogee of this whole cycle in the Paul's repertoire is reached in Chapman's *Bussy D'Ambois* and indeed, if it were played early along with Middleton's *Phoenix*, it may have helped to set the high moral tone of the later plays. Just like the children themselves, Chapman may have been anxious to redeem himself from the smears of *The Old Joiner*. From the outset, Bussy is a man apart, so clear-sighted and uncompromising that he has a Christ-like, rather than a mere human, sense of moral integrity. His views on the corruption of courts are wholly without tolerance for human frailty:

> . . . Alas what should I doe
> With that enchanted Glasse? See divels there?
> Or (like a strumpet) learne to set my lookes
> In an eternall Brake, or practise iuggling,
> To keepe my face still fast, my hart still loose; (A3)
>
> . . .
>
> I am for honest Actions, not for great:
> If I may bring up a new fashion,
> And rise in Court with vertue. (A3ᵛ)

Bussy's relationship with Tamyra which, while wholly innocent, leads to his and her downfall, through the maliciousness of envious courtiers and suspicious husbands, is, of course, an inevitable consequence of his inability to compromise with the subterfuges of mere men. His sacrifice to the cause of virtue, for it is a martyrdom on behalf of innocence, leads to the nearly miraculous conversion of his greatest foe, Montsurry, and the sad and solitary seclusion of Tamyra. The concluding tone of the speech of Umbra is wholly laudatory of Bussy; in

him, the redeemer of the old Adam, a new standard has been set
for human aspiration:

> Farewell brave relicts of a compleat man:
> Looke up and see thy spirit made a star,
> Ioine flames with Hercules: and when thou setst
> Thy radiant forhead in the firmament,
> Make the vast continent, cracke with thy recit,
> Spred to a world of fire: and th'aged skie
> Chere with new sparkes of old humanity. (I4^v)

These examples of human virtue, so frequently repeated on the
Paul's stage in the 1604–6 period, must have done much to alter
the public image of the company: from being impudent, satirical
squibs during the Poetomachia and under Woodford, the Children of Paul's, now more accurately the young men of Paul's,
were, somewhat ironically, much more nearly an ecclesiastical
group, acting out doctrines of which the most conservative of
clerics would hardly disapprove.

It is in *Bussy D'Ambois* that the visible staircase of the last period
in the changing stage design at Paul's is used most effectively.
The latter part of the fourth act seems to have been played in
statuesque or pageant form, with Tamyra above and she, to
music, *'enters with her maid'* (G2); next the direction requires that
'Ascendit Bussy with Comolet' and they rise toward her, followed
shortly afterwards by a spirit who is conjured up; the act ends
with the descent of the spirit (Behemoth) and Comolet. Tamyra's
chamber is located above and the sequential ascent and descent,
demanded by the action both here and elsewhere, stresses the
visible and deliberately unconcealed nature of the relationship
between Bussy and her – no 'back stairs' work here. In the fifth
act Bussy pronounces his unwavering commitment to his virtuous principles from the head of this visible stair:

> Ile not complaine to earth yet, but to heaven,
> And (like a man) looke upwards even in death.
> Proppe me, true sword, as thou hast ever done:
> The equall thought I beare of life and death,
> Shall make me faint on no side; I am up
> Heere like a Roman Statue; I will stand
> Till death hath made me marble. (I2^v)

In this grand and impressive pose, in which the actor would be
required to dominate the set, Bussy is one of Shakespeare's

idealised 'youths' of England aroused by glory and Christian virtue. This speech, virtually a 'set' piece, and others like it would verge dangerously on bathos or parody if pronounced by a child of ten or so. An actor who was extremely young was highly unlikely to have been able to command the stage presence needed for an effective performance, but fortunately by this date (*c.*1604) there appears every probability that the 'children' had become young adults, of nineteen or twenty, and Bussy grows enormously in credibility and stature when performed by a young man of modern university age. The same is true of the more strident satirical outpourings in *West-ward Hoe* and *North-ward Hoe* which are largely 'cony-catching' plays. Perhaps when Maybery tells Bellmont to 'cry *North-ward hoe*, as the boy at Powles saies' (Fᵛ) he is in fact implying what had happened to the Paul's company by about 1604. The senior acting boys, no longer choristers, were dominant perhaps even to the extent of auditioning newcomers, and the choristers (apart from their singing which was becoming a less usual feature of the plays) were relegated to the minor parts of pages and the menial tasks of advertising the name of the play in the middle aisle. It is noticeable that after Marston breaks with the company the use of song is far less pronounced: from an average of seven songs in a play at the beginning of the revival, the incidence gradually declines under Middleton/Woodford to only one.

This period in the history of the Children of Paul's began in a controversy which could easily have led to their permanent closure (the Howe affair), but it ended on a very different note. By 1606 when the children performed *Abuses*, also presumably a play with a strong moralistic tone, their image was almost sedate. While it is true that in *A Trick to Catch the Old-one*, *North-ward Hoe*, *Michaelmas Terme* and elsewhere there is much satire on corruption among merchants and lawyers, the overall tone is admonitory and moralistic and since the boys were becoming older their indulgence in moral exhortation was more easily tolerated. It is probably a sign of their successful rehabilitation after their earlier scandals that they were chosen to provide courtly entertainments on several occasions in 1606.

6

The triumph of profit and Puritanism

During most of 1605, after his falling out with Woodford, Pearce appears to have operated the playhouse alone – the first time he had done so, although he may have had considerable help from Middleton, now principal purveyor of plays. It was probably early in 1606 that he acquired a new partner; he was joined by Edward Kirkham, who was the payee (on 31 March 1606) for two plays (perhaps *The Phoenix* and *A Trick to Catch the Old-one*) at court during the Christmas season or shortly after.[1] Kirkham had previously been associated with the Children of the Queen's Revels at the Blackfriars but he, like Marston, Jonson and Chapman, suffered persecution for offending the King in *Eastward Ho!* (performed at Blackfriars) over the remark, 'as for them [the Scots], there are no greater friends to Englishmen and *England*, when they are out an't, in the world, then they are'.[2] Kirkham moved to Paul's and the offending dramatists tried to keep out of sight and narrowly averted having their ears cut off and their noses slit. Not long after Kirkham arrived and presented plays at court, the spectacles that the Children could offer were eclipsed by a public performance at the west end of Paul's yard. This was the execution of Henry Garnet on 3 May 1606, already preceded by the deaths of Sir Everard Digby and other conspirators; all were condemned for complicity in the Gunpowder Plot. The Dean of Paul's, John Overall, was present when Garnet mounted the scaffold and said to those around him, 'The intention was wicked [the plot] and the fact would have bene cruell, and from his soule he should have abhorred it, had it effected',[3] and to the crowd he continued, 'I am come hither this blessed day . . . to end all my crosses in this life . . . I confesse I have offended the King, and am sory for it, so farre as I was guilty, which was in concealing it [the plot had been revealed to him in confession] . . . I am heartily sorry that any Catholickes ever had so cruell a designe . . .' (Fff2).

The final act of his execution took place upon the gibbet and his last words were 'I commend me to all good Catholickes . . . I pray God [that they] may not fare the worse for my sake, and I exhort them all to take heede they enter not into any Treasons, Rebellions, or Insurrections against the King . . . and fel to praying; And crossing himselfe, said *In nomine Patris et Filii, et Spiritus sancti* . . . and then was turned off, and hung till he was dead' (Fff3). A spectacle like this could hardly be rivalled on stage, but it was undoubtedly good for business for the thronging crowds of the middle aisle would be swelled enormously by the extra spectators who came for a glimpse of the judicial execution of the most wanted man in the England of the reign of James. A later commentator on Garnet's end, Roger Widdrington in 1679, declares that it 'was transacted, not in secret hugger-mugger, but openly, and as it were upon the Stage, partly at his Publick Tryal . . . partly at his Execution in the midst of the City before the gates of *St. Paul's*, to which . . . there was a great conflux of People assembled'.[4]

This thronging of additional crowds to the cathedral was repeated again only two months later during the state visit of Christian IV of Denmark, for on 31 July both kings 'came into *Paules* church-yard, where over against *Pauls* schoole sat al the petty Cannons and singing mē belonging to the great cathedral . . . amongst whō were mingled a cōsort of cornets, Sagbuts and other wind instruments; at *Pauls* schoole doore was a little scaffold reard and covered with cloth of gold from whence was a most eloquent oration made to the two Kings in Latin'.[5] The absence of the choristers is to be accounted for, presumably, by their failure to get back to London from Greenwich in time, for they had performed *Abuses* for the two kings there the previous day.[6] But the playhouse orchestra seems to have been committed here, with the speaking parts performed by the scholars from Colet's grammar school. It is a royal welcome almost identical to those provided by the grammar school in the sixteenth century.[7]

When King Christian visited the interior of the cathedral on the following day, he 'went to the toppe of the steeple, from whence he might take the prospect and full view of the whole Citie, whose outstretched limmits . . . inflamed him both with delight and admiration'.[8] According to Henry Roberts, however, 'he admired most . . . the being of a Horse upon that place, comming up such a way of great danger and so hye, that he tooke very good notice thereof, and wonderfully did admire the same'.[9] This was, of course, Banks' famous performing horse, Morocco, which in 1600 climbed the steps to the steeple. According to Middleton's *Black Booke* this display was merely another example of the iniquities in the church:

I walked in *Powles* to see fashions; to dive into villainous meetings, pernitious Plots, blacke Humours, and a Million of mischiefes, which are bred in that Cathedrall Wombe, and borne within lesse then forty weekes after. But some may obiect and say; What doth the Divell walke in *Powles* then? Why not, Sir, as well as a Seriant, or a Ruffian, or a Murtherer: may not the Divell I pray you walke in *Powles* as well as the Horse goe a toppe of *Powles*, for I am sure I was not farre from his keeper. (B4ᵛ–C)

The fare that Pearce and Kirkham offered the crowds who thronged Paul's both for normal business and for the special free shows provided by the Gunpowder Plot conspirators and King Christian, was characteristic of the well established traditions of the repertoire of the Children of Paul's. When *The Puritaine* opens, the Widow Plus, '*Drawing out her husbands Picture*', bewails his loss:

Deare Copie of my husband, oh let me kisse thee:
How like him is their Model? their briefe Picture
Quickens my tears: my sorrowes are renew'd
At their fresh sight? (A4ᵛ)

The painter among the company, who produced the portraits of Marston and Stanley and played the part of Earl Lassingbergh, may also have produced this likeness of the widow's husband. Similarly talented choristers had made important contributions at first Paul's, with the picture of Wyt (*Wit and Science*) and the painter's studio for Apelles (*Campaspe*). In addition the play offers a re-run of the, by now notorious, resurrection scenes so popular with the second Paul's audience: towards the end of the fourth act, there enters '*the Coffin of the Corporall, the souldier bound, and lead by Officers, the Sheriffe there*' (G4ᵛ). This situation repeats the double reversal in *Antonio and Mellida*, for the Corporal is cured by Pyeboard and his assassins released.

Middleton used the same effect in *Michaelmas Terme* (H3) and, of course, Marston more or less repeated it in *Jacke Drum's Entertainment* (D2). It is possible that Middleton was the author of *The Puritaine*, for the details of the plot certainly reflected a detailed knowledge of the customs of the Paul's playhouse:[10] in the final moments of the play there is a grand procession, when there *'Enter the two Bridegromes Captaine and Scholler after them, Sir* Godfrey *and* Edmond, *Widdow chandge in apparell, mistris* Francis *led between two Knights,* Sir Iohn Pennydub *and* Moll' (H3). This pageant entry recalls the opening of *Antonio and Mellida* with Piero's inspection of his guard, and implies that the Children of Paul's could process on to the stage at least two and perhaps three abreast, probably from the central curtained door on the lower stage. As in Marston's early plays for second Paul's, the author makes extensive and elaborate use of the facilities of the physical structure of the stage throughout the play: the two side doors are used for entry opposed, *'Enter at one doore Corporall* Oth . . . *at the other, three of the Widdow Puritaines Servingmen . . . They meete'* (B2ᵛ), and this door, or the other, has a 'Knocker' on the inside (E2ᵛ); the climactic conjuring scene takes place 'above' in a room visible to the audience, with 'windowes' (G3ᵛ); and this central upper room is flanked by a 'fine Gallery' (E3). The impression created by this play is of an attempt to capitalise on already established habits at Paul's; but it was also a very serious miscalculation, a blunder that was to prove largely responsible for the theatre company's final demise.

On St Valentine's Day 1607/8, a sermon was delivered at Paul's Cross by William Crashawe, a Puritan divine. In its published form this sermon, of some one hundred and seventy-four pages, was sold 'at the great Northgate of S. Paules', and it was directed 'both against Papist, and Brownist'.[11] Its peroration was aimed at the theatre:

> The ungodly Playes and Enterludes so rife in this nation; what are they but a bastard of Babylon, a daughter of error and confusion, a hellish device, (the divels owne recreation to mock at holy things) by him delivered to the Heathen, from them to the Papists, and from them to us? (p. 170)

This general condemnation is usual enough, but he goes on to point out that 'never was there Divine of note and learning . . . that durst so farre prostitute his credite as to write for them' (p.170). In a sense this is a challenge and a warning, for this sermon was as much a performance as Bussy's declaration of lone defiance, delivered to an audience who were seated in much the same pattern as those at the adjacent theatre.[12] Crashawe goes on to rehearse all the conventional grounds for attacking plays:

They know . . . that God accounts it abomination for a man to put on womans apparell [Deuteronomy, 22.5] . . . they know that *Cyprian* resolved (1) *that a Player ought not to come to the Lords table*; and that *hee that teacheth children to play, is not an instructor, but a spoiler and destroyer of children*: they know they have no calling, but are in the State like warts on the hand, or blemishes in the face . . . they know they are defended with the same arguments, as the stewes in Rome bee. (pp. 170–1)

The italics are Crashawe's and they make it clear that this attack is specific: the players he has in mind are Children, their Master and their Priests. He goes on to identify the object of his hatred, beyond all possible doubt:

All this they are daily made to know, but all in vaine, they be children of Babylon that will not bee healed: nay, they grow worse and worse, for now they bring religion and holy things upon the stage . . . Two hypocrites must be brought foorth; and how shall they be described but by these names, *Nicolas S. Antlings, Simon S. Maryoveries*? (p.171)

He is referring to the Children of Paul's and their play *The Puritaine, or the Widdow of Watling-Street*; there enters, in the second scene of the first act, *'at one doore Corporall* Oth, *a Vaine-glorious fellow, and at the other, three of the Widdow Puritaines Servingmen*, Nicholas Saint–Tantlings, Simon Saint Mary-Overies, *and* Frailtie *in blacke scurvie mourning coates, and Bookes at their Girdles, as coming from Church'* (B2ᵛ). Watling Street, where the widow lived, is the continuation of the main thoroughfare out of St Austin's gate from Paul's yard. St Antling's was at this very junction – visible from the main south door of St Paul's or from the Cross, and its parish was notoriously of a Puritan persuasion. St Mary Overys was on the south bank of the river, close to the Clink and the Bear Garden. All three of these parishioners are hypocrites who devise means of evading the commandments:

Nich[olas] Well Corporall, Ile e'en along with you, to visit my Kinsman, if I can do him any good, I will,—but I have nothing

> for him, *Simon* Saint *Mary Overis* and *Fraylty*, pray make a
> lie for me to the Knight my Maister, old Sir *Godfrey*.
> *Cor[poral]* A lie? may you lie then?
> *Fray.* O I, we may lie, but we must not sweare.
> *Sim.* True, wee may lie with our Neighbors wife, but wee must
> not sweare we did so;
> *Cor.* Oh, an excellent Tag of religion? (B3ᵛ)

Their minister, who is priest-in-charge at St Antling's and
whom they call variously 'Maister *Ful-bellie*' (B3ᵛ) or *'Pigman'*
(Hᵛ), for he is 'an excellent feeder' (B3ᵛ) of pork, hates actors and
'railes againe Plaiers mightily I can tel you, because they
brought him drunck upp'oth Stage once, . . . as he will bee
horribly druncke' (C2). The Puritans and their minister are
mercilessly indicted as drunkards, liars, hypocrites and wastrels
and the final insult is to use their 'zealous workes' (G2) to block
up the door, not against devils, but to allow a rogue to cheat Sir
Godfrey. It is a specific attack. The hypocrites are to be found in
Watling Street–less than two minutes' walk from the theatre.

Pearce had not balked at the use of *The Old Joiner* to effect a
form of moral blackmail, and did not, apparently, hesitate to
allow the children to caricature Puritans so outrageously; so
Crashawe (especially if he saw himself in the drunken parson)
might have had a personal motive for his tirade:

> Thus hypocrisie a child of hell must beare the names of two Churches
> of God [St Antling's and St Mary Overys] and two wherein Gods name
> is called on publikely every day in the yeare, and in one of them his
> blessed word preached everie day . . . yet these two, wherein Gods
> name is thus glorified, and our Church and State honoured, shall bee
> by these miscreants thus dishonoured, and that not on the stage only,
> but even in print. (p. 171)

The Puritaine was licensed for publication on 6 August 1607 and
it appeared shortly before this sermon by Crashawe. The
Children of Paul's, therefore, were still operating in February
1608, for there would be no point in attacking an institution
which was already defunct. Not merely are their plays insulting
but their theatrical undertakings are causing some diminution in
the quality of the services in the cathedral, for Crashawe
laments:

> Oh what times are wee cast into, that such a wickednesse should passe
> unpunished! I speake nothing of their continuall prophanesse in their
> phrases, and sometime Atheisme and blasphemie, nor of their conti-

nuall prophaning of the Sabbath, which generally in the countrie is
their play day, and oftentimes Gods divine service hindred, or cut
shorter to make roome and give time for the divels service. (pp. 171–2)

That the choristers shortened evening prayer to end before
4 p.m. to increase their acting time is altogether credible, and
Crashawe confirms Sunday as a play day: in competition with
sermons, Paul's plays won. He reaches his climax with an
emotional appeal for a crusade:

Are they thus incurable? then happie hee that puts his hand to pull
downe this tower of Babel . . . but most happie that Magistrate, who
. . . takes some iust vengeance on that publike dishonour laid upon our
Churches. (p. 172)

This appeal, delivered at the Cross, could hardly have failed to
reach the ears of Pearce, the major and minor canons, and the
new Dean, John Overall, who in 1602 had taken over from the
easy-going Alexander Nowell.

Crashawe concludes his attack against the Children of Paul's
by emphasising his committed sabbatarianism:

The horrible abuse of the Sabbath day . . . is an Impe of *Babylon that will
not be healed*, but rather it creepes as a canker thorow our whole State,
from the foot to the head . . . it will eate out the heart and life of a State
. . . [if we] suffer [God's] Sabbath daily thus to be prophaned; then let
us look for nothing but continuance and increase of these grievous
plagues that have so long lien upon us . . . (pp. 172–3)

The anti-Puritan tirade of *The Puritaine* is invective rather than
satire and it is as personal as was *The Old Joiner of Aldgate*:
Crashawe replied in kind. Just as Howe and Flaskett knew that
they trod the boards in Paul's playhouse, so now the ministers
and leading parishioners of St Antling's are equally conscious of
their caricature on stage. The parish of St Antlin (or St Antholin)
was in the gift of Dean Overall and the Chapter; it is not likely
that they were amused. Crashawe was a powerful and eloquent
champion for the devout of St Antling's, and the pressure he
exerted upon Pearce and the Children of Paul's was undoubtedly considerable. His sermon may, in fact, be the culmination
rather than the commencement of a campaign against them.

It is possible that both Pearce and Kirkham were aware that
The Puritaine was a play which had gone beyond a permissible
licence and, in these last days of the repertoire at Paul's, they
introduced another and quite different style of drama. An

166

apologetical prologue was provided for Beaumont and Fletcher's *Woman Hater*, 'lately Acted by the Children of Paules', and registered for publication on 20 May 1607. The authors, like Marston in *Antonio's Revenge*, dismiss certain categories of spectators:

> *If there be any amongst you, that come to heare lascivious Scenes, let them depart: for I doe pronounce this, to the utter discomfort of all two peny Gallerie men, you shall have no bawdrie in it: or if there bee any lurking amongst you in corners, with Table bookes, who have some hope to find fit matter to feede his—mallice on, let them claspe them up, and slinke away, or stay and be converted. For he that made this Play, meanes to please Auditors so, as hee may bee an Auditor himselfe hereafter, and not purchase them with the deare losse of his eares.* (A2)

The concern over the loss of ears, the punishment for slander and abuse, may not have been an idle fear: Crashawe's denunciation of *The Puritaine* might well have provoked at least an official warning and the *Eastward Ho!* affair was not long stilled. Beaumont and Fletcher are alarmed at the possibility that there may be spies among the spectators, with notebooks poised to report any indiscretion, real or imaginary, to the appropriate authorities. The Children of Paul's were under pressure from powerful enemies.

The Woman Hater was almost certainly a disappointment to those who had their 'table books' ready, as it is a play at which it would be difficult to take offence, for it concerns the undoing of the misogynist, Gondarino, and the triumph of ladies' virtue, while they are still successful in enrapturing the desired object. Unlike *The Puritaine*, where music and song are virtually absent, there is a love lament sung by Oriana in a 'treble' (E), 'a handsome drowsie dittie' (E^v^), and in another play of the Kirkham period, probably brought by him from the Blackfriars, there is a more elaborate musical spectacle. In Marston's *Parasitaster, or The Fawne* there is presented a musical pageant of the deadly sins, probably designed to provoke recall of the show in Marlowe's *Dr Faustus*, '*Cornets playing*. Drunkeness, Sloth, Pride & Plenty *leads* Cupid to his *State, who is followed by* Folly, warre, Beggary *and* Laughter' (H4^v^). This dumb show was designed for the Blackfriars, but in the plays exclusive to Paul's playhouse, it was Pearce who, almost certainly, was responsible for the music.

Pearce's star pupil was Thomas Ravenscroft, a chorister in 1598,[13] the author of *The Urchin's Dance* in *The Maydes Metamorphosis* (D), and probably one of the fairies who performed it, singing

167

'Round about, round about, in a fine Ring a'. He was a child prodigy, possibly beginning his singing career as early as the age of six and graduating 'Bacheler of Musick' at Cambridge in 1607 at the age of fifteen; well might one R.L.L. *Theo-musophilus*, a contributor of commendatory verses to his *Briefe Discourse* of 1614, speak of him as 'Rara avis *Arte Senex* Iuvenis; Sed rarior est, si / *Aetate* est juvenis, *Moribus* ille Senex'.[14] In his *Briefe Discourse* Ravenscroft published two songs by Pearce, 'Of Enamouring' and 'Of Hunting'. Both are written for four parts, treble, tenor, alto and bass, which may be another indication of the range of voices available among the actors. Pearce was also responsible for at least two of the songs in *Blurt Master Constable*. One of these, a setting of the lyric 'Love for such a cherry lip', also appears in this collection by Ravenscroft. The other 'What meate eats the Spaniard', is mainly scored for the alto voice, with the sopranos given only three lines of the lyric; 'none of the vocal parts, however, can easily be executed by the amateur; each presupposes a trained voice and considerable understanding of music'.[15] Pearce was, by Ravenscroft's testimony, an excellent teacher of singing, composition and fingering for lute as well as other instruments.[16] Thomas Piers, a chorister in 1607[17] and perhaps some relation of Ravenscroft's teacher, says that in Pearce 'dwelt . . . perfect Excellence / In Heaven'ly Musicke'.[18]

Ravenscroft, like his predecessor at first Paul's, Thomas Morley, was a staunch advocate of the harmonisation of sound and sense and in this his teacher was Pearce. He says of his master's theme:

Enamoring, a Passion . . . possessing and affecting all, so truely exprest by none, but *Musick*, that is, *Song*, or *Poetry*: the former where of, gives herein both a *relish*, and a *beauty* to the latter, in as much as *Passionate Tunes* make *Amorous Poems*, both willinglier heard, and better remembred. (A3^v)

Under Pearce's influence, then, one may be confident that the songs in the plays were not merely superficial decoration, but integral to the theme and mood. Examples abound: music to augment despair occurs in *Antonio and Mellida* where Antonio commands his page 'Let each note breath the heart of passion, / The sad extracture of extreamest griefe' (G2^v); songs for joy are frequent, as in *What You Will*, with Quadratus' song, '*Musick*,

Tobacco, Sack and Sleepe, / The tide of Sorrow backward keepe' (C3);
and songs of love are usual, as in *Jacke Drums Entertainment*,
'Musick's the quiver of young *Cupids* dart. *The Song with the
Violls'* (G4ᵛ).

Similarly in Middleton's *A Trick to Catch the Old-one*, Audrey,
servant to Dampit the usurer, sings a solo beginning, '*Let the
Usurer cram him, in interest that excell / There's pits enow to dam him,
before he comes to hell'* (G3), as she draws her master's bed
curtains. In this way, she introduces a scene which unmasks
and shames him. Ravenscroft, in *Melismata* (1611) No. 12, has
preserved the music for this song, which is designed for the alto
voice, with a very simple vocal line.[19] Perhaps this was his last
contribution to the company and he played and sang the part of
Audrey before he left Paul's for Cambridge in 1604. While it is
true that the greatest exploitation of music and song in dramatic
contexts was achieved by Marston and the Paul's theatre owes
much of its musical reputation to his personal convictions, the
musical style is largely the product of the ideals of Pearce and
his pupil, Ravenscroft. It may well be that the appreciable
diminution in the musical content of the plays after 1604 was, at
least in part, due to the fact that Ravenscroft went off to
Cambridge to read music.

Pearce trained some of his boys to play the lute, harp and
other instruments and most had, at least originally, been
choristers, so the company had a cadre of professionally trained
singers and instrumentalists. Westcott used a combination of
young trebles and older ex-choristers for his actors. Gyles,
presumably, simply inherited this arrangement and Lyly certainly used boys with broken and unbroken voices. Pearce in
1599 seems to have had no reserve of older talent to draw upon;
the actors for Marston's *Antonio* plays, and the other dramas of
the first years of the revival, were, for Paul's, unusually all very
young, the oldest in the early to mid teens.[20]

The evidence about the acting styles of these performers,
whether children or young men, is meagre, but the children's
companies remained in the forefront of fashion so long as their
music or their scandals could attract audiences. When music
was allowed to wane, notoriety was all they had left. As far as
ability was concerned the children were clearly superior as
musicians, but probably inferior to the adults as actors and

when they became more adult themselves they lost ground. This does not necessarily presume that their style remained formal and mannered, merely that as actors they were not as good as Burbage, Kempe or Alleyn. The most serious hidden reason for the ultimate demise of the children's companies was their miscalculation that they could compete on equal terms with the adult companies by producing similar plays, presented in largely the same way. The rather frantic efforts in *The Puritaine* and *The Woman Hater* to find a special niche in which they could outshine all others is surely indicative of this problem. The children simply did not have enough actors of exceptional talent to challenge the adult companies successfully at their own game.

Under Pearce, during the opening of the revival period, the audience was at first rather limited. The impression given by Marston is that the spectators were of his own social standing or above it: minor aristocracy, Inns of Court students, some clerics – Marston turned to the church in his later life and certainly most of the minor canons would hardly have hesitated to go to the plays, whatever the foundation statutes dictated. This audience was presumed to be regular in its attendance and knowledgeable about contemporary theatre. In *Antonio's Revenge* the dumb show which begins Act III required Piero to 'tear open his breast', as he proposes marriage to Andrugio's widow, Maria. There is, however, no explanatory dialogue, yet the ensuing act assumes that the audience are aware that Maria has accepted him. This can only be understood by an audience familiar with Richard of Gloucester's wooing of Anne: the audience were expected to know their Shakespeare. Similarly Marston re-uses his successful interruption technique four times in as many plays: he expects the effect to be remembered and the new variation noted. This, then, was an exclusive audience possibly personally invited by Marston, Stanley and Pearce and for a while at least they were loyal and supportive, as the Prologue to *Antonio's Revenge* attests. This audience may have had a collective consciousness of itself as a club. The situation, however, changed drastically as a result of the Poets' War: notoriety bred commercial success and Woodford arrived to manage the theatre. Woodford was a speculator in the theatre business and stayed involved only so long as there was a good chance of a profit.[21] Marston's personal credibility was destroyed by the Poetomachia but, in a sense, this dispute was only a resurgence of the kind of local scandal for which Paul's was already famous, as with the Goulding–Maicocke quarrel. The Poetomachia was dramatic journalism: it humiliated Marston.

In the same way, *The Old Joiner* destroyed the credibility of those involved in the Howe affair. Paul's playhouse was taking on the character of a tabloid newspaper, known for its sensational revelations about the private lives of prominent local residents. *The Old Joiner of Aldgate* involved local people: residents of Newgate Street, Knightrider Street, and the churchyard, all give evidence. Flaskett, one of the principals, was relatively well-to-do; his shop was worth 'twoe or three hundred pounds'[22] and he 'doth live by his trade & is not a very poore man for he is worthe one hundred mks [£66 13s 4d] his detts being paid'.[23] He was a tradesman and yet he could both obtain entry to the theatre, without let or hindrance, and take a guest (John Howe). While Flaskett had special reason to see *The Old Joiner*, there is nothing to suggest that a visit to the playhouse was in any way an unusual event.

There would obviously have been a strong appeal to those living in the immediate area of the theatre, for many would recognise the local inhabitants who were being satirised, especially if a prologue was devised and presented containing the words:

> . . . followe thou
> That will sue to have a woman for thy wife
> And yet seeke her disgrace . . .[24]

Paul's audience at the time of this *Old Joiner* prologue cannot reasonably be considered a coterie of the same type which was found under Marston; by now it contained a large element of local citizens. This local audience was recognised by Pearce, Woodford and Kirkham, for in *The Puritaine* the emphasis is again on the specific local identity of the plot. Nicholas St Antlings, the comic butt of the piece, was a church visible to the inhabitants of the cathedral neighbourhood as they went about their daily business. Similarly the setting in Paul's middle aisle is common in plays after 1602, as in *West-ward Hoe; North-ward Hoe; Michaelmas Terme*. This local audience and those who were attracted by the advertising of the plays in the main aisles were Woodford's contribution to the commercial exploitation of the children's theatre.

Why, then, did the Children of Paul's decline? The explanation is probably to be found not in a single cause but in a combination of overlapping circumstances. They appeared at court for the last time on 30 July 1606, but Crashawe speaks of them, on 14 February 1608, as still playing on Sundays. It seems likely, however, that from late in 1606 they gradually began to play intermittently, for most of their known texts came on the market between August 1606 and October 1608. Like the other playhouses, Paul's had been troubled by very frequent official stoppages after 1602. They had always been closed during Lent, but when the old Queen became ill on 19 March 1603 all the playhouses were shut, and the very severe plague visitation that ensued caused them to remain closed until 9 April 1604 (although perhaps they were open for a brief period prior to Lent, 22 February, in that winter). For the first time the aisles of Paul's were deserted, for in 1603

this middle of Pawles lookes strange and bare, like a long-hayrde Gentleman new powlde, washt and shaved, and I may fitly say shaved, for there was never a lusty Shaver seene walking here this half yeare: especially if he loved his life, hee would revolt from Duke Humphrey, and rather bee a Wood-cleaver in the Countrey, then a chest-breaker in London.[25]

There was another plague restraint from 5 October 1605 to 15 December; again in 1606 and in 1607 plague almost certainly caused plays to cease during the middle and later summer. This would certainly have interrupted the appeal the playhouse was seeking to make to establish a regular local audience: indeed a significant fraction would be lost annually to the disease. They were also under Puritan attack, as Crashawe demonstrates, and the Dean and Chapter no doubt could vividly recall the *Old Joiner* affair and the ensuing scandal in the courts.

Some of the supporters of the playhouse had drifted away; Marston was with the Children of the Queen's Revels at the Blackfriars and Woodford had fallen out with Pearce; Ambrose Goulding, Senior Cardinal, died in November 1606 and his place was taken by William Maicocke, his arch-enemy and not a likely supporter of the playhouse for he appears to have been friendly with Dr White, who caused the 1603 closure.[26] The Children of Paul's, too, had themselves grown older and lost some of their distinctive character; they had become like the other London playhouses but could not directly compete with them because of their small capacity and, probably, weaker acting. Perhaps most important of all, Pearce never seems to have been content to run the playhouse alone: his interest was the music; he needed a manager for the plays and Kirkham may not have proved a congenial associate.

Fashion had changed too and the children, who were now men, could no longer command the following they had once enjoyed, but there were some speculators who believed a profitable market still existed for children's companies, despite the fact that, like Paul's, the Blackfriars was also in serious difficulty.[27] In the spring of 1609 Robert Keysar and Philip Rossiter moved with some of their company from the Blackfriars to the new Whitefriars playhouse. This had been originally founded by a syndicate led by Thomas Woodford in 1606, but it failed within eighteen months, and, in an attempt to ensure the success of this new venture there, Rossiter sought to guarantee a monopoly for performances by children.[28] In the Rejoinder of Richard Burbage, Cuthbert Burbage, John Heming and Henry Condell to the Replication of Robert Keysar of 19 June 1610 in a suit over the Blackfriars theatre property, it is affirmed that 'One Mr Roseter a partner of the said Comp^{lts} delt for Compounded wth . . . Mr Pierce to the onely benefytt of him the said Roseter the now Comp^{lts} the rest of theire partners & Company . . . that thereby they . . . might advance their gaines & profitt to be had & made in theire . . . howse in the white ffryers That there might be a Cessation of playeinge & playes to be acted in the . . . howse neere St Paules Church . . . for w^{ch} . . . Roceter Compounded with . . . Pierce to give him . . . twenty poundes per Annum'.[29] This document makes it clear that when Pearce was offered the £20 'dead rente' the playhouse was inactive, but clearly Rossiter and Keysar regarded this cessation as purely temporary. Paul's playhouse ceased operation in mid to late 1608, possibly as a direct consequence of Crashawe's attack. Pearce, early in 1609, was offered a bribe to remain shut and the bribe is of a similar amount to the minimum £22 income Gyles had previously enjoyed when letting the cloisters to trunkmakers.[30] Burbage and his associates, when they took over the Blackfriars, were 'content to beare & paye one halfe of the Charge of the said rent of twenty poundes per Annum'. This bribe may have had positive as well as negative aspects for both the Whitefriars and the new Blackfriars managements; not merely did they want to avoid damaging competition from Paul's, but perhaps also they wished to retain the allegiance of the local audience cultivated so assiduously at the house in the shrouds.

The sixteenth statute of the minor canons concerns '*suspecte women and unhonest playes and sightes to be shunnede*'. The minor canons are threatened with a fine of 3s 4d if they shall 'bringe in . . . any wemen . . . notorios for evell lyfe, into o^r howses'; for a second offence, 6s 8d and for the third, expulsion 'owt of the comone haule'. The statute continues, 'In lyke sorte it is also concluded, that as often as any of the . . . Petie Canons doo frequent or haunt the stues or taverns publickly, with harlottes, or any other unhonest playes and spectacles prohibited to clerkes, whereby an offence may growe of the state of the Peticannons, and of o^r . . . Colledge, except they, being once warned, do shewe themselves to be reclaymed, they shall incurr the lyke punishment as hath byn before declared.'[31] Perhaps the closure of the Paul's playhouse would be welcomed among at least some of the minor canons, probably by William Maicocke for one, and certainly, among the major canons, by Dr White. Pearce's £20 per annum, from the managements of the Whitefriars and the Blackfriars, may have continued until his death, for on 15 June 1612 in St Gregory's church, was buried 'Edward Pierce maister of the children of Paules'. The playhouse became the choristers' 'singing school',[32] and in 1633 Dugdale reports that 'the Houses adjoyning to, and nere the churche . . . [were] compounded for and pulled down'.[33] Whether or not the house in the shrouds was included in this demolition, the whole cloister precinct had succumbed to complete decay by 1657.

William Crashawe and Thomas White would not have mourned the passing of Paul's playhouse. For them its demise was a just retribution for its sins. It is Dekker, however, who offers the most appropriate epitaph for the Children of Paul's and the house in the shrouds, in a lament he ascribes to the steeple of Paul's itself:

What damnable bargaines of unmercifull Brokery, of unmeasurable Usury are there clapt up? What swearing is there: yea, what swaggering, what facing and out-facing? What shuffling, what shouldering, what Justling, what Jeering, what byting of Thumbs to beget quarels, what holding uppe of fingers to remember drunken meetings, what braving with Feathers, what bearding with Mustachoes, what casting open of cloakes to publish new clothes, what muffling in cloakes to hyde broken Elbows, so that when I heare such trampling up and downe, suche spetting, such halking, and such humming . . . I verily beleeve that I am the *Tower of Babell* newly to be builded up, but presentlie despaire of ever being finished, because there is in me such a confusion of languages . . . my lamentations are scattered with the winds, my sighes are lost in the Ayre, and I my selfe not thought worthy to stand high in the love of those that are borne and nourished by mee. [34]

Such was the complaint from within the cathedral, of neglect, decay and unsuitable usage. From one point of view, at least, the decline and eventual collapse of the cathedral church of St Paul was a fit punishment for its guilt; and the same for Paul's playhouse. It fell as the first victim of the new Puritanism, which demanded the expulsion of plays from sacred precincts. Crashawe, like Malvolio, had his revenge on the 'whole pack' of the harlotry players.

APPENDIX 1

Documents

(a) and (b) are from *The Visitation Report of Bishop Bancroft, 1598* [Guildhall MS. 9537/9]. (c) is from St Gregory's, Guildhall MS. 10,231; St Martin's, Guildhall MS. 10,213; St Anne Blackfriars, Guildhall MSS. 4508/1, 4509/1, 4510/1; St Augustine, Guildhall MS. 8872/1; St Andrew Wardrobe, Guildhall MSS. 4502/1, 4503/1, 4507/1; St Vedast, *Registers of St. Vedast*, ed. W. A. Littledale, Harleian Society, *Registers*, Vol. XXIX, 1902, 2 vols.

(a) The choristers and their Master

. . . from the visitation questions of Bishop Bancroft:

3 Whether doe they [the officers of the church at the services] and every of them there, continewe and remaine the whole tyme of divine service, and there singe distinctly in an audible voyce accordinge to the order of the said Churche, and whether doe any of them depart from thence before the end of service wth owt licence first asked of Mr Deane, or the antient Resedentiarie there pnte [present], and whoe doe offend herein, or have offended herein, and when and howe often.

4 Whether doe the petticannons and vicars Chorall, Vergers, bellring-ers & Choristers frequent the divinitie lecture, and other Sundaie and holiday sermons by the fowdation thereof especially erected for increase of knowledge of these inferiour ministers of the Churche, and wch of them bee most negligent therein.

5 Whether is that decree and ordinaunce of yours observed, that all the peticannons and vicars of the Churche should diligently attend in the quier the whole tyme of all sermons on Sundaies and holidaies in the afternoones from whence none of them should depart wth out leave askinge of the Subdeane or Chauntor of your Churche and what be their names that bee, or have bynn most offensive therein and when and howe often they have offended.

[f.7^v

6 Whether is that good and godly ordinaunce of the Churche ob-served for the better bringinge upp of the Children and Queristers of this Cathedrall Churche in the feare of god, and the Cardinalls shall weekely or att the least monthly teach them their Catechisme, and examine them in the principles of Religion, and shall once a

176

yeare deliver unto Mr Deane a note of those whoe doe nott profitt, or whoe bynn negligent or stubborne in attendinge that good and Christiane exercise, and what bee their names, and when and howe often they have bynn so negligent, either of the Cardinalls in not Catechisinge, or of the Children in not learninge.

. . . from the supplementary questions:

6 Whether be there or have theire bynn any of the petycannons, vicars or other inferiour ministers in the Churche or any of them goers unto or haunters of Tavernes or typling howses, and whether be any of them, or have there bynn any geven to immoderate drinkinge, or fighters, quarelers, or otherwise destempered by their over common and unseasonable hauntinge of tavernes, and what be their names of those whoe are or have bynn most noted to offend herein: and when and where, and howe often have they or ether of them offended since the first of December 1595. [f.8

21 how many Choristers ought there to be maineteyned for divine service in the Churche

22 Whether are they well instructed and fitt for their places

23 Whether doe they keepe the accustomed howers of repayringe to divine service

24 In their reparinge to the Churche whether come they two and two in devout order in their gownes lyned as the manner hath bynn and in their surplices cleane washed and whether is their apparrell decent wthowt tearinge and totters as decency requireth

25 Whether have the said Choristers convenient allowaunce of meate and drink and sett downe what you know meete or Convenient towchinge any thinge belonginge unto the Choristers to be in your opinion reformed. [f.21

. . . at the formal hearing:

Quibus die et loco facta publica preconizatione ec comparuerunt personatr omnes Canonici Minores et Vicarij Chorales, exceptis Thoma Gyles et Roberto Browne egrotis et Roberto Ennsley lectore Evangelij quos dictus Reverendus pater accusavit necnon comparuerunt personata omnes Choriste virgiferarij et campanarum pulsatores, et dictos Choristas dictus Reverendus pater pro hoc tempore dimissit usque ad et in Septimum diem mense Junij prox

. . .

[On which day and in which place a public preliminary hearing having been held and there appeared in person all the Minor Canons and the Vicars Choral with the exception of Thomas Gyles and Robert Browne who were sick and Robert Ennsley reader of the Gospel whom the said reverend father charged and likewise there appeared in person all the choristers the vergers and the bellringers and the said reverend father dismissed the said Choristers for this time until and on the seventh day of June next . . .]

[f.18

. . . from the reply of William Maicocke and Thomas Langley:

177

6 To the sixt, we Answere that the twoe Cardinalls doe not wickely examine the Quoristers in there Catachesime, but they doe goe often to them and instructe them.   [f.43

12 We thinke it a verye necessare thinge that every Quorister should bringe wth him to Churche a testament in Inglishe, and tourne to every Chapter as it is daylie read or some other good and godlie praye^r booke rather then spend their tyme in talke and huntinge after spurr money where on they sett their whole mindes, and doe often abuse dive^rs yf they will not bestowe some what on them.
[f.44

. . . from the reply of John Phetibone:

4 Item at the tyme of divine service the Children of the queere, either they use them selves very unreverently in their seats talkinge & playinge or else they be runninge aboute the quiere to gentlemen, and other poore men for spurr money, not lightlie leavinge them till they have mony or drive them oute of the quier wch many fynde falte at yt.   [f.44^v

. . . from the reply of Richard Smythe, verger:

8 Item the vaultes under the Churche are lett unto M^r ffinche ye Carpenter and those uppon the north side, the petticannons have the use of. and m^r Gyles hath one of them on the sowthe side & under the Chancell & quier Mr Lawes & petley the Carpenter hath the use of, those under the Churche were lett by the B: those under the Chauncell & queer by the Deane and Chapter lycense and further I can saie nothinge.

10 Item the names of them that are in possession of them under ye Chauncell and queere are Mr Cawgal Mr Norton Mr Petley & M^r lownes & under the Churche M^r ffinche Mr Gyles and the petty cannons they are in good repayre & be not offensive   [f.47

. . .

20 Item that as I have heard there is dive^rs psons have keyes [to the Church] M^r gouldinge M^r gyles and soper that was sometymes meeke man but by whose authority I can saie nothinge.

21 Item there are X Quoristers accordinge to the first foundacon as I have heard

22 Item that they are sufficientlie instructed their places as I have hard by those that have skill in musicke.   [f.47^v

23 Item that they doe keepe the accustomed howers of repayringe to divine service some of them & sometimes all.

24 Item in their Repayringe to Churche they sometimes Come two & twoe & in their gownes but not lyned and in their surplyces washed and their apparrell fitt for Children

25 Item that the said Quoristers M^r have fiftie powndes a yere payd by the Deane and Chapter & Rec in rent of howes belonginge to the Almner as I have hard XX^l by the yere.   [f.48

. . . from the reply of John Sharpe, Zachery Alley and John Howe:

Mr Gyles M^r of Quoristers hath the possession of a great vaute under ye south side of the Churche wch he useth to laie in wood and other old lumber [f.55

John Greene is in possession of a howse adioyininge to the west end of ye same wall [the Chapter House wall] by demise in pte from the Deane and Chapter and in pte from Mr Gilles wch hath byn incroched uppon the Churche yarde.

There ix shedds incroched in the Alley wch leadeth to the Churche at the little sowthe dore wch straights the passage on both sides of the waie, the Tenaunts in possession of them are John Martin, William Lane, Nicholas Willson, Nicholas Stevenson and Edward Beacon all wch hold by demise from Mr Gylles. In possession of the other are Richard Whaley William Stepnall Edmund Sweten, and Richard Bynnie all wch doe hould by demise from the Deane and Chapter [f.56

21, 22, 23 Item to the xxj xxij xxiij xxiiij et xxvth articles we saie there 24 et 25 ought to be ten Quoristers mayntained for divine service in the churche who are now well instructed and fitt for their places and they doe diligentlie keepe their accustomed howers in repayringe unto divine service, they come to the Churche in decent order, but they have not their gownes lyned as in former tymes was used, ther surplice are most Comenlie uncleane, and their apparrell not in suche sorte as decencie becometh as we are informed they have sufficient allowance of meat and drinke [f.56^v

. . . from the reply of the Vicars Choral:

. . . we answer that both petticannons and vicars doe Come to divine service for none and afternone ordely in their gownes and surplics excepte Mr Harrold for he doth often offend therein wch by meanes of his shorte Cominge Goeth upp to the organ wth his Cloke but yf any Come late after the second toulinge they are putt into the booke of pdition by one of the Cardinalls and are Contrould on satterdaie followinge by the Deane and Chapter accordinge to the offence.

To the third article we answer that the wholl quier gen^reallie doth offend for the wch they are putt into the booke of absence aforesaid and so Contrould by the Deane and Chapter

To the 4th we doe not knowe whether the wholl quier are tyed by the statutes of the Churche to Come to the divinitie lecture, but the pettycannons by Course ought to saie at those times the Confession and begyn the psalm wch is pformed by one of them savinge of late it was neglected once or twice, by whome we knowe not. [f.58

To this vth as to the iijth that the wholl quier offendeth for many tymes and verie oft they goe forth wthout askinge leave either of the Subdeane or Subchanter, and morover it is a generall faulte amongst us all, and we doe wishe it might be reformed of everie one of us that at the Confession of o^r synnes and askinge Mercy and pdon at gods handes for o^r offences at the beginninge of service that everie one should kneele and turne his face towards the east and likewise at the Creed to stand upp wth his face towardes the east and alsoe to kneele at the rest of the prayers, and not to sett, on our tailes as Comenlie we doe w^thout any Reverence at all wch is verie scandall to those that be [f.58] present and especiallie to those that shewe Reverence and are well disposed in the service of god

To the vjth the Cardinalls have neglected of late Cathekisinge of the Children

. . .

To the vjth we have not knowen any drunckeness amongst them of late but for goinge to taverns any of the quier or all sometimes doth frequente neither hath it byn of late any quarrellinge amongst them as we understand   [f.58^v

. . . from the reply of Thomas Harrould:

There is a disorder amonge the quier men, in that they use not to light their Candles at service tyme in the darke evenings, for whereas they have everie one a Candle they seldome lighte above 3 or 4 on a side when there should be 9, to the great disgrace of the Churche and their owne hinderaunce

The Quoiristers alsoe doe the like and use moreover wth great impudence to importune men to give them monye for their spurres w^thout regard either of pson or time or place & trouble them in their prayers   [f.61^v

(b) The house in the 'shrowdes'

. . . from the Visitation questions:

11 how is the upper Cloyster by the Chapter howse imployed, and wheather is theire any extraordinary doore for any private mans use made into it, by whome and by whose consent.

12 In whose custody are the lower Cloisters, and the place Caled the shrowdes how are they imployd, and by whome and whose license and whether is there any doore of any pryvate mans use made into them, and for whose use.   [f.20^v

. . . from the reply of Richard Smythe, verger:

11 Item the upper cloister in the Chapter howse are not imployed to any use at this presente neither is there any dore for any private manns use but suche as were made at the buildinge of the same as I have hard

12 Item the lower cloisters and the place called the shrowdes are in the Custodie of M^r gyles and by the license of the Dean and Chapter as I have hard   [f.47

14 . . . one little howse was builte by Mr Heydon in the lower place Called ye shrowdes wch howse Raynold Chunell Inioyeth by license of Mr Gyles wch howse was built by the Consent of Mr Benbowe beinge then Almner: and the said Mr Heydon one of the petticannons.   [f.47^v

. . . from the reply of John Sharpe, Zachery Alley and John Howe:

11 Item to the xi[th] Article we saie that the upper Cloister by the Chapter howse is not imployed wth any thinge nether is there any extraordinairie dore made into them for any mans private use, but onelie the dore to goe into the leades to clense and repaier them of which dore Mr Gyles hath a keye as we are informed

12 Item to the 12th Article we saie that the lower cloyster and the place called the shrowdes are in the keepinge of Mr Gyles which have a longe tyme byn used of the master of the Quoristers, there is not now any dore into them for any mans private use but there is a house builte in the shrowdes by Mr Haydon sometyme petticannon of this churche which howse we take to be verie offensive in that it is close adioyinnge [adjoining] to the upper end of the chapter howse wall.   [f.55

. . . from the reply of John Howe, verger:

 4 Item I present that the Shrowdes and Cloyster under the Convocation howse were not longe since the Sermons in fowle weather were wont to be preached are made a Comon laystall for boardes trunckes and Chests beinge lett out unto trunckmakers, whereby meanes of their dailie knockinge and noyse, the Churche is greatlie disturbed
                                                              [f.60

(c) Graphs of baptism/marriage and burial statistics from parishes adjacent to St Paul's

See graphs on pp. 182–3.

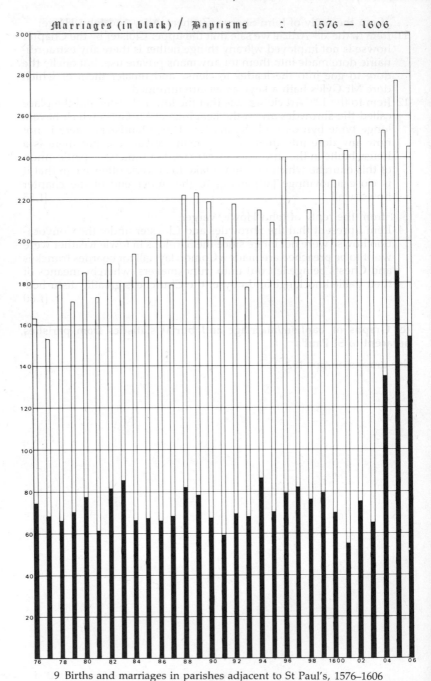

9 Births and marriages in parishes adjacent to St Paul's, 1576–1606

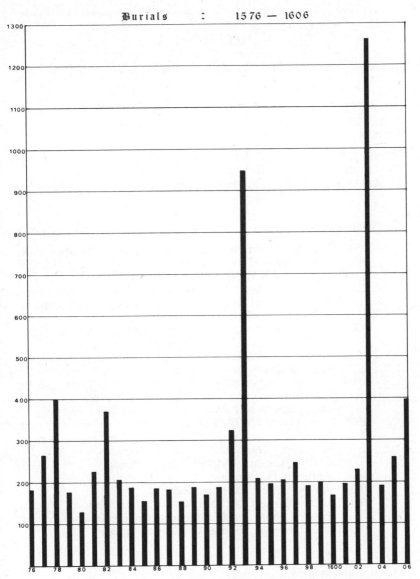

10 Deaths in parishes adjacent to St Paul's, 1576–1606

Personalia

Masters of the Choristers

1 Feb. 1553–April 1582   Sebastian Westcott
22 May 1584–July 1600   Thomas Gyles
11 May 1599–June 1612   Edward Pearce

Chorister/actors

1554   John Burde; Simon Burde; Richard Hewse; George More; John Alkok; Gilbert Maxsey; Roger Stakhouse; Richard Prynce; John Farmer; Robert Chofe

1574   George Bowring; Thomas Morley; Peter Phillipp; Henry Nation; Robert Knight; Thomas Brande; Edward Pattmie; Robert Baker; Thomas Johnson

1582   Nicolas Carlton; Bromeham; Baylye; Richard Huse; Robert Knight; [Henry] Nasion; Gregorye Bowringe

1593–4   William Noblett [alias Loblee]; William Rawlyns; Thomas Quiddington; Giles Jennynges

1594   Edward Buckeredge; William Thayer; John Taylor; Germaine Wilson; Richard Badlowe; Thomas Weste; Humphrey Weste; William Maycocke; Giles Jennynges

1598   John Taylor; William Thaire; Richard Brackenbury; John Norwood; Robert Coles; John Thomkins; Samuel Marcupp; Thomas Rainescroft [Ravenscroft]; Russell Gyrdler; Carolus Pytcher; Charles Pendry

1598   Anthonie Hitchman

1600   Alvery Trussel; Solomon Pavy

1607   Henry Burnett; Richard Kenede; John Mansell; Thomas Peers; Richard Patrick; Nicholas Crosse; Thomas Waters; John Dawson; Thomas Codbolt; Lightfoot Codbolt

Playhouse managers

1553–82   Sebastian Westcott
1582–4   Henry Evans; [?] John Lyly
1584–91   Thomas Gyles
1599–1603   John Marston

184

Appendix 2: Personalia

1603–04 Thomas Woodford
1604–06 Edward Kirkham
1606–08 Edward Pearce

Plays

Those marked* are lost.

c.1545	*Wit and Science* – Redford
c.1568	*The Marriage of Wit and Science*
1567–8	*As Playne as Canne Be*
1567–8	*The Paynfull Pillgrimage*
1567–8	*Jack and Jyll*
1567–8	*Wit and Will* [this may be the same as *The Marriage of Wit and Science*]
1567–8	*Orestes*
1567–8	*Tragedy of the King of Scots*
1567–8	*Six Fooles*
1567–8	*The Contention betweene Liberalitie and Prodigalitie*
1571/2	*Effiginia*
1573	*Alkmeon*
c.1575	*Meleager*
1577	*The History of Error*
1577	*The History of Titus and Gesippus*
1579	*A Morall of the Marryage of Mynde and Measure*
1580	*Scipio Africanus*
1581	*A Story of Pompey*
1583/4	*Campaspe* – Lyly
1583/4	*Sapho and Phao* – Lyly
1584	*Agamemnon and Ulysses*
1585	*Gallathea* – Lyly
1588	*Endimion* – Lyly
1589	*Midas* – Lyly
1589	*Mother Bombie* – Lyly
1599	*Antonio and Mellida* – Marston
1599	*[?] The Plays of William Stanley
1600	*Jacke Drums Entertainment* – Marston
1600	*The Wisdome of Doctor Dodypoll*
1600	*The Maydes Metamorphosis*
1600/1	*Antonio's Revenge* – Marston
1601	*Blurt Master Constable* – Middleton
1601	*What You Will* – Marston
1601	*Satiro-mastix* – Dekker
1601	*Arabia Sitiens* – Percy
1601	*The Cuckqueanes and Cuckolds Errants* – Percy

Appendix 3: Plays

1601 *Loves Metamorphosis*
1602 *A Forrest Tragedy in Vacunium* – Percy
1602 *The Aphrodysial* – Percy
1603 *The Faery Pastorall* – Percy
1603 *The Old Joiner of Aldgate* – Chapman
1603 *The Phoenix* – Middleton
1604 *A Trick to Catch the Old-one* – Middleton
1604 *Bussy D'Ambois* – Chapman
1604 *West-ward Hoe* – Dekker and Webster
1605 *North-ward Hoe* – Dekker and Webster
1605 *Family of Love* – Middleton
1605 *The Fawne* – Marston
1605 *Michaelmas Terme* – Middleton
1605 *A Mad World, My Masters* – Middleton
1606 *The Woman Hater* – Beaumont and Fletcher
1606 *The Puritaine* – [?] Middleton
1606 *Abuses*

Notes

Introduction: The Children of Paul's and the English drama

1. Sir E. K. Chambers, *The Mediaeval Stage*, 1903, II, 380 (citing R. Dodsley, *Collection of Old Plays*, 1744, I, xii). To E. K. Chambers, A. Gurr (*The Shakespearean Stage 1574–1642*, 1970), and T. W. Craik (compiler of the year charts in *The Revels History of Drama in English*), I am indebted for much of the substance of this compilation.
2. William Malim, *Consuetudinarium Vetus Scholae Etonensis . . . 1560*, in Sir Edward Creasy, *Memoirs of Eminent Etonians*, 1850, pp. 77–84: 'Circiter festum D. Andreae ludimagister eligere solet pro suo arbitrio, scaenicas fabulas optimas et quam accommodatissimas, quas pueri feriis natalitiis subsequentibus non sine ludorum elegantia, populo spectante, publice aliquando peragant. Histrionum levis ars est, ad actionem tamen oratorum, et gestum motumque corporis decentem, tantopere facit, ut nihil magis. Interdum etiam exhibet Anglico sermone contextas fabulas, quae habeant acumen et leporem', p. 80n.
3. W. C. Hazlitt, *The English Drama and Stage*, 1869, pp. 5–6.
4. *Ibid.*, pp. 22–3.
5. *Ibid.*, pp. 25–6.
6. *Ibid.*, pp. 27–31.
7. Thomas White, *A Sermon preached at Pawles Crosse . . .*, 1578, pp. 47–8.
8. White may be thinking of the very popular *Contention betweene Liberalitie and Prodigalitie*, probably being played at Paul's at about this time; see Chapter 3, pp. 93–4.
9. Sir E. K. Chambers, *The Elizabethan Stage*, 1923, IV, 295.
10. *Ibid.*, p. 313.
11. *Ibid.*, p. 316.
12. *Ibid.*, p. 323.
13. *Ibid.*, p. 334.
14. *Ibid.*, p. 336.
15. *Ibid.*, p. 339.
16. *Ibid.*, p. 320.

1. The decay of St Paul's

1. Guildhall, MS. 7784/15, f. 38.

2. Guildhall, MS. 1336/1, f. 1ᵛ (St Gregory's vestry minute book).
3. William Dugdale, *The History of St. Paul's Cathedral*, 1658, p. 192.
4. *Ibid.*
5. P.R.O., MS. SP 18/179/X/K2370, dated 12 November 1657.
6. St Paul's, *Dean and Chapter Registers, Nowell* I, f. 171; dated 10 August 1566.
7. *The True Report of the burning of the Steeple and Church of Paul's in London*, 1561, ed. E. Arber in *An English Garner*, VIII, 1896, pp. 111ff.
8. *Ibid.*, p. 111.
9. *Ibid.*, p. 112.
10. *Ibid.*
11. J. Stowe, *Survay of London*, 1598, p. 264.
12. Arber, *True Report*, pp. 112–13.
13. *Ibid.*, p. 114.
14. Dugdale, *St. Paul's*, p. 134.
15. Stowe, *Survay*, p. 269.
16. St Paul's, MS. W.D. 32, f. 12.
17. *Ibid.*, f. 13.
18. Dugdale, *St. Paul's*, p. 134.
19. *The Visitation Report of Bishop Bancroft*, Guildhall, MS. 9537/9, f. 20ᵛ: this MS. is hereafter referred to as *V.R.*, followed by a folio number.
20. *V.R.*, f. 47ᵛ.
21. *Ibid.*, f. 47.
22. *Ibid.*, f. 55.
23. St Paul's, *Dean and Chapter Registers, Sampson*, f. 150.
24. *Ibid.*, f. 241.
25. See *Sampson* and *Nowell* leases *passim* from *Dean and Chapter Registers*.
26. H. H. Milman, *Annals of St. Paul's Cathedral*, 1869, 2nd edn, p. 271.
27. *Nowell* II, ff. 209ᵛ–210.
28. *V.R.*, f. 55ᵛ.
29. Dugdale, *St. Paul's*, p. 134.
30. *Sampson*, f. 343ᵛ.
31. *Ibid.*, ff. 360ᵛ–361.
32. *Ibid.*, f. 377ᵛ.
33. H. N. Hillebrand, *The Child Actors*, Urbana, 1926, pp. 327–8.
34. *Nowell* III, f. 100.
35. *V.R.*, f. 56.
36. See W. R. Gair, 'The Conditions of Appointment for Masters of Choristers at Paul's (1553–1613)', *N. & Q.*, 27 (1980) 116–24.
37. *Nowell* III, f. 219.
38. Stowe, *Survay*, p. 263.
39. *V.R.*, f. 53.
40. *Ibid.*, f. 55.
41. *Ibid.*
42. Stowe, *Survay*, pp. 302–3.

43. W. B. Rye, *England as Seen by Foreigners*, New York, 1967, p. 8 (from The Diary of the Duke of Wurtemberg, 1592).
44. *V.R.*, f. 55^v.
45. *Ibid.*, f. 56^v.
46. *Ibid.*, f. 57.
47. *The Diary of Henry Mackyn*, ed. J. G. Nichols, Camden Society, 1846, pp. 287–8.
48. Guildhall, MS. 10,231 (by date).
49. *Ibid.*
50. *V.R.*, f. 57.
51. *Ibid.*, f. 58.
52. For the quarrel, see Chapter 4.
53. *V.R.*, f. 48^v.
54. *Ibid.*, f. 58.
55. *Ibid.*, f. 59.
56. *Certain Sermons or Homilies*, 1562, p. 290.
57. *V.R.*, f. 59^v.
58. *Ibid.*
59. *Ibid.*, f. 45.
60. *Ibid.*, f. 52.
61. *Ibid.*, f. 59.
62. *Ibid.*, f. 61.
63. *Ibid.*, f. 45.
64. *Ibid.*, f. 61.
65. *Ibid.*, f. 42^v.
66. *Ibid.*, f. 44^v.
67. *Ibid.*
68. *Ibid.*, f. 45.
69. *Ibid.*
70. *Ibid.*, f. 59.
71. Dekker, *The Guls Horne Book*, 1609, p. 21.
72. *V.R.*, f. 45.
73. J. Hall, *Virgidemiarum*, 1597, Bk II (Satire V).
74. *V.R.*, f. 60.
75. *The Anatomie of Abuses*, ed. J. P. Collier, 1870, III, 139; see also G. Lell, '"Ganymede" on the Elizabethan Stage: Homosexual Implications of the Use of Boy Actors', *Aegis*, I (1973) 5–15.
76. I.H., *The House of Correction, Certaine Characters, called Par Pari*, 1619, sig. D2^v.
77. *V.R.*, f. 44.
78. Stowe, *Survay*, p. 274.
79. Dekker, *Guls Horne Book*, p. 20.
80. F. Osborn, *Traditionall Memoryes on the Reign of King James*, Oxford, 1658, p. 47.
81. W. Dugdale, *Origines Juridiciales*, 1680, p. 142.
82. Dekker, *Guls Horne Book*, p. 19.
83. R. Greene, *Life and Works*, ed. A. B. Grosart, re-issue 1964, X, 215; XI, 24; X, 105.

84. W. S. Simpson, *Gleanings from Old S. Paul's*, 1889, pp. 226–7.
85. *V.R.*, f. 45.
86. *Ibid.*, f. 60.
87. *Ibid.*, f. 46ᵛ.
88. *Ibid.*, f. 52ᵛ.
89. T. Dekker, 'Paules Steeples Complaint' in *The Dead Tearme or Westministers Complaint for long vacations*, 1608, sig. e.
90. Cited W. Benham, *Old St. Paul's Cathedral*, 1902, pp. 46–7.
91. *V.R.*, f. 61ᵛ.
92. The warrant is printed by T. H. Vail Motter, *The School Drama in England*, New York, 1929, p. 144n; for Westcott's, see A. Brown, 'Sebastian Westcott at York', *Modern Language Review*, 47 (1952) 49–50.
93. *Five Hundredth Pointes of Good Husbandrie*, 1573.
94. British Library, MS. *Addl.* 15,233, f. 49ᵛ.
95. *Sampson*, f. 377ᵛ; Westcott was appointed 'for the period of his natural life, under exactly the same terms as' John Redford.
96. *Ibid.*
97. Sir M. McDonnell, *The Annals of St. Paul's School*, 1959, p. 16.
98. *Ibid.*, p. 25.
99. See p. 33.
100. See my article, *N. & Q.*, NS 25 (1978) 440–1.
101. McDonnell, pp. 25–6, 27, 29, 99.
102. *V.R.*, 47ᵛ.
103. See my article, *N. & Q.*, NS 27 (1980) 116–24, where the documents of appointment of Westcott, Gyles and Pearce are printed in full.
104. Preface, sig. A2–A2ᵛ.
105. See n. 103 above.
106. *V.R.*, f. 19. On 23 November 1598 'Thomas Gyles et Roberto Brown' failed to appear before Bishop Bancroft, but both were excused, as being 'egrotis'. Gyles never did complete a report on the choir for Bancroft's visitation and it is from other witnesses that the information about the state of the choir derives. Gyles never recovered and Pearce was appointed in May 1599 to take over his duties.
107. See n. 103 above.
108. See my article, under n. 100 above.
109. W. S. Simpson, *Registrum Statutorum et Consuetudinum Ecclesiae Cathedralis Sancti Pauli*, 1873, p. 449.
110. *Ibid.*, p. 457.
111. *V.R.*, f. 43.
112. See n. 103 above.
113. Simpson, *Registrum*, p. 228.
114. See McDonnell, Chapter I *passim*.
115. See n. 103 above.
116. McDonnell, pp. 76–7.
117. *Ibid.*, p. 90.

118. *Ibid.*, p. 88.
119. *Ibid.*, p. 129.
120. *Ibid.*
121. *V.R.*, f. 60.
122. *Ibid.*, f. 48.
123. *Ibid.*, f. 21.
124. *Ibid.*, f. 56ᵛ.
125. *Ibid.*, f. 58ᵛ.
126. *Ibid.*, f. 58.
127. *Ibid.*, f. 52ᵛ.
128. *Ibid.*, f. 48.
129. *Ibid.*, f. 56.
130. *Nowell* II, f. 281.
131. *Ibid.*, III, f. 101.
132. *V.R.*, f. 60.
133. See n. 103 above.
134. *Privy Council Registers, Elizabeth*, II, 408 (3 December 1575). Hillebrand cites this document, p. 124n.

2. Paul's playhouse

1. *Repertories* 18 Elizabeth, cited by Hillebrand p. 123.
2. See Chapter 3.
3. Hillebrand, pp. 112, 114.
4. See Chapter 1.
5. See Chapter 5.
6. See Chapter 1, n. 103.
7. *V.R.*, f. 20ᵛ.
8. *Ibid.*, f. 47.
9. *Ibid.*
10. See *N. & Q.*, NS 27 (1980) 121.
11. *V.R.*, f. 60.
12. See p. 183.
13. *V.R.*, f. 55.
14. *Ibid.*
15. *Ibid.*, f. 59ᵛ.
16. P.R.O., MS. SP 18/179/X/K2370.
17. *V.R.*, f. 55ᵛ.
18. *Ibid.*, f. 47ᵛ.
19. In Dugdale's *St. Paul's*.
20. See F. C. Penrose, 'Notes on St. Paul's Cathedral', *Royal Institute of British Architects, Trans.* 29 (1878–9) 94.
21. The children were baptised in St Gregory's; Mary 22 April 1597 and Thomas 27 June 1599 (Guildhall, MS. 10, 231).
22. *V.R.*, f. 56.
23. See G. Hennessy, *Novum Repertorium Ecclesiasticum Parochiale Londinense*, 1898 (by name, office and church).
24. St Gregory's parish register, Guildhall, MS. 10, 231, f. 141ᵛ.

25. E. F. Rimbault, *The Old Cheque Book of the Chapel Royal (1561–1744)*, Camden Society, NS III, 1875, 5. It is, of course, possible that this is a different Thomas Benbowe, but to move from St Paul's to the Chapel Royal is a likely promotion.
26. See Chapter 3.
27. Hennessy, *Repertorium*, p. 134; there was a John Haydon, Sheriff of London in 1582. The minor canons 'must be priests'.
28. Stephen Gosson, *Plays Confuted in Five Actions*, 1582, sig. D4^v.
29. *The Works of Thomas Nashe*, ed., R. B. McKerrow, III, 46.
30. M. Shapiro, *N. & Q.*, NS 18 (1971) 14, argues that this reference establishes that Paul's was revived in 1597 but (1) Gyles was ill and (2) out of over forty witnesses in the *Visitation Report* not one mentions it. The reference is to be explained as either a report of an amateur performance (like the masque of Slegg, or a play at Paul's Grammar School) or it is merely an old reference, not up-dated.
31. McKerrow, *Nashe*, III, 46.
32. This statement occurs only in the Huntington Library copy of the Percy MSS. It is to be found on f. 191, after the play *Necromantes* (which is dated 1632). While it was J. P. Collier who was the first to print it (*The History of English Dramatic Poetry*, 1831, 3, 377n), the MS. belonged to Haslewood and Collier misreads 'five and foremost' as 'fine and formost' – Percy is in fact referring to the first five plays in the volume: I am, therefore, satisfied that it is not a forgery. This is the most precise surviving evidence for times of performance at Paul's; plays began shortly after 4 p.m. and concluded at 6 p.m., or thereabouts, and Westcott left a legacy to 'Pole the keper of the gate' (Hillebrand, p. 330). It was Percy's habit to make additional notations to his dramatic works over a period of years, often on odd leaves. The Huntington MS. is dedicated by Percy to the Paul's Boys 'de affectibus' and there are numerous marginal notes throughout all MSS., which make it clear that whether or not his plays were staged in the 'shrowdes', Percy, at least imaginatively, prepared them for presentation there. His knowledge, therefore, of the interior of the Paul's playhouse is at least as accurate as that of others, like Marston, who certainly had plays presented there.
33. C. Sisson, *Lost Plays of Shakespeare's Age*, Cambridge, 1936, pp. 77, 61.
34. Cited by C. W. Wallace, 'Shakespeare and his London Associates', *University Studies*, Nebraska, 10, 4 (1910) 355.
35. *V.R.*, f. 55^v.
36. Sisson, p. 61.
37. Chambers, *Stage*, IV, 369.
38. Hillebrand, p. 330.
39. Huntington MS., f. 92^v (subsequent references are given only by a bracketed folio number).
40. See illustration no. 6.
41. Alnwick Castle, MS. 508 (unfoliated).
42. Herford and Simpson, Jonson, *Works*, Oxford, 1947, VIII, 77; and see Hillebrand, p. 161.

43. *The King of Denmarkes welcome,* 1606, p. 23. Many of the following deductions about the use of music and instruments at Paul's are drawn from the studies by J. Manifold, 'Theatre Music in the Sixteenth and Seventeenth Centuries', *Music and Letters,* 29 (1948) 366–97, and the same author's *The Music in English Drama from Shakespeare to Purcell,* 1956.
44. W. L. Woodfill, *Musicians in English Society from Elizabeth to Charles I,* Princeton, 1953, p. 242.
45. The smallest was that of Trinity Church (14 feet wide by 32 feet long); see R. Hosley, 'Three Renaissance Indoor Playhouses', *English Literary Renaissance,* 3, 1 (1973) 176–9.
46. Penrose, 'Notes on St. Paul's Cathedral', p. 94.
47. Millar Maclure, *The Paul's Cross Sermons, 1534–1642,* Toronto, 1958, p. 4.
48. *V.R.,* f. 52.
49. The following commentary on the parishes in the immediate area of the Cathedral is based upon (a) an analysis of the parish registers of St Gregory's, St Martin's Ludgate, St Vedast, St Augustine, St Anne Blackfriars, St Andrew Wardrobe (the originals are in the Guildhall Library and they are illustrated graphically in Appendix 1(c)) and (b) comments by Stowe (*Survay*) and some remarks from the *Visitation Report.* The parish records were analysed, correlated and statistically smoothed by a computer program devised by Professor R. Ellerton of the University of New Brunswick. Spearman's rank correlation coefficient was used in the analysis (see W. W. Daniel, *Applied Non-parametric Statistics,* Boston, 1978, pp. 298–304). While Professor Ellerton suggested much of the basis of my interpretation of the figures, the actual description that has emerged is strictly my responsibility.
50. St Martin's Ludgate, Register (MS. 10,213).
51. P. Laslett, *The World We Have Lost,* 1965, p. 102, points out that even a ratio of 5 was dangerously low.
52. Guildhall, MS. 8872/1, by date.
53. Laslett, citing Gregory King, uses 32 as the expectation of life in 1690 for both sexes; I have, arbitrarily, deducted 2 years to allow for endemic plague.
54. *V.R.,* f. 59ᵛ.
55. H. Hall, *Society in the Elizabethan Age,* 1888, pp. 101, 211 and pp. 206–33, where Darrell's accounts are printed.
56. See Chapter 5, pp. 147–51.
57. For further discussion of prices, see pp. 72–3 and 88–9.
58. The baker's accounts are cited by A. J. Cook, 'The Audience of Shakespeare's Plays: A Reconsideration', *Shakespeare Studies,* VII (1974) 293–4.
59. Woodford was manager 1603–4 and Kirkham 1604–6, for further discussion of the local appeal of Paul's, see Chapter 5.

3. The business of theatre in court and city

1. *C.S.P. Venetian*, IV (1527–33) 225.
2. The Pope, Clement VII, had been besieged in Rome by the forces of Charles V: his captivity began on 6 May 1527, but on 8 or 9 December, of the same year, he escaped. The mottos celebrated Wolsey's initiative; 'War gives way to diplomacy'; 'The peace treaty will not be overturned'; 'In honour and praise of the peacemaker'; 'Peacemaker Cardinal'.
3. J. Nichols, *The Progresses and Public Processions of Queen Elizabeth*, 1823, I, 74.
4. See Chapter 1, pp. 33, 35.
5. It has been suggested that John Heywood was an associate director of the Paul's plays and on two occasions (at Hatfield House 1551/2 and at Nonsuch, August 1559) his name appears next to Westcott's in the list of payments. In addition Heywood was paid by the Princess Mary in 1537/8 for 'playing an interlude with his children' (A. Brown, 'Two Notes on John Redford', *Modern Language Review*, 43 (1948) 510). Brown argues for a close association between Redford, Westcott and Heywood and Hillebrand (pp. 116–17) feels that Heywood acted as a presenter for the Paul's plays either alone or as an assistant to Westcott. It is an attractive conjecture to link the author of interludes like *The Four Ps* and *The Play of the Wether* with the children of Paul's, for it would add a whole group of plays to their known repertoire. The evidence is, however, largely conjectural and associative: the linking of his name with Westcott's in lists of payments may be accidental. I am inclined to believe that Heywood was involved with the Paul's company in its formative years, perhaps as a dramatic assistant or even as a provider of plays, but both Redford and Westcott were strong enough personalities to allow him no more than a subordinate role. Paul's may have performed Heywood's Interludes, but his association with them terminated after 1564 (he left England on 20 July, as a Catholic refugee: see A. W. Reed, *Early Tudor Drama*, 1926, p. 68). He was not associated with the Children of Paul's when their professional period began in the 1570s.
6. British Library, MS. *Addl*. 15,233: published by the Malone Society, 1951.
7. See P. Ariès, *Centuries of Childhood* (tr. R. Baldick), 1962, p. 16 and *passim*.
8. Glynne Wickham, *Early English Stages 1300 to 1600*, Volume 3, *Plays and Their Makers to 1576*, 1981, p. 116, suggests that Wyt's face was blackened while he slept in Idleness' lap, and when Lady Science meets him she understandably refuses to recognise him.
9. Westcott leaves viols to the choristers in his will; see Chapter 1, p. 21.
10. A Thomas Morley is among the list of choristers in 1574; a see Hillebrand, p. 111.

11. *Household Accounts of Princess Elizabeth, 1551–2*, Camden Miscellany II (1853) 37.
12. Grindal to Cecil, 12 August 1563, 'My L. Robert [Dudley] wrote to me earnestly for *Sebastiane* . . .' (MS. *Lansdowne*, 6, No, 69) and *C.S.P. Rome*, Elizabeth I (1558–71) I, 67, 'Sebastian, Organist at St Paul's, London, did not shrink from ejectment; but Elizabeth was so loath to part with him, that without in any way complying with schisme, he keeps his place in the church.'
13. See A. Feuillerat, *Documents Relating to the Office of the Revels*, 1908, pp. 218–19.
14. Cited by T. N. S. Lennam, *Sebastian Westcott, The children of Paul's and The Marriage of Wit and Science*, Toronto, 1975, p. 61.
15. Lennam, pp. 62–9.
16. The plot of *Meleager* was first reported by B. Dobell (*Athenaeum*, 14 September 1901, p. 349): at this time Dobell owned the MS. but subsequently mislaid it. It remained lost until 1969 when it was sold at Sotheby's: it is now MS. *Eng.* 1285 in the Houghton Library at Harvard. The argument of Meleager is on ff. 3–4 and a transcription of it is to be found in A. Freeman, 'The Argument of *Meleager*', *English Literary Renaissance*, I, 2 (1971) 122–31.
17. Some editors have emended 'uppe on' to 'upon', but T. Craik (*The Tudor Interlude*, Leicester, 1958, p. 16) suggests an upper window of Science's house and Lennam (p. 108) finds no textual reason to suspect a corrupt reading here.
18. See my Revels edition of this play, Manchester, 1978, IV.v.74–7n.
19. This notion of rehearsal for court performance, which is frequently cited as the raison d'être of the children's companies at this time, has been exaggerated in importance. It was a convenient fiction and it would be highly unlikely that such a successful businessman as Westcott would fail to recognise it.
20. This play has been identified as the 'prodigallitie' played before the Queen at Whitehall at Christmas/Shrovetide 1567/8: see Hillebrand, pp. 128–30 and Lennam, pp. 64–5.
21. Lennam, pp. 64–5.
22. The ascription of the performance of this play to the Chapel Children in 1601 rests on flimsy evidence: the date 4 February 1601 is given in the text for Prodigalitie's trial (1260) and the nearest recorded court performance by a children's company is 22 February 1601. The presumption is that it was planned for 4 February and postponed. It is as likely that Paul's revived it as the Chapel Children, and the performance was either not recorded or simply not given: Elizabeth may not have wished to see it for a third time.
23. This is substantially the same analysis of the action as that arrived at by Lennam, p. 109.
24. Shepard is named in Westcott's will; see Chapter 1, p. 56.
25. R. W. Bond, *The Complete Works of John Lyly*, 1902, III, 408.
26. Hall, *Society*, pp. 101, 211.
27. See Chapter 1, p. 42.

28. M. S. Steele, *Plays and Masques at Court*, New York, 1968, *passim*.
29. MS. *Lansdowne* 30, No. 55: cited by Lennam, p. 51.
30. Lennam, p. 53.
31. Hillebrand prints the will in full, pp. 327–30.
32. *Nowell* III, f. 154: and see Chapter 1 above.
33. *Nowell* II, f. 188: and see Chapter 1 above.
34. A. B. Grosart, *The Works of Gabriel Harvey*, 1884, II, 212.
35. See Chapter 1 above, pp. 40–2.
36. These three performances are described in the Revels accounts as by 'the Earl of Oxford's Company' or 'The Children of the Earl of Oxford' (see Steele, pp. 89–91). Oxford was patron of a provincial group of nine boys and a man in the 80s (see Hillebrand, p. 136n) and the Revels accounts have confused this group with the joint Paul's and Chapel Children Company. I see no reason to assume that here the description 'Oxford's Company' is more than a collective term, celebrating their sponsor, for the temporary amalgamation of the Paul's and Blackfriars players.
37. See n. 5 above.
38. In his will (see Reed, *Tudor Drama*, p. 55) Westcott is named as his sole executor and residuary legatee. In addition his sister, Margaret, in her will of 30 September 1556, concludes 'the rest of my goodes whatsoever they be I gyve to Sebastian Westcote who I ordeyne and make my sole executor . . . he to see my bodye honestly browght to the earthe, And do therin and all other thinges as he shall thinke good for my sowle', (A. Brown, 'Two Notes on John Redford', *Modern Language Review*, 43 (1948) 509).
39. Hillebrand, pp. 132–7.
40. P. Saccio, *The Court Comedies of John Lyly*, Princeton, 1969, p. 79.
41. *Ibid.*, p. 63.
42. *Defence of Poesie* (1595), ed. A. Feuillerat, 1962, III, 40–1.
43. *Musica Transalpina*, 1588, Dedication, Aij.
44. Saccio, p. 121n.
45. The song does not occur in the Quarto (1594); it, and others, were added by Blount (*Six Court Comedies*, 1632). I believe that these are Lyly's original songs kept separately with the children's music (as G. Hunter, *John Lyly: The Humanist as Courtier*, 1962, pp. 367–72, surmised) and thus not published at first with the play quartos.
46. Hunter, p. 229.
47. *Ibid.*, pp. 186–8.
48. Harvey, *Works*, ed. Grosart, II, 213.
49. Bodleian, MS. *Tanner* 169, f. 69^v; Hunter, p. 75.
50. Cited by Maclure, *Paul's Cross Sermons*, p. 74.
51. See G. R. Hibbard, *Thomas Nashe*, 1962, p. 27: the whole of his second chapter concerns the Marprelate affair (pp. 19–48).
52. Bond, *Lyly*, III, 408.
53. *Ibid.*
54. *Ibid.*, 585n.
55. *Ibid.*, I, 52–4.

56. *An Introductory Sketch to the Martin Marprelate Controversy (1588–90)*, ed. E. Arber, 1879, p. 113.
57. Steele, p. 99.

4. Interregnum and new departures

1. *V.R.*, f. 20.
2. For further details of this quarrel see *V.R.*, ff. 46–57 *passim* and *Elizabethan Theatre VII*, ed. G. R. Hibbard, Port Credit, 1980, pp. 26–9.
3. Robert Barnes was arrested on 5 June 1594 and accused of harbouring the Jesuit priest, John Jones: his examination took place between 30 June and 31 July 1598. In order to obtain additional evidence, his elderly servant John Harrison was also arrested and put to the torture. Barnes and Harrison, however, may well have both been innocent for on 12 July 1598 Henry Lok reported to Robert Cecil 'the Prest [Jones] todaye . . . hath chardged his soul with clering . . . Barnes for ever knowing him a prest' (*Unpublished Documents relating to the English Martyrs*, ed. J. H. Pollen, 1908, I, 362, 370). Slegg, if he did give refuge to Harrison, was hardly as black as he was painted, but clearly both Barnes and Harrison had Catholic sympathies, even if they were not actually guilty of harbouring Jesuits.
4. *V.R.*, f. 58^v.
5. *N. & Q.*, NS 27 (1980) 121.
6. *Ibid.*, pp. 121–2.
7. *C.S.P. Dom.* (Elizabeth I) 1598–1601, 227.
8. This is the theory of P. J. Finkelpearl, with which I concur ('John Marston's *Histrio-Mastix* as an Inns of Court Play: A Hypothesis', *Huntington Library Quarterly*, 29 (1966) 223–34).
9. *Henslowe's Diary*, ed. W. W. Greg, 1904, I, 112.
10. P. J. Finkelpearl, *John Marston of the Middle Temple*, Harvard, 1969, p. 84.
11. *V.R.*, f. 43. Maicocke became Junior Cardinal on 10 December 1597.
12. St Paul's, MS. A53/17/f. 6.
13. His will is dated 20 November 1606, *Prob.* II. 108. f. 91.
14. *V.R.*, ff. 48, 56^v.
15. *Historical Manuscripts Commission, Lord de L'Isle and Dudley* (Penshurst Place), II, 415.
16. See Chapter 2, p. 58.
17. See Chapter 1, p. 17.
18. *V.R.*, f. 55.
19. See Chapter 1, p. 19.
20. It was produced late in 1599, probably in October, after 28 September, when Marston was still dealing with the Admiral's Men, and before 13 November.
21. Marston directs, '*Exeunt all on the lower Stage*' (B4^v), implying that the upper acting area was called 'the upper stage' and the main acting area 'the lower stage': these terms I have adopted.

22. See D. Mehl, *The Elizabethan Dumb Show*, 1965, p. 124.
23. *O.E.D.* lists this as the first use of this adverb.
24. At F4ᵛ (IV.i.) Marston directs, '*Enter Andrugio, Lucio, Cole, and Norwod*'; since only Andrugio, Lucio and Antonio (who is already on stage) speak in this scene, and the only other character on stage is Antonio's page (also already there), then Coles probably played Andrugio and Norwood Lucio and the prompt book read, '*Enter Andrugio, Lucio, (Cole and Norwod)*'. Robert Coles and John Norwood are listed as choristers in 1598 (Hillebrand, p. 111).
25. This incident serves as a reminder that Antonio needs to be accompanied by a singing page, for his own voice is '*virago*-like' – see page 119.
26. Cited by R. B. Sharpe, *The Real War of the Theatres*, Boston, 1935, p. 155.
27. The quotation is from *Wily Beguiled* (1606, Q., A2): it has been claimed that this too was a Paul's play (anon., c.1602), but the Malone editor (1912) suggests that it is 'a Cambridge piece of the circle of Parnassus' (p. vii). With this view I agree, for it is a tissue of allusions to other plays as in its Prologue, which copies the Inductions to *Antonio and Mellida* and *Jacke Drums Entertainment*.
28. See the Introduction to my Revels edition, pp. 27–41: A. Caputi, *John Marston, Satirist*, New York, 1961, p. 115 similarly argues that the Blackfriars boys aged.
29. My Revels edition lists these in the commentary.
30. The date of *Hamlet* is 1600/1 (see my *Antonio's Revenge*, pp. 12–19); thus the 1603 bad Quarto reading is an almost contemporary report on the reactions to the Poets' War and the Folio text a more studied, and probably later, reflection.
31. I. Smith, *Shakespeare's Blackfriars Playhouse*, New York, 1964, p. 180.
32. See further my *Antonio's Revenge*, pp. 12–16.
33. *The Complete Poems*, ed. A. B. Grosart, Edinburgh, 1878, II, 37.
34. *V.R.*, ff. 35, 54.
35. A. Caputi, *John Marston, Satirist*, p. 113.
36. R. Foakes, 'John Marston's Fantastical Plays: *Antonio and Mellida* and *Antonio's Revenge*', *Philological Quarterly*, 41 (1962) 236.

5. New management: new methods

1. P.R.O., MS. STAC 8.8/2, f. 163; while some details of the affair have been gleaned from this MS., most of the substance of this account is derived from C. J. Sisson, *Lost Plays of Shakespeare's Age*, Cambridge, 1936, pp. 12–79.
2. MS. STAC 8.8/2, f. 176.
3. Hillebrand, p. 213.
4. *V.R.*, f. 49.
5. See pp. 72–3, 88–9.
6. See Chapter 6, pp. 163–6.
7. *The King of Denmarkes Welcome*, 1606, p. 16.

8. O.E.D., 'youth' 6: Marston, in the epistle to the reader, in *Sophonisbu* (*Q.*, 1606) speaks of the play (for the Blackfriars) as being 'presented by youthes'.
9. Hillebrand, p. 143.

6. The triumph of profit and Puritanism

1. Steele, p. 148.
2. *The Plays of John Marston*, ed. H. H. Wood, Edinburgh, 1934–9, III, 128.
3. *A True and Perfect Relation of the Whole proceedings . . . against . . . Garnet a Iesuite*, 1606, Fff–Fff^v.
4. *The Tryall and Execution of Father Henry Garnet*, 1679, p. 8.
5. *The King of Denmarkes Welcome*, pp. 23–4.
6. See Chapter 5, pp. 154–5.
7. See Chapter 3, p. 76 and S. Anglo, *Spectacle, Pageantry and Early Tudor Policy*, Oxford, 1969, *passim*.
8. *The King of Denmarkes Welcome*, p. 12.
9. *Englands Farewell to Christian the fourth*, 1606, B2.
10. See W. D. Dunkel, 'The Authorship of *The Puritan*', *PMLA*, XLV (1930) 804–8.
11. *The Sermon preached at the Crosse, Feb. xiiij 1607*, W. Crashawe, 1608.
12. See illustration no. 8.
13. Hillebrand, p. 111 and see my note, 'Chorister-Actors at Paul's', *N. & Q.*, NS 25 (1978) 440–1.
14. 'A young man who is an old man in his skill is a rare bird, but what is rarer still is if a man is young in years, but old in moral character'.
15. A. J. Sabol, 'Two Songs with Accompaniment for an Elizabethan Choirboy Play', *Studies in the Renaissance*, 5 (1958) 149.
16. *Briefe Discourse*, A2^v; cited in Chapter 1, p. 36.
17. Hillebrand, p. 112.
18. *Briefe Discourse*, il il il^v.
19. A. Sabol, 'Ravenscroft's "Melismata" and the Children of Paul's', *Renaissance News*, XII (1959) 6.
20. Marston also attempted to use the fact of the gradual maturing of the children, as a feature of the relationship between *Antonio and Mellida* and *Antonio's Revenge*. The trial and torment of the latter play turned the children of the former into men: see the introduction to my Revels edition, pp. 27–39.
21. Hillebrand, p. 236.
22. MS. STAC 8.8/2, f. 35.
23. *Ibid.*, f. 27.
24. An interrogatory addressed to Woodford, Pearce and Chapman was sufficiently detailed to imply that these words were the actual words of the prologue, although all three denied its existence (*ibid.*, f. 175).
25. *The Meeting of Gallants at an Ordinarie*, 1604 (ed. J. Halliwell, Percy Society, V. 1841), p. 11.

26. *V.R.*, f. 43^v.
27. Cf. Hillebrand, pp. 236–7.
28. *Ibid.*, pp. 211–37.
29. Printed by Wallace, 'Shakespeare and his London Associates', pp. 352–7.
30. See Chapter 1 above, pp. 41–2.
31. Simpson, *Registrum*, p. 345.
32. John Stowe, *Annales*, continued by E. Howes, 1631, p. 104; but the pagination is incorrect and the correct page number is 1016; p. 104 occurs after a page numbered 1003.
33. Dugdale, *St. Paul's*, p. 159.
34. T. Dekker, *Paules Steeples Complaint*, D4^v.

Select bibliography

The place of publication is London unless otherwise stated.

Manuscripts

Parish records: The Guildhall Library

St Andrew Wardrobe, MSS., 4502/1; 4503/1; 4507/1.
St Anne Blackfriars, MSS., 4508/1; 4509/1; 4510/1.
St Augustine, MS., 8872/1.
St Gregory, MS., 10,231.
St Martin, MS., 10,213.
St Vedast, MS., Lost; Registers ed. W. A. Littledale, Harleian Society, *Registers* Vol. XXIX (1902).
The Visitation Report of Bishop Bancroft, 1598, MS., 9537/9.

Public Record Office

MS., SP 18/179/X/K2370.
MS., STAC 8.8/2.

St Paul's Cathedral

The Registers of the Dean and Chapter (for Sampson, Nowell and Overall).

Books and articles

Anglo, Sidney, *Spectacle, Pageantry and Early Tudor Policy*, Oxford, 1969.
Arber, E., *An Introductory Sketch to the Martin Marprelate Controversy, (1588–90)*, 1879.
   The True Report of the burning of the Steeple and Church of Paul's in London, 1561, in *An English Garner*, VIII, 1896.
Ariès, Phillipe, *Centuries of Childhood*, tr. R. Baldick, 1962.
Armstrong, William A., 'The Audience of the Elizabethan Private Theatres', *Review of English Studies*, NS 10 (1959), 234–49.
   'Actors and Theatres', *Shakespeare Survey*, 17 (1964), 191–204.

202

Bains, Yashdip S., 'Thomas Middleton's *Blurt, Master Constable* as a Burlesque on Love', in *Essays Presented to Amy G. Stock*, ed. R. K. Kaul, Jaipur, 1965.

Ball, Roma, 'The Choir-Boy Actors of St. Paul's Cathedral', *Emporia State Research Studies*, 10 (June 1962), 5–16.

Berringer, Ralph W., 'Jonson's *Cynthia's Revels* and the War of the Theatres', *Philological Quarterly*, 22 (1943), 1–22.

Best, Michael, 'A Note on The Songs in Lyly's Plays', *N. & Q.*, NS 12 (1965), 93–4.

'The staging and production of the plays of John Lyly', *Theatre Research*, 9 (1968), 104–17.

Bond, R. Warwick, *The Complete Works of John Lyly*, 4 vols., 1902.

'Lyly's Songs', *Review of English Studies*, 6 (1930), 295–98.

Bradbrook, M. C., *The Rise of the Common Player: A Study of Actor and Society in Shakespeare's England*, Cambridge, 1962.

' "Silk? Satin? Kersey? Rags?" The Chorister's Theatre under Elizabeth and James', *Studies in English Literature*, I (1961), 53–64.

Brawner, James Paul, 'Early Classical Narrative Plays by Sebastian Westcott and Richard Mulcaster', *Modern Language Quarterly*, 4 (1943), 455–64.

Brown, Arthur, 'Two Notes on John Redford', *Modern Language Review* 43 (1948), 508–10.

'Three Notes on Sebastian Westcott', *Modern Language Review*, 44 (1949), 229–32.

'A Note on Sebastian Westcott and the Plays Presented by the Children of Paul's', *Modern Language Quarterly*, 12 (1951), 134–6.

'Sebastian Westcott at York', *Modern Language Review*, 47 (1952), 49–50.

Caputi, Anthony, *John Marston, Satirist*, New York, 1961.

Certaine Sermons or Homilies, 1562.

Chambers, Sir E. K., *The Mediaeval Stage*, 2 vols., Oxford, 1903.

The Elizabethan Stage, 4 vols., Oxford, 1923.

Charney, Maurice, 'The Children's Plays in Performance', *Research Opportunities in Renaissance Drama*, 18 (1975), 19–23.

Colley, John Scott, 'Music in the Elizabethan Private Theatres', *Yearbook of English Studies*, 4 (1974), 62–9.

Contention Between Liberality and Prodigalitie, Malone Society, 1913.

Cook, Ann J., 'The London Theatre Audience, 1576–1642', Ph.D. dissertation, Vanderbilt, 1972 (DA1 33: 4337A).

Cope, Jackson I., 'Marlowe's *Dido* and the Titillating Children', *English Literary Renaissance*, 4 (1974), 315–25.

Craik, T. W., *The Tudor Interlude*, Leicester, 1958.

Crashawe, William, *The Sermon preached at the Crosse, Feb. xiiij 1607*, 1608.

Creasy, Sir Edward, *Memoirs of Eminent Etonians*, 1850.

Davies, John, of Hereford, *The Complete Poems*, ed. A. B. Grosart, Edinburgh, 1878.

Dekker, Thomas, *The Dead Tearme or Westministers Complaint for long vacations*, 1608.

The Guls Horne Book, 1609.

Dugdale, William, *The History of St Paul's Cathedral*, 1658.

Origines Juridiciales, 1680.

Dunkel, W. D., 'The Authorship of *The Puritan'*. *PMLA*, XLV (1930), 804–8.

Feuillerat, A., *Documents Relating to the Office of the Revels*, 1908.

Finkelpearl, Philip J., *John Marston of the Middle Temple: An Elizabethan Dramatist in His Social Setting*, Harvard, 1969.

Foakes, R. A., 'John Marson's Fantastical Plays: *Antonio and Mellida* and *Antonio's Revenge'*, *Philological Quarterly* 41 (1962) 229–39.

'Tragedy at the Children's Theatres after 1600: A Challenge to the Adult Stage', *The Elizabethan Theatre II*, ed. D. Galloway, Toronto, 1970, pp. 37–59.

Freeman, A., 'The Argument of *Meleager'*, *English Literary Renaissance*, I, 2 (1971), 122–31.

Gair, W. Reavley, 'La Compagnie des Enfants de St Paul (1599–1606), *Dramaturgie et Société*, ed. J. Jacquot, Paris, 1968, II, 655–74.

'Marston's Vocabulary', *N. & Q.*, NS 19 (1972), 386.

'Masters of the Choristers at Paul's', *N. & Q.*, NS 24 (1977), 521.

'The Staging of Plays at Second Paul's: the Early Phase, 1599–1602', *The Elizabethan Theatre VI*, ed. G. Hibbard, Toronto, 1977, pp. 21–47.

'Chorister-Actors at Paul's' *N. & Q.*, NS 25 (1978), 440–1.

Antonio's Revenge, The Revels Plays, Manchester, 1978.

'The Conditions of Appointment for Masters of Choristers at Paul's (1553–1613)', *N. & Q.*, NS 27 (1980), 116–24.

'Second Paul's; its theatre and personnel: its later repertoire and audience (1602–06)', *The Elizabethan Theatre VII*, ed. G. Hibbard, Port Credit, 1980, pp. 21–46.

Gosson, Stephen, *Plays Confuted in Five Actions*, 1582.

Greene, Robert, *Life and Works*, ed. A. B. Grosart, 15 vols., 1881–6.

Gurr, Andrew, *The Shakespearian Stage 1574–1642*, Cambridge, 1970.

Hall, H., *Society in the Elizabethan Age*, 1888.

Hall, Joseph, *Virgidemiarum*, 1597.

Harbage, Alfred, *Shakespeare and the Rival Traditions*, New York, 1952.

'Elizabethan Acting', *PMLA*, LIV (1939), 685–708.

Harvey, Gabriel, *Works*, ed. A. B. Grosart, 1884.

Hazlitt, W. C., *The English Drama and Stage . . . 1543–1664*, 1869.

Hennessy, G., *Novum Repertorium Ecclesiasticum Parochiale Londinense*, 1898.

Henslowe, Philip, *Diary*, ed. W. W. Greg, 1904.

Hibbard, G. R., *Thomas Nashe*, 1962.

Hillebrand, Harold Newcomb, *The Child Actors: A Chapter in Elizabethan Stage History*, University of Illinois Studies in Language and Literature, II, Nos. 1 and 2, Urbana, 1926.

Hosley, Richard, 'Three Renaissance Indoor Playhouses', *English Literary Renaissance*, 3, 1 (1973), 166–82.

Hunter, G. K., *John Lyly: The Humanist as Courtier*, 1962.

Select bibliography

I. H., *The House of Correction, Certaine Characters, called Par Pari*, 1619.

Ingram, R. W., 'The Use of Music in the Plays of Marston', *Music and Letters*, 37 (1956), 154–164.

Jensen, Ejner J., 'The Style of the Boy Actors', *Comparative Drama*, 2 (1968), 100–11.

'The Boy Actors: Plays and Playing', *Research Opportunities in Renaissance Drama*, 18 (1975), 5–11.

Kolin, Philip C., 'A Bibliography of Children's Companies', *Research Opportunities in Renaissance Drama*, 19 (1976), 57–82.

Laslett, Peter, *The World We Have Lost*, 1965.

Lell, Gordon, ' "Ganymede" on the Elizabethan Stage: Homosexual Implications of the Use of Boy-Actors', *Aegis*, I (1973), 5–15.

Lennam, Trevor, 'The Children of Paul's, 1551–1582', *The Elizabethan Theatre II*, ed. D. Galloway, Toronto, 1970, pp. 20–36.

Sebastian Westcott, The Children of Paul's and The Marriage of Wit and Science, Toronto, 1975.

McDonnell, Michael, *The Annals of St. Paul's School*, 1959.

Mackyn, Henry, *Diary*, ed. J. G. Nichols, Camden Society, 1846.

Maclure, Millar, *The Paul's Cross Sermons, 1534–1642*, Toronto, 1958.

Manifold, John, *The Music in English Drama from Shakespeare to Purcell*, 1956.

'Theatre Music in the Sixteenth and Seventeenth Centuries', *Music and Letters*, 29 (1948), 366–97.

Matson, Marshall N., 'A Critical Edition of *The Wisdom of Doctor Dodypoll* (1600) with a Study of *Dodypoll's* Place in the Repertory of Paul's Boys', Ph.D. dissertation, Northwestern, 1967 (DA 28: 2213A-2214A).

Mehl, D., *The Elizabethan Dumb Show*, 1965.

Milman, H. H., *Annals of St. Paul's Cathedral*, 1869.

Motter, T. H. Vail, *The School Drama in England*, New York, 1929.

Nashe, Thomas, *Works*, ed. R. B. McKerrow, 1905.

Nichols, J., *The Progresses and Public Processions of Queen Elizabeth*, 1823.

Osborn, Francis, *Traditionall Memoryes on the Reign of King James*, Oxford, 1658.

Penrose, F. C., 'Notes on St. Paul's Cathedral', *Royal Institute of British Architects, Trans.* 29 (1878–9), 93–104.

Redford, John, *Wit and Science*, ed. A. Brown, Malone Society, 1951.

Reed, A. W., *Early Tudor Drama*, 1926.

Reese, Gustave, *Music in the Renaissance*, New York, 1954 (revised 1959).

Rimbault, E. F., *The Old Cheque Book of the Chapel Royal (1561–1744)*, Camden Society, NS III, 1875.

Roberts, Charles W., 'The Authorship of Gammer Gurton's Needle', *Philological Quarterly*, 19 (1940), 97–113.

Rye, W. B., *England as Seen by Foreigners*, New York, 1967.

Sabol, Andrew J., 'A Newly Discovered Contemporary Song Setting for Jonson's *Cynthia's Revels*', *N. & Q.*, 203 (1958), 384–5.

205

'Two Songs with Accompaniment for an Elizabethan Choirboy Play', *Studies in the Renaissance*, 5 (1958), 145–59.

'Ravenscroft's "Melismata" and the Children of Paul's', *Renaissance News*, XII (1959), 3–9.

Saccio, P. *The Court Comedies of John Lyly*, Princeton, 1969.

Shapiro, Michael, *Children of the Revels: The Boy Companies of Shakespeare's Time and Their Plays*, New York, 1977.

'Children's Troupes: Dramatic Illusion and Acting Styles', *Comparative Drama*, 3 (1967), 42–53.

'Music and Song in Plays Acted by Children's Companies during the English Renaissance', *Current Musicology*, 7 (1968), 97–110.

'Three Notes on The Theatre at Paul's, *c*.1569–*c*.1607', *Theatre Notebook*, 24 (1970), 147–54.

' "Le Prince D'Amour" and the Resumption of Playing at Paul's', *N. & Q.*, NS 18 (1971), 14–16.

'Towards a Reappraisal of the Children's Troupes', *Theatre Survey*, 13 (1972), 1–19.

'Audience vs. Dramatist in Jonson's *Epicoene* and Other Plays of the Children's Troupes', *English Literary Renaissance*, 3 (1973), 400–17.

'Theatrical Perspectives of Children's Companies., *Research Opportunities in Renaissance Drama*, 18 (1975), 13–18.

Sharpe, Robert B., *The Real War of the Theatres*, Boston, 1935.

Simpson, W. S., *Registrum Statutorum et Consuetudinum Ecclesiae Cathedralis Sancti Pauli*, 1873.

Gleanings from Old S. Paul's, 1889.

Sisson, C. J., *Lost Plays of Shakespeare's Age*, Cambridge, 1936.

'A Note on Sebastian Westcott', *Review of English Studies*, 19 (1943), 204–5.

Smith, Alan, 'The Cultivation of Music in English Cathedrals in the Reign of Elizabeth I', *Proceedings of the Royal Music Association*, 1967–8, pp. 37–49.

Smith, Irwin, *Shakespeare's Blackfriars Playhouse: Its History and its Design*, New York, 1964.

Southern, Richard, 'The Contribution of the Interlude to Elizabethan Staging', in *Essays on Shakespeare and Elizabethan Drama in Honor of Hardin Craig*, ed. R. Hosley, Columbia, 1962, pp. 3–14.

The Staging of Plays before Shakespeare, 1973.

'The "Houses" of the Westminster Play', *Theatre Notebook*, 3 (1949), 46–52.

Steele, Mary Susan, *Plays and Masques at Court During the Reigns of Elizabeth, James and Charles*, 1926; reprinted New York, 1968.

Stowe, John, *A Survay of London*, 1598.

Stubbes, John, *The Anatomie of Abuses*, ed. J. P. Collier, 1870.

Tusser, Thomas, *Five Hundredth Pointes of Good Husbandrie*, 1573.

Wallace, Charles William, *The Children of the Chapel at Blackfriars, 1597–1603*, University of Nebraska Studies, 8 Nos. 2 and 3, Lincoln, 1908.

Select bibliography

The Evolution of the English Drama Up to Shakespeare with a History of the First Blackfriars Theatre, Berlin, 1912.

'Shakespeare and his London Associates', *University Studies*, Nebraska, 10, 4 (1910), 261–360.

Woodfill, Walter L., *Musicians in English Society from Elizabeth to Charles I*, Princeton, 1953.

Yonge, Nicholas, *Musica Transalpina*, 1588.

Zwager, N., *Glimpses of Ben Jonson's London*, Amsterdam, 1926.

Index